CUDA by Example

CUDA by Example

AN INTRODUCTION TO GENERAL-PURPOSE GPU PROGRAMMING

JASON SANDERS
EDWARD KANDROT

✦✦Addison-Wesley

Upper Saddle River, NJ • Boston • Indianapolis • San Francisco
New York • Toronto • Montreal • London • Munich • Paris • Madrid
Capetown • Sydney • Tokyo • Singapore • Mexico City

The publisher offers excellent discounts on this book when ordered in quantity for bulk purchases or special sales, which may include electronic versions and/or custom covers and content particular to your business, training goals, marketing focus, and branding interests. For more information, please contact:

U.S. Corporate and Government Sales
(800) 382-3419
corpsales@pearsontechgroup.com

For sales outside the United States, please contact:

International Sales
international@pearson.com

Visit us on the Web: informit.com/aw

Library of Congress Cataloging-in-Publication Data

Sanders, Jason.
 CUDA by example : an introduction to general-purpose GPU programming / Jason Sanders, Edward Kandrot.
    p.   cm.
 Includes index.
 ISBN 978-0-13-138768-3 (pbk. : alk. paper)
 1. Application software—Development. 2. Computer architecture. 3. Parallel programming (Computer science) I. Kandrot, Edward. II. Title.
 QA76.76.A65S255 2010
 005.2'75—dc22

                                                                2010017618

ISBN-13: 978-0-13-138768-3
ISBN-10:   0-13-138768-5
Text printed in the United States on recycled paper at Edwards Brothers in Ann Arbor, Michigan.
First printing, July 2010

To our families and friends, who gave us endless support.
To our readers, who will bring us the future.
And to the teachers who taught our readers to read.

Contents

8   GRAPHICS INTEROPERABILITY   139

9   ATOMICS   163

Foreword

Recent activities of major chip manufacturers such as NVIDIA make it more evident than ever that future designs of microprocessors and large HPC systems will be hybrid/heterogeneous in nature. These heterogeneous systems will rely on the integration of two major types of components in varying proportions:

- **Multi- and many-core CPU technology**: The number of cores will continue to escalate because of the desire to pack more and more components on a chip while avoiding the power wall, the instruction-level parallelism wall, and the memory wall.

- **Special-purpose hardware and massively parallel accelerators**: For example, GPUs from NVIDIA have outpaced standard CPUs in floating-point performance in recent years. Furthermore, they have arguably become as easy, if not easier, to program than multicore CPUs.

The relative balance between these component types in future designs is not clear and will likely vary over time. There seems to be no doubt that future generations of computer systems, ranging from laptops to supercomputers, will consist of a composition of heterogeneous components. Indeed, the *petaflop* (10^{15} floating-point operations per second) performance barrier was breached by such a system.

And yet the problems and the challenges for developers in the new computational landscape of hybrid processors remain daunting. Critical parts of the software infrastructure are already having a very difficult time keeping up with the pace of change. In some cases, performance cannot scale with the number of cores because an increasingly large portion of time is spent on data movement rather than arithmetic. In other cases, software tuned for performance is delivered years after the hardware arrives and so is obsolete on delivery. And in some cases, as on some recent GPUs, software will not run at all because programming environments have changed too much.

CUDA by Example addresses the heart of the software development challenge by leveraging one of the most innovative and powerful solutions to the problem of programming the massively parallel accelerators in recent years.

This book introduces you to programming in CUDA C by providing examples and insight into the process of constructing and effectively using NVIDIA GPUs. It presents introductory concepts of parallel computing from simple examples to debugging (both logical and performance), as well as covers advanced topics and issues related to using and building many applications. Throughout the book, programming examples reinforce the concepts that have been presented.

The book is required reading for anyone working with accelerator-based computing systems. It explores parallel computing in depth and provides an approach to many problems that may be encountered. It is especially useful for application developers, numerical library writers, and students and teachers of parallel computing.

I have enjoyed and learned from this book, and I feel confident that you will as well.

Jack Dongarra
University Distinguished Professor, University of Tennessee Distinguished Research Staff Member, Oak Ridge National Laboratory

Preface

This book shows how, by harnessing the power of your computer's graphics process unit (GPU), you can write high-performance software for a wide range of applications. Although originally designed to render computer graphics on a monitor (and still used for this purpose), GPUs are increasingly being called upon for equally demanding programs in science, engineering, and finance, among other domains. We refer collectively to GPU programs that address problems in nongraphics domains as *general-purpose*. Happily, although you need to have some experience working in C or C++ to benefit from this book, you need not have any knowledge of computer graphics. None whatsoever! GPU programming simply offers you an opportunity to build—and to build mightily—on your existing programming skills.

To program NVIDIA GPUs to perform general-purpose computing tasks, you will want to know what CUDA is. NVIDIA GPUs are built on what's known as the *CUDA Architecture*. You can think of the CUDA Architecture as the scheme by which NVIDIA has built GPUs that can perform *both* traditional graphics-rendering tasks *and* general-purpose tasks. To program CUDA GPUs, we will be using a language known as *CUDA C*. As you will see very early in this book, CUDA C is essentially C with a handful of extensions to allow programming of massively parallel machines like NVIDIA GPUs.

We've geared *CUDA by Example* toward experienced C or C++ programmers who have enough familiarity with C such that they are comfortable reading and writing code in C. This book builds on your experience with C and intends to serve as an example-driven, "quick-start" guide to using NVIDIA's CUDA C programming language. By no means do you need to have done large-scale software architecture, to have written a C compiler or an operating system kernel, or to know all the ins and outs of the ANSI C standards. However, we do not spend time reviewing C syntax or common C library routines such as `malloc()` or `memcpy()`, so we will assume that you are already reasonably familiar with these topics.

You will encounter some techniques that can be considered general parallel programming paradigms, although this book does not aim to teach general parallel programming techniques. Also, while we will look at nearly every part of the CUDA API, this book does not serve as an extensive API reference nor will it go into gory detail about every tool that you can use to help develop your CUDA C software. Consequently, we highly recommend that this book be used in conjunction with NVIDIA's freely available documentation, in particular the *NVIDIA CUDA Programming Guide* and the *NVIDIA CUDA Best Practices Guide*. But don't stress out about collecting all these documents because we'll walk you through everything you need to do.

Without further ado, the world of programming NVIDIA GPUs with CUDA C awaits!

Acknowledgments

It's been said that it takes a village to write a technical book, and *CUDA by Example* is no exception to this adage. The authors owe debts of gratitude to many people, some of whom we would like to thank here.

Ian Buck, NVIDIA's senior director of GPU computing software, has been immeasurably helpful in every stage of the development of this book, from championing the idea to managing many of the details. We also owe Tim Murray, our always-smiling reviewer, much of the credit for this book possessing even a modicum of technical accuracy and readability. Many thanks also go to our designer, Darwin Tat, who created fantastic cover art and figures on an extremely tight schedule. Finally, we are much obliged to John Park, who helped guide this project through the delicate legal process required of published work.

Without help from Addison-Wesley's staff, this book would still be nothing more than a twinkle in the eyes of the authors. Peter Gordon, Kim Boedigheimer, and Julie Nahil have all shown unbounded patience and professionalism and have genuinely made the publication of this book a painless process. Additionally, Molly Sharp's production work and Kim Wimpsett's copyediting have utterly transformed this text from a pile of documents riddled with errors to the volume you're reading today.

Some of the content of this book could not have been included without the help of other contributors. Specifically, Nadeem Mohammad was instrumental in researching the CUDA case studies we present in Chapter 1, and Nathan Whitehead generously provided code that we incorporated into examples throughout the book.

We would be remiss if we didn't thank the others who read early drafts of this text and provided helpful feedback, including Genevieve Breed and Kurt Wall. Many of the NVIDIA software engineers provided invaluable technical assistance during the course of developing the content for *CUDA by Example*, including Mark Hairgrove who scoured the book, uncovering all manner of inconsistencies—technical, typographical, and grammatical. Steve Hines, Nicholas Wilt, and Stephen Jones consulted on specific sections of the CUDA API, helping elucidate nuances that the authors would have otherwise over-looked. Thanks also go out to Randima Fernando who helped to get this project off the ground and to Michael Schidlowsky for acknowledging Jason in his book.

And what acknowledgments section would be complete without a heartfelt expression of gratitude to parents and siblings? It is here that we would like to thank our families, who have been with us through everything and have made this all possible. With that said, we would like to extend special thanks to loving parents, Edward and Kathleen Kandrot and Stephen and Helen Sanders. Thanks also go to our brothers, Kenneth Kandrot and Corey Sanders. Thank you all for your unwavering support.

About the Authors

Jason Sanders is a senior software engineer in the CUDA Platform group at NVIDIA. While at NVIDIA, he helped develop early releases of CUDA system software and contributed to the OpenCL 1.0 Specification, an industry standard for heterogeneous computing. Jason received his master's degree in computer science from the University of California Berkeley where he published research in GPU computing, and he holds a bachelor's degree in electrical engineering from Princeton University. Prior to joining NVIDIA, he previously held positions at ATI Technologies, Apple, and Novell. When he's not writing books, Jason is typically working out, playing soccer, or shooting photos.

Edward Kandrot is a senior software engineer on the CUDA Algorithms team at NVIDIA. He has more than 20 years of industry experience focused on optimizing code and improving performance, including for Photoshop and Mozilla. Kandrot has worked for Adobe, Microsoft, and Google, and he has been a consultant at many companies, including Apple and Autodesk. When not coding, he can be found playing World of Warcraft or visiting Las Vegas for the amazing food.

Chapter 1

Why CUDA? Why Now?

There was a time in the not-so-distant past when parallel computing was looked upon as an "exotic" pursuit and typically got compartmentalized as a specialty within the field of computer science. This perception has changed in profound ways in recent years. The computing world has shifted to the point where, far from being an esoteric pursuit, nearly every aspiring programmer *needs* training in parallel programming to be fully effective in computer science. Perhaps you've picked this book up unconvinced about the importance of parallel programming in the computing world today and the increasingly large role it will play in the years to come. This introductory chapter will examine recent trends in the hardware that does the heavy lifting for the software that we as programmers write. In doing so, we hope to convince you that the parallel computing revolution has *already* happened and that, by learning CUDA C, you'll be well positioned to write high-performance applications for heterogeneous platforms that contain both central and graphics processing units.

1.1 Chapter Objectives

Through the course of this chapter, you will accomplish the following:

- You will learn about the increasingly important role of parallel computing.

- You will learn a brief history of GPU computing and CUDA.

- You will learn about some successful applications that use CUDA C.

1.2 The Age of Parallel Processing

In recent years, much has been made of the computing industry's widespread shift to parallel computing. Nearly all consumer computers in the year 2010 will ship with multicore central processors. From the introduction of dual-core, low-end netbook machines to 8- and 16-core workstation computers, no longer will parallel computing be relegated to exotic supercomputers or mainframes. Moreover, electronic devices such as mobile phones and portable music players have begun to incorporate parallel computing capabilities in an effort to provide functionality well beyond those of their predecessors.

More and more, software developers will need to cope with a variety of parallel computing platforms and technologies in order to provide novel and rich experiences for an increasingly sophisticated base of users. Command prompts are out; multithreaded graphical interfaces are in. Cellular phones that only make calls are out; phones that can simultaneously play music, browse the Web, and provide GPS services are in.

1.2.1 CENTRAL PROCESSING UNITS

For 30 years, one of the important methods for the improving the performance of consumer computing devices has been to increase the speed at which the processor's clock operated. Starting with the first personal computers of the early 1980s, consumer central processing units (CPUs) ran with internal clocks operating around 1MHz. About 30 years later, most desktop processors have clock speeds between 1GHz and 4GHz, nearly 1,000 times faster than the clock on the original personal computer. Although increasing the CPU clock speed is certainly not the only method by which computing performance has been improved, it has always been a reliable source for improved performance.

In recent years, however, manufacturers have been forced to look for alternatives to this traditional source of increased computational power. Because of various fundamental limitations in the fabrication of integrated circuits, it is no longer feasible to rely on upward-spiraling processor clock speeds as a means for extracting additional power from existing architectures. Because of power and heat restrictions as well as a rapidly approaching physical limit to transistor size, researchers and manufacturers have begun to look elsewhere.

Outside the world of consumer computing, supercomputers have for decades extracted massive performance gains in similar ways. The performance of a processor used in a supercomputer has climbed astronomically, similar to the improvements in the personal computer CPU. However, in addition to dramatic improvements in the performance of a single processor, supercomputer manufacturers have also extracted massive leaps in performance by steadily increasing the *number* of processors. It is not uncommon for the fastest supercomputers to have tens or hundreds of thousands of processor cores working in tandem.

In the search for additional processing power for personal computers, the improvement in supercomputers raises a very good question: Rather than solely looking to increase the performance of a single processing core, why not put more than one in a personal computer? In this way, personal computers could continue to improve in performance without the need for continuing increases in processor clock speed.

In 2005, faced with an increasingly competitive marketplace and few alternatives, leading CPU manufacturers began offering processors with two computing cores instead of one. Over the following years, they followed this development with the release of three-, four-, six-, and eight-core central processor units. Sometimes referred to as the *multicore revolution*, this trend has marked a huge shift in the evolution of the consumer computing market.

Today, it is relatively challenging to purchase a desktop computer with a CPU containing but a single computing core. Even low-end, low-power central processors ship with two or more cores per die. Leading CPU manufacturers have already announced plans for 12- and 16-core CPUs, further confirming that parallel computing has arrived for good.

1.3 The Rise of GPU Computing

In comparison to the central processor's traditional data processing pipeline, performing general-purpose computations on a graphics processing unit (GPU) is a new concept. In fact, the GPU itself is relatively new compared to the computing field at large. However, the idea of computing on graphics processors is not as new as you might believe.

1.3.1 A BRIEF HISTORY OF GPUS

We have already looked at how central processors evolved in both clock speeds and core count. In the meantime, the state of graphics processing underwent a dramatic revolution. In the late 1980s and early 1990s, the growth in popularity of graphically driven operating systems such as Microsoft Windows helped create a market for a new type of processor. In the early 1990s, users began purchasing 2D display accelerators for their personal computers. These display accelerators offered hardware-assisted bitmap operations to assist in the display and usability of graphical operating systems.

Around the same time, in the world of professional computing, a company by the name of Silicon Graphics spent the 1980s popularizing the use of three-dimensional graphics in a variety of markets, including government and defense applications and scientific and technical visualization, as well as providing the tools to create stunning cinematic effects. In 1992, Silicon Graphics opened the programming interface to its hardware by releasing the OpenGL library. Silicon Graphics intended OpenGL to be used as a standardized, platform-independent method for writing 3D graphics applications. As with parallel processing and CPUs, it would only be a matter of time before the technologies found their way into consumer applications.

By the mid-1990s, the demand for consumer applications employing 3D graphics had escalated rapidly, setting the stage for two fairly significant developments. First, the release of immersive, first-person games such as Doom, Duke Nukem 3D, and Quake helped ignite a quest to create progressively more realistic 3D environments for PC gaming. Although 3D graphics would eventually work their way into nearly all computer games, the popularity of the nascent first-person shooter genre would significantly accelerate the adoption of 3D graphics in consumer computing. At the same time, companies such as NVIDIA, ATI Technologies, and 3dfx Interactive began releasing graphics accelerators that were affordable enough to attract widespread attention. These developments cemented 3D graphics as a technology that would figure prominently for years to come.

The release of NVIDIA's GeForce 256 further pushed the capabilities of consumer graphics hardware. For the first time, transform and lighting computations could be performed directly on the graphics processor, thereby enhancing the potential for even more visually interesting applications. Since transform and lighting were already integral parts of the OpenGL graphics pipeline, the GeForce 256 marked the beginning of a natural progression where increasingly more of the graphics pipeline would be implemented directly on the graphics processor.

From a parallel-computing standpoint, NVIDIA's release of the GeForce 3 series in 2001 represents arguably the most important breakthrough in GPU technology. The GeForce 3 series was the computing industry's first chip to implement Microsoft's then-new DirectX 8.0 standard. This standard required that compliant hardware contain both programmable vertex and programmable pixel shading stages. For the first time, developers had some control over the exact computations that would be performed on their GPUs.

1.3.2 EARLY GPU COMPUTING

The release of GPUs that possessed programmable pipelines attracted many researchers to the possibility of using graphics hardware for more than simply OpenGL- or DirectX-based rendering. The general approach in the early days of GPU computing was extraordinarily convoluted. Because standard graphics APIs such as OpenGL and DirectX were still the only way to interact with a GPU, any attempt to perform arbitrary computations on a GPU would still be subject to the constraints of programming within a graphics API. Because of this, researchers explored general-purpose computation through graphics APIs by trying to make their problems appear to the GPU to be traditional rendering.

Essentially, the GPUs of the early 2000s were designed to produce a color for every pixel on the screen using programmable arithmetic units known as *pixel shaders*. In general, a pixel shader uses its (x, y) position on the screen as well as some additional information to combine various inputs in computing a final color. The additional information could be input colors, texture coordinates, or other attributes that would be passed to the shader when it ran. But because the arithmetic being performed on the input colors and textures was completely controlled by the programmer, researchers observed that these input "colors" could actually be *any* data.

So if the inputs were actually numerical data signifying something other than color, programmers could then program the pixel shaders to perform arbitrary computations on this data. The results would be handed back to the GPU as the final pixel "color," although the colors would simply be the result of whatever computations the programmer had instructed the GPU to perform on their inputs. This data could be read back by the researchers, and the GPU would never be the wiser. In essence, the GPU was being tricked into performing nonrendering tasks by making those tasks appear as if they were a standard rendering. This trickery was very clever but also very convoluted.

Because of the high arithmetic throughput of GPUs, initial results from these experiments promised a bright future for GPU computing. However, the programming model was still far too restrictive for any critical mass of developers to form. There were tight resource constraints, since programs could receive input data only from a handful of input colors and a handful of texture units. There were serious limitations on how and where the programmer could write results to memory, so algorithms requiring the ability to write to arbitrary locations in memory (scatter) could not run on a GPU. Moreover, it was nearly impossible to predict how your particular GPU would deal with floating-point data, if it handled floating-point data at all, so most scientific computations would be unable to use a GPU. Finally, when the program inevitably computed the incorrect results, failed to terminate, or simply hung the machine, there existed no reasonably good method to debug any code that was being executed on the GPU.

As if the limitations weren't severe enough, anyone who *still* wanted to use a GPU to perform general-purpose computations would need to learn OpenGL or DirectX since these remained the only means by which one could interact with a GPU. Not only did this mean storing data in graphics textures and executing computations by calling OpenGL or DirectX functions, but it meant writing the computations themselves in special graphics-only programming languages known as *shading languages*. Asking researchers to both cope with severe resource and programming restrictions as well as to learn computer graphics and shading languages before attempting to harness the computing power of their GPU proved too large a hurdle for wide acceptance.

1.4 CUDA

It would not be until five years after the release of the GeForce 3 series that GPU computing would be ready for prime time. In November 2006, NVIDIA unveiled the industry's first DirectX 10 GPU, the GeForce 8800 GTX. The GeForce 8800 GTX was also the first GPU to be built with NVIDIA's CUDA Architecture. This architecture included several new components designed strictly for GPU computing and aimed to alleviate many of the limitations that prevented previous graphics processors from being legitimately useful for general-purpose computation.

1.4.1 WHAT IS THE CUDA ARCHITECTURE?

Unlike previous generations that partitioned computing resources into vertex and pixel shaders, the CUDA Architecture included a unified shader pipeline, allowing each and every arithmetic logic unit (ALU) on the chip to be marshaled by a program intending to perform general-purpose computations. Because NVIDIA intended this new family of graphics processors to be used for general-purpose computing, these ALUs were built to comply with IEEE requirements for single-precision floating-point arithmetic and were designed to use an instruction set tailored for general computation rather than specifically for graphics. Furthermore, the execution units on the GPU were allowed arbitrary read and write access to memory as well as access to a software-managed cache known as *shared memory*. All of these features of the CUDA Architecture were added in order to create a GPU that would excel at computation in addition to performing well at traditional graphics tasks.

1.4.2 USING THE CUDA ARCHITECTURE

The effort by NVIDIA to provide consumers with a product for both computation and graphics could not stop at producing hardware incorporating the CUDA Architecture, though. Regardless of how many features NVIDIA added to its chips to facilitate computing, there continued to be no way to access these features without using OpenGL or DirectX. Not only would this have required users to continue to disguise their computations as graphics problems, but they would have needed to continue writing their computations in a graphics-oriented shading language such as OpenGL's GLSL or Microsoft's HLSL.

To reach the maximum number of developers possible, NVIDIA took industry-standard C and added a relatively small number of keywords in order to harness some of the special features of the CUDA Architecture. A few months after the launch of the GeForce 8800 GTX, NVIDIA made public a compiler for this language, CUDA C. And with that, CUDA C became the first language specifically designed by a GPU company to facilitate general-purpose computing on GPUs.

In addition to creating a language to write code for the GPU, NVIDIA also provides a specialized hardware driver to exploit the CUDA Architecture's massive computational power. Users are no longer required to have any knowledge of the OpenGL or DirectX graphics programming interfaces, nor are they required to force their problem to look like a computer graphics task.

1.5 Applications of CUDA

Since its debut in early 2007, a variety of industries and applications have enjoyed a great deal of success by choosing to build applications in CUDA C. These benefits often include orders-of-magnitude performance improvement over the previous state-of-the-art implementations. Furthermore, applications running on NVIDIA graphics processors enjoy superior performance per dollar and performance per watt than implementations built exclusively on traditional central processing technologies. The following represent just a few of the ways in which people have put CUDA C and the CUDA Architecture into successful use.

1.5.1 MEDICAL IMAGING

The number of people who have been affected by the tragedy of breast cancer has dramatically risen over the course of the past 20 years. Thanks in a large part to the tireless efforts of many, awareness and research into preventing and curing this terrible disease has similarly risen in recent years. Ultimately, every case of breast cancer should be caught early enough to prevent the ravaging side effects of radiation and chemotherapy, the permanent reminders left by surgery, and the deadly consequences in cases that fail to respond to treatment. As a result, researchers share a strong desire to find fast, accurate, and minimally invasive ways to identify the early signs of breast cancer.

The mammogram, one of the current best techniques for the early detection of breast cancer, has several significant limitations. Two or more images need to be taken, and the film needs to be developed and read by a skilled doctor to identify potential tumors. Additionally, this X-ray procedure carries with it all the risks of repeatedly radiating a patient's chest. After careful study, doctors often require further, more specific imaging—and even biopsy—in an attempt to eliminate the possibility of cancer. These false positives incur expensive follow-up work and cause undue stress to the patient until final conclusions can be drawn.

Ultrasound imaging is safer than X-ray imaging, so doctors often use it in conjunction with mammography to assist in breast cancer care and diagnosis. But conventional breast ultrasound has its limitations as well. As a result, TechniScan Medical Systems was born. TechniScan has developed a promising, three-dimensional, ultrasound imaging method, but its solution had not been put into practice for a very simple reason: computation limitations. Simply put, converting the gathered ultrasound data into the three-dimensional imagery required computation considered prohibitively time-consuming and expensive for practical use.

The introduction of NVIDIA's first GPU based on the CUDA Architecture along with its CUDA C programming language provided a platform on which TechniScan could convert the dreams of its founders into reality. As the name indicates, its Svara ultrasound imaging system uses ultrasonic waves to image the patient's chest. The TechniScan Svara system relies on two NVIDIA Tesla C1060 processors in order to process the 35GB of data generated by a 15-minute scan. Thanks to the computational horsepower of the Tesla C1060, within 20 minutes the doctor can manipulate a highly detailed, three-dimensional image of the woman's breast. TechniScan expects wide deployment of its Svara system starting in 2010.

1.5.2 COMPUTATIONAL FLUID DYNAMICS

For many years, the design of highly efficient rotors and blades remained a black art of sorts. The astonishingly complex movement of air and fluids around these devices cannot be effectively modeled by simple formulations, so accurate simulations prove far too computationally expensive to be realistic. Only the largest supercomputers in the world could hope to offer computational resources on par with the sophisticated numerical models required to develop and validate designs. Since few have access to such machines, innovation in the design of such machines continued to stagnate.

The University of Cambridge, in a great tradition started by Charles Babbage, is home to active research into advanced parallel computing. Dr. Graham Pullan and Dr. Tobias Brandvik of the "many-core group" correctly identified the potential in NVIDIA's CUDA Architecture to accelerate computational fluid dynamics unprecedented levels. Their initial investigations indicated that acceptable levels of performance could be delivered by GPU-powered, personal workstations. Later, the use of a small GPU cluster easily outperformed their much more costly supercomputers and further confirmed their suspicions that the capabilities of NVIDIA's GPU matched extremely well with the problems they wanted to solve.

For the researchers at Cambridge, the massive performance gains offered by CUDA C represent more than a simple, incremental boost to their supercomputing resources. The availability of copious amounts of low-cost GPU computation empowered the Cambridge researchers to perform rapid experimentation. Receiving experimental results within seconds streamlined the feedback process on which researchers rely in order to arrive at breakthroughs. As a result, the use of GPU clusters has fundamentally transformed the way they approach their research. Nearly interactive simulation has unleashed new opportunities for innovation and creativity in a previously stifled field of research.

1.5.3 ENVIRONMENTAL SCIENCE

The increasing need for environmentally sound consumer goods has arisen as a natural consequence of the rapidly escalating industrialization of the global economy. Growing concerns over climate change, the spiraling prices of fuel, and the growing level of pollutants in our air and water have brought into sharp relief the collateral damage of such successful advances in industrial output. Detergents and cleaning agents have long been some of the most necessary yet potentially calamitous consumer products in regular use. As a result, many scientists have begun exploring methods for reducing the environmental impact of such detergents without reducing their efficacy. Gaining something for nothing can be a tricky proposition, however.

The key components to cleaning agents are known as *surfactants*. Surfactant molecules determine the cleaning capacity and texture of detergents and shampoos, but they are often implicated as the most environmentally devastating component of cleaning products. These molecules attach themselves to dirt and then mix with water such that the surfactants can be rinsed away along with the dirt. Traditionally, measuring the cleaning value of a new surfactant would require extensive laboratory testing involving numerous combinations of materials and impurities to be cleaned. This process, not surprisingly, can be very slow and expensive.

Temple University has been working with industry leader Procter & Gamble to use molecular simulation of surfactant interactions with dirt, water, and other materials. The introduction of computer simulations serves not just to accelerate a traditional lab approach, but it extends the breadth of testing to numerous variants of environmental conditions, far more than could be practically tested in the past. Temple researchers used the GPU-accelerated Highly Optimized Object-oriented Many-particle Dynamics (HOOMD) simulation software written by the Department of Energy's Ames Laboratory. By splitting their simulation across two

NVIDIA Tesla GPUs, they were able achieve equivalent performance to the 128 CPU cores of the Cray XT3 and to the 1024 CPUs of an IBM BlueGene/L machine. By increasing the number of Tesla GPUs in their solution, they are already simulating surfactant interactions at 16 times the performance of previous platforms. Since NVIDIA's CUDA has reduced the time to complete such comprehensive simulations from several weeks to a few hours, the years to come should offer a dramatic rise in products that have both increased effectiveness and reduced environmental impact.

1.6 Chapter Review

The computing industry is at the precipice of a parallel computing revolution, and NVIDIA's CUDA C has thus far been one of the most successful languages ever designed for parallel computing. Throughout the course of this book, we will help you learn how to write your own code in CUDA C. We will help you learn the special extensions to C and the application programming interfaces that NVIDIA has created in service of GPU computing. You are *not* expected to know OpenGL or DirectX, nor are you expected to have any background in computer graphics.

We will not be covering the basics of programming in C, so we do not recommend this book to people completely new to computer programming. Some familiarity with parallel programming might help, although we do not *expect* you to have done any parallel programming. Any terms or concepts related to parallel programming that you will need to understand will be explained in the text. In fact, there may be some occasions when you find that knowledge of traditional parallel programming will cause you to make assumptions about GPU computing that prove untrue. So in reality, a moderate amount of experience with C or C++ programming is the only prerequisite to making it through this book.

In the next chapter, we will help you set up your machine for GPU computing, ensuring that you have both the hardware and the software components necessary get started. After that, you'll be ready to get your hands dirty with CUDA C. If you already have some experience with CUDA C or you're sure that your system has been properly set up to do development in CUDA C, you can skip to Chapter 3.

Chapter 2

Getting Started

We hope that Chapter 1 has gotten you excited to get started learning CUDA C. Since this book intends to teach you the language through a series of coding examples, you'll need a functioning development environment. Sure, you could stand on the sideline and watch, but we think you'll have more fun and stay interested longer if you jump in and get some practical experience hacking CUDA C code as soon as possible. In this vein, this chapter will walk you through some of the hardware and software components you'll need in order to get started. The good news is that you can obtain all of the software you'll need for free, leaving you more money for whatever tickles your fancy.

2.1 Chapter Objectives

Through the course of this chapter, you will accomplish the following:

- You will download all the software components required through this book.

- You will set up an environment in which you can build code written in CUDA C.

2.2 Development Environment

Before embarking on this journey, you will need to set up an environment in which you can develop using CUDA C. The prerequisites to developing code in CUDA C are as follows:

- A CUDA-enabled graphics processor

- An NVIDIA device driver

- A CUDA development toolkit

- A standard C compiler

To make this chapter as painless as possible, we'll walk through each of these prerequisites now.

2.2.1 CUDA-ENABLED GRAPHICS PROCESSORS

Fortunately, it should be easy to find yourself a graphics processor that has been built on the CUDA Architecture because every NVIDIA GPU since the 2006 release of the GeForce 8800 GTX has been CUDA-enabled. Since NVIDIA regularly releases new GPUs based on the CUDA Architecture, the following will undoubtedly be only a partial list of CUDA-enabled GPUs. Nevertheless, the GPUs are all CUDA-capable.

For a complete list, you should consult the NVIDIA website at www.nvidia.com/cuda, although it is safe to assume that all recent GPUs (GPUs from 2007 on) with more than 256MB of graphics memory can be used to develop and run code written with CUDA C.

Table 2.1 CUDA-enabled GPUs

GeForce GTX 480	GeForce 8300 mGPU	Quadro FX 5600
GeForce GTX 470	GeForce 8200 mGPU	Quadro FX 4800
GeForce GTX 295	GeForce 8100 mGPU	Quadro FX 4800 for Mac
GeForce GTX 285	Tesla S2090	Quadro FX 4700 X2
GeForce GTX 285 for Mac	Tesla M2090	Quadro FX 4600
GeForce GTX 280	Tesla S2070	Quadro FX 3800
GeForce GTX 275	Tesla M2070	Quadro FX 3700
GeForce GTX 260	Tesla C2070	Quadro FX 1800
GeForce GTS 250	Tesla S2050	Quadro FX 1700
GeForce GT 220	Tesla M2050	Quadro FX 580
GeForce G210	Tesla C2050	Quadro FX 570
GeForce GTS 150	Tesla S1070	Quadro FX 470
GeForce GT 130	Tesla C1060	Quadro FX 380
GeForce GT 120	Tesla S870	Quadro FX 370
GeForce G100	Tesla C870	Quadro FX 370 Low Profile
GeForce 9800 GX2	Tesla D870	Quadro CX
GeForce 9800 GTX+	**QUADRO MOBILE PRODUCTS**	Quadro NVS 450
GeForce 9800 GTX		Quadro NVS 420
GeForce 9800 GT	Quadro FX 3700M	Quadro NVS 295
GeForce 9600 GSO	Quadro FX 3600M	Quadro NVS 290
GeForce 9600 GT	Quadro FX 2700M	Quadro Plex 2100 D4
GeForce 9500 GT	Quadro FX 1700M	Quadro Plex 2200 D2
GeForce 9400GT	Quadro FX 1600M	Quadro Plex 2100 S4
GeForce 8800 Ultra	Quadro FX 770M	Quadro Plex 1000 Model IV
GeForce 8800 GTX	Quadro FX 570M	**GEFORCE MOBILE PRODUCTS**
GeForce 8800 GTS	Quadro FX 370M	
GeForce 8800 GT	Quadro FX 360M	GeForce GTX 280M
GeForce 8800 GS	Quadro NVS 320M	GeForce GTX 260M
GeForce 8600 GTS	Quadro NVS 160M	GeForce GTS 260M
GeForce 8600 GT	Quadro NVS 150M	GeForce GTS 250M
GeForce 8500 GT	Quadro NVS 140M	GeForce GTS 160M
GeForce 8400 GS	Quadro NVS 135M	GeForce GTS 150M
GeForce 9400 mGPU	Quadro NVS 130M	GeForce GT 240M
GeForce 9300 mGPU	Quadro FX 5800	GeForce GT 230M

Continued

Table 2.1 CUDA-enabled GPUs (Continued)

GeForce GT 130M	GeForce 9700M GTS	GeForce 9200M GS
GeForce G210M	GeForce 9700M GT	GeForce 9100M G
GeForce G110M	GeForce 9650M GS	GeForce 8800M GTS
GeForce G105M	GeForce 9600M GT	GeForce 8700M GT
GeForce G102M	GeForce 9600M GS	GeForce 8600M GT
GeForce 9800M GTX	GeForce 9500M GS	GeForce 8600M GS
GeForce 9800M GT	GeForce 9500M G	GeForce 8400M GT
GeForce 9800M GTS	GeForce 9300M GS	GeForce 8400M GS
GeForce 9800M GS	GeForce 9300M G	

2.2.2 NVIDIA DEVICE DRIVER

NVIDIA provides system software that allows your programs to communicate with the CUDA-enabled hardware. If you have installed your NVIDIA GPU properly, you likely already have this software installed on your machine. It never hurts to ensure you have the most recent drivers, so we recommend that you visit www.nvidia.com/cuda and click the *Download Drivers* link. Select the options that match the graphics card and operating system on which you plan to do development. After following the installation instructions for the platform of your choice, your system will be up-to-date with the latest NVIDIA system software.

2.2.3 CUDA DEVELOPMENT TOOLKIT

If you have a CUDA-enabled GPU and NVIDIA's device driver, you are ready to run compiled CUDA C code. This means that you can download CUDA-powered applications, and they will be able to successfully execute their code on your graphics processor. However, we assume that you want to do more than just run code because, otherwise, this book isn't really necessary. If you want to *develop* code for NVIDIA GPUs using CUDA C, you will need additional software. But as promised earlier, none of it will cost you a penny.

You will learn these details in the next chapter, but since your CUDA C applications are going to be computing on two different processors, you are consequently going to need two compilers. One compiler will compile code for your GPU, and one will compile code for your CPU. NVIDIA provides the compiler for your GPU code. As with the NVIDIA device driver, you can download the *CUDA Toolkit* at http://developer.nvidia.com/object/gpucomputing.html. Click the CUDA Toolkit link to reach the download page shown in Figure 2.1.

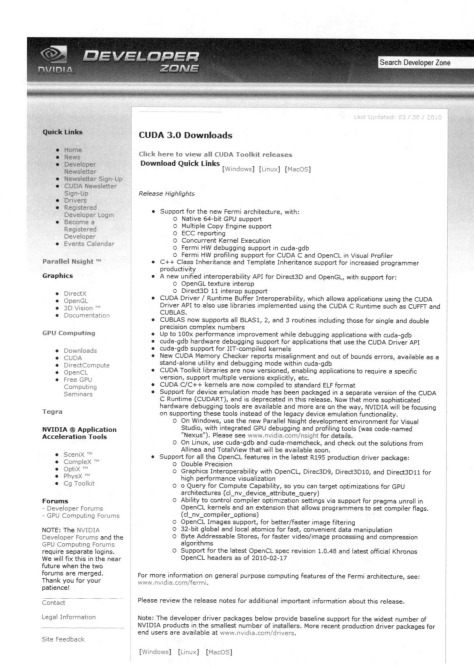

Figure 2.1 The CUDA download page

You will again be asked to select your platform from among 32- and 64-bit versions of Windows XP, Windows Vista, Windows 7, Linux, and Mac OS. From the available downloads, you need to download the CUDA Toolkit in order to build the code examples contained in this book. Additionally, you are encouraged, although not required, to download the GPU Computing SDK code samples, which contains dozens of helpful example programs. The GPU Computing SDK code samples will not be covered in this book, but they nicely complement the material we intend to cover, and as with learning any style of programming, the more examples, the better. You should also take note that although nearly all the code in this book will work on the Linux, Windows, and Mac OS platforms, we have targeted the applications toward Linux and Windows. If you are using Mac OS X, you will be living dangerously and using unsupported code examples.

2.2.4 STANDARD C COMPILER

As we mentioned, you will need a compiler for GPU code and a compiler for CPU code. If you downloaded and installed the CUDA Toolkit as suggested in the previous section, you have a compiler for GPU code. A compiler for CPU code is the only component that remains on our CUDA checklist, so let's address that issue so we can get to the interesting stuff.

WINDOWS

On Microsoft Windows platforms, including Windows XP, Windows Vista, Windows Server 2008, and Windows 7, we recommend using the Microsoft Visual Studio C compiler. NVIDIA currently supports both the Visual Studio 2005 and Visual Studio 2008 families of products. As Microsoft releases new versions, NVIDIA will likely add support for newer editions of Visual Studio while dropping support for older versions. Many C and C++ developers already have Visual Studio 2005 or Visual Studio 2008 installed on their machine, so if this applies to you, you can safely skip this subsection.

If you do not have access to a supported version of Visual Studio and aren't ready to invest in a copy, Microsoft does provide free downloads of the Visual Studio 2008 Express edition on its website. Although typically unsuitable for commercial software development, the Visual Studio Express editions are an excellent way to get started developing CUDA C on Windows platforms without investing money in software licenses. So, head on over to www.microsoft.com/visualstudio if you're in need of Visual Studio 2008!

LINUX

Most Linux distributions typically ship with a version of the GNU C compiler (gcc) installed. As of CUDA 3.0, the following Linux distributions shipped with supported versions of gcc installed:

- Red Hat Enterprise Linux 4.8

- Red Hat Enterprise Linux 5.3

- OpenSUSE 11.1

- SUSE Linux Enterprise Desktop 11

- Ubuntu 9.04

- Fedora 10

If you're a die-hard Linux user, you're probably aware that many Linux software packages work on far more than just the "supported" platforms. The CUDA Toolkit is no exception, so even if your favorite distribution is not listed here, it may be worth trying it anyway. The distribution's kernel, gcc, and glibc versions will in a large part determine whether the distribution is compatible.

MACINTOSH OS X

If you want to develop on Mac OS X, you will need to ensure that your machine has at least version 10.5.7 of Mac OS X. This includes version 10.6, Mac OS X "Snow Leopard." Furthermore, you will need to install gcc by downloading and installing Apple's Xcode. This software is provided free to Apple Developer Connection (ADC) members and can be downloaded from http://developer.apple.com/tools/Xcode. The code in this book was developed on Linux and Windows platforms but should work without modification on Mac OS X systems.

2.3 Chapter Review

If you have followed the steps in this chapter, you are ready to start developing code in CUDA C. Perhaps you have even played around with some of the NVIDIA GPU Computing SDK code samples you downloaded from NVIDIA's website. If so, we applaud your willingness to tinker! If not, don't worry. Everything you need is right here in this book. Either way, you're probably ready to start writing your first program in CUDA C, so let's get started.

Chapter 3

Introduction to CUDA C

If you read Chapter 1, we hope we have convinced you of both the immense computational power of graphics processors and that you are just the programmer to harness it. And if you continued through Chapter 2, you should have a functioning environment set up in order to compile and run the code you'll be writing in CUDA C. If you skipped the first chapters, perhaps you're just skimming for code samples, perhaps you randomly opened to this page while browsing at a bookstore, or maybe you're just dying to get started; that's OK, too (we won't tell). Either way, you're ready to get started with the first code examples, so let's go.

3.1 Chapter Objectives

Through the course of this chapter, you will accomplish the following:

- You will write your first lines of code in CUDA C.

- You will learn the difference between code written for the *host* and code written for a *device*.

- You will learn how to run device code from the host.

- You will learn about the ways device memory can be used on CUDA-capable devices.

- You will learn how to query your system for information on its CUDA-capable devices.

3.2 A First Program

Since we intend to learn CUDA C by example, let's take a look at our first example of CUDA C. In accordance with the laws governing written works of computer programming, we begin by examining a "Hello, World!" example.

3.2.1 HELLO, WORLD!

```
#include "../common/book.h"

int main( void ) {
    printf( "Hello, World!\n" );
    return 0;
}
```

At this point, no doubt you're wondering whether this book is a scam. Is this just C? Does CUDA C even exist? The answers to these questions are both in the affirmative; this book is not an elaborate ruse. This simple "Hello, World!" example is meant to illustrate that, at its most basic, there is no difference between CUDA C and the standard C to which you have grown accustomed.

The simplicity of this example stems from the fact that it runs entirely on the *host*. This will be one of the important distinctions made in this book; we refer to the CPU and the system's memory as the *host* and refer to the GPU and its memory as the *device*. This example resembles almost all the code you have ever written because it simply ignores any computing devices outside the host.

To remedy that sinking feeling that you've invested in nothing more than an expensive collection of trivialities, we will gradually build upon this simple example. Let's look at something that uses the GPU (a *device*) to execute code. A function that executes on the device is typically called a *kernel*.

3.2.2 A KERNEL CALL

Now we will build upon our example with some code that should look more foreign than our plain-vanilla "Hello, World!" program.

```
#include <iostream>


__global__ void kernel( void ) {
}


int main( void ) {
    kernel<<<1,1>>>();
    printf( "Hello, World!\n" );
    return 0;
}
```

This program makes two notable additions to the original "Hello, World!" example:

• An empty function named kernel() qualified with __global__

• A call to the empty function, embellished with <<<1,1>>>

As we saw in the previous section, code is compiled by your system's standard C compiler by default. For example, GNU gcc might compile your host code on Linux operating systems, while Microsoft Visual C compiles it on Windows systems. The NVIDIA tools simply feed this host compiler your code, and everything behaves as it would in a world without CUDA.

Now we see that CUDA C adds the `__global__` qualifier to standard C. This mechanism alerts the compiler that a function should be compiled to run on a device instead of the host. In this simple example, `nvcc` gives the function `kernel()` to the compiler that handles device code, and it feeds `main()` to the host compiler as it did in the previous example.

So, what is the mysterious call to `kernel()`, and why must we vandalize our standard C with angle brackets and a numeric tuple? Brace yourself, because this is where the magic happens.

We have seen that CUDA C needed a linguistic method for marking a function as device code. There is nothing special about this; it is shorthand to send host code to one compiler and device code to another compiler. The trick is actually in calling the device code from the host code. One of the benefits of CUDA C is that it provides this language integration so that device function calls look very much like host function calls. Later we will discuss what actually happens behind the scenes, but suffice to say that the CUDA compiler and runtime take care of the messy business of invoking device code from the host.

So, the mysterious-looking call invokes device code, but why the angle brackets and numbers? The angle brackets denote arguments we plan to pass to the runtime system. These are not arguments to the device code but are parameters that will influence how the runtime will launch our device code. We will learn about these parameters to the runtime in the next chapter. Arguments to the device code itself get passed within the parentheses, just like any other function invocation.

3.2.3 PASSING PARAMETERS

We've promised the ability to pass parameters to our kernel, and the time has come for us to make good on that promise. Consider the following enhancement to our "Hello, World!" application:

```
#include <iostream>
#include "book.h"


__global__ void add( int a, int b, int *c ) {
    *c = a + b;
}


int main( void ) {
    int c;
    int *dev_c;
    HANDLE_ERROR( cudaMalloc( (void**)&dev_c, sizeof(int) ) );

    add<<<1,1>>>( 2, 7, dev_c );

    HANDLE_ERROR( cudaMemcpy( &c,
                              dev_c,
                              sizeof(int),
                              cudaMemcpyDeviceToHost ) );
    printf( "2 + 7 = %d\n", c );
    cudaFree( dev_c );

    return 0;
}
```

You will notice a handful of new lines here, but these changes introduce only two concepts:

• We can pass parameters to a kernel as we would with any C function.

• We need to allocate memory to do anything useful on a device, such as return values to the host.

There is nothing special about passing parameters to a kernel. The angle-bracket syntax notwithstanding, a kernel call looks and acts exactly like any function call in standard C. The runtime system takes care of any complexity introduced by the fact that these parameters need to get from the host to the device.

The more interesting addition is the allocation of memory using cudaMalloc().
This call behaves very similarly to the standard C call malloc(), but it tells
the CUDA runtime to allocate the memory on the device. The first argument
is a pointer to the pointer you want to hold the address of the newly allocated
memory, and the second parameter is the size of the allocation you want to make.
Besides that your allocated memory pointer is not the function's return value,
this is identical behavior to malloc(), right down to the void* return type. The
HANDLE_ERROR() that surrounds these calls is a utility macro that we have
provided as part of this book's support code. It simply detects that the call has
returned an error, prints the associated error message, and exits the application
with an EXIT_FAILURE code. Although you are free to use this code in your own
applications, it is highly likely that this error-handling code will be insufficient in
production code.

This raises a subtle but important point. Much of the simplicity and power of
CUDA C derives from the ability to blur the line between host and device code.
However, it is the responsibility of the programmer not to dereference the pointer
returned by cudaMalloc() from code that executes on the host. Host code may
pass this pointer around, perform arithmetic on it, or even cast it to a different
type. But you cannot use it to read or write from memory.

Unfortunately, the compiler cannot protect you from this mistake, either. It will
be perfectly happy to allow dereferences of device pointers in your host code
because it looks like any other pointer in the application. We can summarize the
restrictions on the usage of device pointer as follows:

You *can* pass pointers allocated with cudaMalloc() to functions that
execute on the device.

You *can* use pointers allocated with cudaMalloc() to read or write
memory from code that executes on the device.

You *can* pass pointers allocated with cudaMalloc() to functions that
execute on the host.

You *cannot* use pointers allocated with cudaMalloc() to read or write
memory from code that executes on the host.

If you've been reading carefully, you might have anticipated the next lesson: We
can't use standard C's free() function to release memory we've allocated with
cudaMalloc(). To free memory we've allocated with cudaMalloc(), we need
to use a call to cudaFree(), which behaves exactly like free() does.

We've seen how to use the host to allocate and free memory on the device, but we've also made it painfully clear that you cannot modify this memory from the host. The remaining two lines of the sample program illustrate two of the most common methods for accessing device memory—by using device pointers from within device code and by using calls to `cudaMemcpy()`.

We use pointers from within device code exactly the same way we use them in standard C that runs on the host code. The statement `*c = a + b` is as simple as it looks. It adds the parameters `a` and `b` together and stores the result in the memory pointed to by `c`. We hope this is almost too easy to even be interesting.

We listed the ways in which we can and cannot use device pointers from within device and host code. These caveats translate exactly as one might imagine when considering host pointers. Although we are free to pass host pointers around in device code, we run into trouble when we attempt to use a host pointer to access memory from within device code. To summarize, host pointers can access memory from host code, and device pointers can access memory from device code.

As promised, we can also access memory on a device through calls to `cudaMemcpy()` from host code. These calls behave exactly like standard C `memcpy()` with an additional parameter to specify which of the source and destination pointers point to device memory. In the example, notice that the last parameter to `cudaMemcpy()` is `cudaMemcpyDeviceToHost`, instructing the runtime that the source pointer is a device pointer and the destination pointer is a host pointer.

Unsurprisingly, `cudaMemcpyHostToDevice` would indicate the opposite situation, where the source data is on the host and the destination is an address on the device. Finally, we can even specify that *both* pointers are on the device by passing `cudaMemcpyDeviceToDevice`. If the source and destination pointers are both on the host, we would simply use standard C's `memcpy()` routine to copy between them.

3.3 Querying Devices

Since we would like to be allocating memory and executing code on our device, it would be useful if our program had a way of knowing how much memory and what types of capabilities the device had. Furthermore, it is relatively common for people to have more than one CUDA-capable device per computer. In situations like this, we will definitely want a way to determine which processor is which.

For example, many motherboards ship with integrated NVIDIA graphics processors. When a manufacturer or user adds a discrete graphics processor to this computer, it then possesses two CUDA-capable processors. Some NVIDIA products, like the GeForce GTX 295, ship with two GPUs on a single card. Computers that contain products such as this will also show two CUDA-capable processors.

Before we get too deep into writing device code, we would love to have a mechanism for determining which devices (if any) are present and what capabilities each device supports. Fortunately, there is a very easy interface to determine this information. First, we will want to know how many devices in the system were built on the CUDA Architecture. These devices will be capable of executing kernels written in CUDA C. To get the count of CUDA devices, we call cudaGetDeviceCount(). Needless to say, we anticipate receiving an award for Most Creative Function Name.

```
int count;
HANDLE_ERROR( cudaGetDeviceCount( &count ) );
```

After calling cudaGetDeviceCount(), we can then iterate through the devices and query relevant information about each. The CUDA runtime returns us these properties in a structure of type cudaDeviceProp. What kind of properties can we retrieve? As of CUDA 3.0, the cudaDeviceProp structure contains the following:

```
struct cudaDeviceProp {
    char name[256];
    size_t totalGlobalMem;
    size_t sharedMemPerBlock;
    int regsPerBlock;
    int warpSize;
    size_t memPitch;
    int maxThreadsPerBlock;
    int maxThreadsDim[3];
    int maxGridSize[3];
    size_t totalConstMem;
    int major;
```

```
        int minor;
        int clockRate;
        size_t textureAlignment;
        int deviceOverlap;
        int multiProcessorCount;
        int kernelExecTimeoutEnabled;
        int integrated;
        int canMapHostMemory;
        int computeMode;
        int maxTexture1D;
        int maxTexture2D[2];
        int maxTexture3D[3];
        int maxTexture2DArray[3];
        int concurrentKernels;
    }
```

Some of these are self-explanatory; others bear some additional description (see Table 3.1).

Table 3.1 CUDA Device Properties

DEVICE PROPERTY	DESCRIPTION
char name[256];	An ASCII string identifying the device (e.g., "GeForce GTX 280")
size_t totalGlobalMem	The amount of global memory on the device in bytes
size_t sharedMemPerBlock	The maximum amount of shared memory a single block may use in bytes
int regsPerBlock	The number of 32-bit registers available per block
int warpSize	The number of threads in a warp
size_t memPitch	The maximum pitch allowed for memory copies in bytes

Continued

Table 3.1 Caption needed (Continued)

DEVICE PROPERTY	DESCRIPTION
`int maxThreadsPerBlock`	The maximum number of threads that a block may contain
`int maxThreadsDim[3]`	The maximum number of threads allowed along each dimension of a block
`int maxGridSize[3]`	The number of blocks allowed along each dimension of a grid
`size_t totalConstMem`	The amount of available constant memory
`int major`	The major revision of the device's compute capability
`int minor`	The minor revision of the device's compute capability
`size_t textureAlignment`	The device's requirement for texture alignment
`int deviceOverlap`	A boolean value representing whether the device can simultaneously perform a `cudaMemcpy()` and kernel execution
`int multiProcessorCount`	The number of multiprocessors on the device
`int kernelExecTimeoutEnabled`	A boolean value representing whether there is a runtime limit for kernels executed on this device
`int integrated`	A boolean value representing whether the device is an integrated GPU (i.e., part of the chipset and not a discrete GPU)
`int canMapHostMemory`	A boolean value representing whether the device can map host memory into the CUDA device address space
`int computeMode`	A value representing the device's computing mode: default, exclusive, or prohibited
`int maxTexture1D`	The maximum size supported for 1D textures

Table 3.1 CUDA Device Properties (Continued)

DEVICE PROPERTY	DESCRIPTION
`int maxTexture2D[2]`	The maximum dimensions supported for 2D textures
`int maxTexture3D[3]`	The maximum dimensions supported for 3D textures
`int maxTexture2DArray[3]`	The maximum dimensions supported for 2D texture arrays
`int concurrentKernels`	A boolean value representing whether the device supports executing multiple kernels within the same context simultaneously

We'd like to avoid going too far, too fast down our rabbit hole, so we will not go into extensive detail about these properties now. In fact, the previous list is missing some important details about some of these properties, so you will want to consult the *NVIDIA CUDA Programming Guide* for more information. When you move on to write your own applications, these properties will prove extremely useful. However, for now we will simply show how to query each device and report the properties of each. So far, our device query looks something like this:

```
#include "../common/book.h"

int main( void ) {
    cudaDeviceProp  prop;

    int count;
    HANDLE_ERROR( cudaGetDeviceCount( &count ) );
    for (int i=0; i< count; i++) {
        HANDLE_ERROR( cudaGetDeviceProperties( &prop, i ) );

        //Do something with our device's properties


    }
}
```

Now that we know each of the fields available to us, we can expand on the ambiguous "Do something..." section and implement something marginally less trivial:

```c
#include "../common/book.h"

int main( void ) {
    cudaDeviceProp  prop;

    int count;
    HANDLE_ERROR( cudaGetDeviceCount( &count ) );
    for (int i=0; i< count; i++) {
        HANDLE_ERROR( cudaGetDeviceProperties( &prop, i ) );
        printf( "   --- General Information for device %d ---\n", i );
        printf( "Name:  %s\n", prop.name );
        printf( "Compute capability:  %d.%d\n", prop.major, prop.minor );
        printf( "Clock rate:  %d\n", prop.clockRate );
        printf( "Device copy overlap:  " );
        if (prop.deviceOverlap)
            printf( "Enabled\n" );
        else
            printf( "Disabled\n" );
        printf( "Kernel execition timeout :  " );
        if (prop.kernelExecTimeoutEnabled)
            printf( "Enabled\n" );
        else
            printf( "Disabled\n" );

        printf( "   --- Memory Information for device %d ---\n", i );
        printf( "Total global mem:  %ld\n", prop.totalGlobalMem );
        printf( "Total constant Mem:  %ld\n", prop.totalConstMem );
        printf( "Max mem pitch:  %ld\n", prop.memPitch );
        printf( "Texture Alignment:  %ld\n", prop.textureAlignment );
```

```
        printf( "   --- MP Information for device %d ---\n", i );
        printf( "Multiprocessor count:  %d\n",
                prop.multiProcessorCount );
        printf( "Shared mem per mp:  %ld\n", prop.sharedMemPerBlock );
        printf( "Registers per mp:  %d\n", prop.regsPerBlock );
        printf( "Threads in warp:  %d\n", prop.warpSize );
        printf( "Max threads per block:  %d\n",
                prop.maxThreadsPerBlock );
        printf( "Max thread dimensions:  (%d, %d, %d)\n",
                prop.maxThreadsDim[0], prop.maxThreadsDim[1],
                prop.maxThreadsDim[2] );
        printf( "Max grid dimensions:  (%d, %d, %d)\n",
                prop.maxGridSize[0], prop.maxGridSize[1],
                prop.maxGridSize[2] );
        printf( "\n" );
    }
}
```

3.4 Using Device Properties

Other than writing an application that handily prints every detail of every CUDA-capable card, why might we be interested in the properties of each device in our system? Since we as software developers want everyone to think our software is fast, we might be interested in choosing the GPU with the most multiprocessors on which to run our code. Or if the kernel needs close interaction with the CPU, we might be interested in running our code on the integrated GPU that shares system memory with the CPU. These are both properties we can query with `cudaGetDeviceProperties()`.

Suppose that we are writing an application that depends on having double-precision floating-point support. After a quick consultation with Appendix A of the *NVIDIA CUDA Programming Guide*, we know that cards that have compute capability 1.3 or higher support double-precision floating-point math. So to successfully run the double-precision application that we've written, we need to find at least one device of compute capability 1.3 or higher.

Based on what we have seen with cudaGetDeviceCount() and cudaGetDeviceProperties(), we could iterate through each device and look for one that either has a major version greater than 1 or has a major version of 1 and minor version greater than or equal to 3. But since this relatively common procedure is also relatively annoying to perform, the CUDA runtime offers us an automated way to do this. We first fill a cudaDeviceProp structure with the properties we need our device to have.

```
cudaDeviceProp  prop;
memset( &prop, 0, sizeof( cudaDeviceProp ) );
prop.major = 1;
prop.minor = 3;
```

After filling a cudaDeviceProp structure, we pass it to cudaChooseDevice() to have the CUDA runtime find a device that satisfies this constraint. The call to cudaChooseDevice() returns a device ID that we can then pass to cudaSetDevice(). From this point forward, all device operations will take place on the device we found in cudaChooseDevice().

```
#include "../common/book.h"

int main( void ) {
    cudaDeviceProp  prop;
    int dev;

    HANDLE_ERROR( cudaGetDevice( &dev ) );
    printf( "ID of current CUDA device:  %d\n", dev );

    memset( &prop, 0, sizeof( cudaDeviceProp ) );
    prop.major = 1;
    prop.minor = 3;
    HANDLE_ERROR( cudaChooseDevice( &dev, &prop ) );
    printf( "ID of CUDA device closest to revision 1.3:  %d\n", dev );
    HANDLE_ERROR( cudaSetDevice( dev ) );
}
```

Systems with multiple GPUs are becoming more and more common. For example, many of NVIDIA's motherboard chipsets contain integrated, CUDA-capable GPUs. When a discrete GPU is added to one of these systems, you suddenly have a multi-GPU platform. Moreover, NVIDIA's SLI technology allows multiple discrete GPUs to be installed side by side. In either of these cases, your application may have a preference of one GPU over another. If your application depends on certain features of the GPU or depends on having the fastest GPU in the system, you should familiarize yourself with this API because there is no guarantee that the CUDA runtime will choose the best or most appropriate GPU for your application.

3.5 Chapter Review

We've finally gotten our hands dirty writing CUDA C, and ideally it has been less painful than you might have suspected. Fundamentally, CUDA C is standard C with some ornamentation to allow us to specify which code should run on the device and which should run on the host. By adding the keyword `__global__` before a function, we indicated to the compiler that we intend to run the function on the GPU. To use the GPU's dedicated memory, we also learned a CUDA API similar to C's `malloc()`, `memcpy()`, and `free()` APIs. The CUDA versions of these functions, `cudaMalloc()`, `cudaMemcpy()`, and `cudaFree()`, allow us to allocate device memory, copy data between the device and host, and free the device memory when we've finished with it.

As we progress through this book, we will see more interesting examples of how we can effectively use the device as a massively parallel coprocessor. For now, you should know how easy it is to get started with CUDA C, and in the next chapter we will see how easy it is to execute parallel code on the GPU.

Chapter 4

Parallel Programming in CUDA C

In the previous chapter, we saw how simple it can be to write code that executes on the GPU. We have even gone so far as to learn how to add two numbers together, albeit just the numbers 2 and 7. Admittedly, that example was not immensely impressive, nor was it incredibly interesting. But we hope you are convinced that it is easy to get started with CUDA C and you're excited to learn more. Much of the promise of GPU computing lies in exploiting the massively parallel structure of many problems. In this vein, we intend to spend this chapter examining how to execute parallel code on the GPU using CUDA C.

4.1 Chapter Objectives

Through the course of this chapter, you will accomplish the following:

- You will learn one of the fundamental ways CUDA exposes its parallelism.

- You will write your first parallel code with CUDA C.

4.2 CUDA Parallel Programming

Previously, we saw how easy it was to get a standard C function to start running on a device. By adding the __global__ qualifier to the function and by calling it using a special angle bracket syntax, we executed the function on our GPU. Although this was extremely simple, it was also extremely inefficient because NVIDIA's hardware engineering minions have optimized their graphics processors to perform hundreds of computations in parallel. However, thus far we have only ever launched a kernel that runs serially on the GPU. In this chapter, we see how straightforward it is to launch a device kernel that performs its computations in parallel.

4.2.1 SUMMING VECTORS

We will contrive a simple example to illustrate threads and how we use them to code with CUDA C. Imagine having two lists of numbers where we want to sum corresponding elements of each list and store the result in a third list. Figure 4.1 shows this process. If you have any background in linear algebra, you will recognize this operation as summing two vectors.

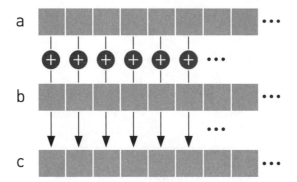

Figure 4.1 Summing two vectors

CPU VECTOR SUMS

First we'll look at one way this addition can be accomplished with traditional C code:

```
#include "../common/book.h"

#define N    10

void add( int *a, int *b, int *c ) {
    int tid = 0;    // this is CPU zero, so we start at zero
    while (tid < N) {
        c[tid] = a[tid] + b[tid];
        tid += 1;    // we have one CPU, so we increment by one
    }
}

int main( void ) {
    int a[N], b[N], c[N];

    // fill the arrays 'a' and 'b' on the CPU
    for (int i=0; i<N; i++) {
        a[i] = -i;
        b[i] = i * i;
    }

    add( a, b, c );
```

```
// display the results
for (int i=0; i<N; i++) {
    printf( "%d + %d = %d\n", a[i], b[i], c[i] );
}

return 0;
}
```

Most of this example bears almost no explanation, but we will briefly look at the add() function to explain why we overly complicated it.

```
void add( int *a, int *b, int *c ) {
    int tid = 0;    // this is CPU zero, so we start at zero
    while (tid < N) {
        c[tid] = a[tid] + b[tid];
        tid += 1;   // we have one CPU, so we increment by one
    }
}
```

We compute the sum within a while loop where the index tid ranges from 0 to N-1. We add corresponding elements of a[] and b[], placing the result in the corresponding element of c[]. One would typically code this in a slightly simpler manner, like so:

```
void add( int *a, int *b, int *c ) {
    for (i=0; i < N; i++) {
        c[i] = a[i] + b[i];
    }
}
```

Our slightly more convoluted method was intended to suggest a potential way to parallelize the code on a system with multiple CPUs or CPU cores. For example, with a dual-core processor, one could change the increment to 2 and have one core initialize the loop with tid = 0 and another with tid = 1. The first core would add the even-indexed elements, and the second core would add the odd-indexed elements. This amounts to executing the following code on each of the two CPU cores:

CPU CORE 1	CPU CORE 2
```void add(int *a, int *b, int *c) { int tid = 0; while (tid < N) { c[tid] = a[tid] + b[tid]; tid += 2; } }```	```void add(int *a, int *b, int *c) { int tid = 1; while (tid < N) { c[tid] = a[tid] + b[tid]; tid += 2; } }```

Of course, doing this on a CPU would require considerably more code than we have included in this example. You would need to provide a reasonable amount of infrastructure to create the worker threads that execute the function add() as well as make the assumption that each thread would execute in parallel, a scheduling assumption that is unfortunately not always true.

GPU VECTOR SUMS

We can accomplish the same addition very similarly on a GPU by writing add() as a device function. This should look similar to code you saw in the previous chapter. But before we look at the device code, we present main(). Although the GPU implementation of main() is different from the corresponding CPU version, nothing here should look new:

```
#include "../common/book.h"

#define N   10

int main( void ) {
    int a[N], b[N], c[N];
    int *dev_a, *dev_b, *dev_c;

    // allocate the memory on the GPU
    HANDLE_ERROR( cudaMalloc( (void**)&dev_a, N * sizeof(int) ) );
    HANDLE_ERROR( cudaMalloc( (void**)&dev_b, N * sizeof(int) ) );
    HANDLE_ERROR( cudaMalloc( (void**)&dev_c, N * sizeof(int) ) );

    // fill the arrays 'a' and 'b' on the CPU
    for (int i=0; i<N; i++) {
        a[i] = -i;
        b[i] = i * i;
    }
```

```
    // copy the arrays 'a' and 'b' to the GPU
    HANDLE_ERROR( cudaMemcpy( dev_a, a, N * sizeof(int),
                              cudaMemcpyHostToDevice ) );
    HANDLE_ERROR( cudaMemcpy( dev_b, b, N * sizeof(int),
                              cudaMemcpyHostToDevice ) );

    add<<<N,1>>>( dev_a, dev_b, dev_c );

    // copy the array 'c' back from the GPU to the CPU
    HANDLE_ERROR( cudaMemcpy( c, dev_c, N * sizeof(int),
                              cudaMemcpyDeviceToHost ) );

    // display the results
    for (int i=0; i<N; i++) {
        printf( "%d + %d = %d\n", a[i], b[i], c[i] );
    }

    // free the memory allocated on the GPU
    cudaFree( dev_a );
    cudaFree( dev_b );
    cudaFree( dev_c );

    return 0;
}
```

You will notice some common patterns that we employ again:

- We allocate three arrays on the device using calls to `cudaMalloc()`: two arrays, `dev_a` and `dev_b`, to hold inputs, and one array, `dev_c`, to hold the result.

- Because we are environmentally conscientious coders, we clean up after ourselves with `cudaFree()`.

- Using `cudaMemcpy()`, we copy the input data to the device with the parameter `cudaMemcpyHostToDevice` and copy the result data back to the host with `cudaMemcpyDeviceToHost`.

- We execute the device code in `add()` from the host code in `main()` using the triple angle bracket syntax.

As an aside, you may be wondering why we fill the input arrays on the CPU. There is no reason in particular why we *need* to do this. In fact, the performance of this step would be faster if we filled the arrays on the GPU. But we intend to show how a particular operation, namely, the addition of two vectors, can be implemented on a graphics processor. As a result, we ask you to imagine that this is but one step of a larger application where the input arrays a[] and b[] have been generated by some other algorithm or loaded from the hard drive by the user. In summary, it will suffice to pretend that this data appeared out of nowhere and now we need to do something with it.

Moving on, our add() routine looks similar to its corresponding CPU implementation:

```
__global__ void add( int *a, int *b, int *c ) {
    int tid = blockIdx.x;     // handle the data at this index
    if (tid < N)
        c[tid] = a[tid] + b[tid];
}
```

Again we see a common pattern with the function add():

- We have written a function called add() that executes on the device. We accomplished this by taking C code and adding a __global__ qualifier to the function name.

So far, there is nothing new in this example except it can do more than add 2 and 7. However, there *are* two noteworthy components of this example: The parameters within the triple angle brackets and the code contained in the kernel itself both introduce new concepts.

Up to this point, we have always seen kernels launched in the following form:

```
kernel<<<1,1>>>( param1, param2, … );
```

But in this example we are launching with a number in the angle brackets that is not 1:

```
add<<<N,1>>>( dev_a, dev_b, dev_c );
```

What gives?

Recall that we left those two numbers in the angle brackets unexplained; we stated vaguely that they were parameters to the runtime that describe how to launch the kernel. Well, the first number in those parameters represents the number of parallel blocks in which we would like the device to execute our kernel. In this case, we're passing the value N for this parameter.

For example, if we launch with `kernel<<<2,1>>>()`, you can think of the runtime creating two copies of the kernel and running them in parallel. We call each of these parallel invocations a *block*. With `kernel<<<256,1>>>()`, you would get 256 *blocks* running on the GPU. Parallel programming has never been easier.

But this raises an excellent question: The GPU runs N copies of our kernel code, but how can we tell from within the code which block is currently running? This question brings us to the second new feature of the example, the kernel code itself. Specifically, it brings us to the variable `blockIdx.x`:

```
__global__ void add( int *a, int *b, int *c ) {
    int tid = blockIdx.x;      // handle the data at this index
    if (tid < N)
        c[tid] = a[tid] + b[tid];
}
```

At first glance, it looks like this variable should cause a syntax error at compile time since we use it to assign the value of `tid`, but we have never defined it. However, there is no need to define the variable `blockIdx`; this is one of the built-in variables that the CUDA runtime defines for us. Furthermore, we use this variable for exactly what it sounds like it means. It contains the value of the block index for whichever block is currently running the device code.

Why, you may then ask, is it not just `blockIdx`? Why `blockIdx.x`? As it turns out, CUDA C allows you to define a group of blocks in two dimensions. For problems with two-dimensional domains, such as matrix math or image processing, it is often convenient to use two-dimensional indexing to avoid annoying translations from linear to rectangular indices. Don't worry if you aren't familiar with these problem types; just know that using two-dimensional indexing can sometimes be more convenient than one-dimensional indexing. But you never *have* to use it. We won't be offended.

When we launched the kernel, we specified N as the number of parallel blocks. We call the collection of parallel blocks a *grid*. This specifies to the runtime system that we want a one-dimensional *grid* of N blocks (scalar values are interpreted as one-dimensional). These threads will have varying values for blockIdx.x, the first taking value 0 and the last taking value N-1. So, imagine four blocks, all running through the same copy of the device code but having different values for the variable blockIdx.x. This is what the actual code being executed in each of the four parallel blocks looks like after the runtime substitutes the appropriate block index for blockIdx.x:

BLOCK 1

```
__global__ void
add( int *a, int *b, int *c ) {
    int tid = 0;
    if (tid < N)
        c[tid] = a[tid] + b[tid];
}
```

BLOCK 2

```
__global__ void
add( int *a, int *b, int *c ) {
    int tid = 1;
    if (tid < N)
        c[tid] = a[tid] + b[tid];
}
```

BLOCK 3

```
__global__ void
add( int *a, int *b, int *c ) {
    int tid = 2;
    if (tid < N)
        c[tid] = a[tid] + b[tid];
}
```

BLOCK 4

```
__global__ void
add( int *a, int *b, int *c ) {
    int tid = 3;
    if (tid < N)
        c[tid] = a[tid] + b[tid];
}
```

If you recall the CPU-based example with which we began, you will recall that we needed to walk through indices from 0 to N-1 in order to sum the two vectors. Since the runtime system is already launching a kernel where each block will have one of these indices, nearly all of this work has already been done for us. Because we're something of a lazy lot, this is a good thing. It affords us more time to blog, probably about how lazy we are.

The last remaining question to be answered is, why do we check whether tid is less than N? It *should* always be less than N, since we've specifically launched our kernel such that this assumption holds. But our desire to be lazy also makes us paranoid about someone breaking an assumption we've made in our code. Breaking code assumptions means broken code. This means bug reports, late nights tracking down bad behavior, and generally lots of activities that stand between us and our blog. If we didn't check that `tid` is less than `N` and subsequently fetched memory that wasn't ours, this would be bad. In fact, it could possibly kill the execution of your kernel, since GPUs have sophisticated memory management units that kill processes that seem to be violating memory rules.

If you encounter problems like the ones just mentioned, one of the `HANDLE_ ERROR()` macros that we've sprinkled so liberally throughout the code will detect and alert you to the situation. As with traditional C programming, the lesson here is that functions return error codes for a reason. Although it is always tempting to ignore these error codes, we would love to save *you* the hours of pain through which *we* have suffered by urging that you *check the results of every operation that can fail*. As is often the case, the presence of these errors will not prevent you from continuing the execution of your application, but they will most certainly cause all manner of unpredictable and unsavory side effects downstream.

At this point, you're running code in parallel on the GPU. Perhaps you had heard this was tricky or that you had to understand computer graphics to do general-purpose programming on a graphics processor. We hope you are starting to see how CUDA C makes it much easier to get started writing parallel code on a GPU. We used the example only to sum vectors of length 10. If you would like to see how easy it is to generate a massively parallel application, try changing the 10 in the line `#define N 10` to 10000 or 50000 to launch tens of thousands of parallel blocks. Be warned, though: No dimension of your launch of blocks may exceed 65,535. This is simply a hardware-imposed limit, so you will start to see failures if you attempt launches with more blocks than this. In the next chapter, we will see how to work within this limitation.

4.2.2 A FUN EXAMPLE

We don't mean to imply that adding vectors is anything less than fun, but the following example will satisfy those looking for some flashy examples of parallel CUDA C.

The following example will demonstrate code to draw slices of the Julia Set. For the uninitiated, the Julia Set is the boundary of a certain class of functions over complex numbers. Undoubtedly, this sounds even less fun than vector addition and matrix multiplication. However, for almost all values of the function's parameters, this boundary forms a fractal, one of the most interesting and beautiful curiosities of mathematics.

The calculations involved in generating such a set are quite simple. At its heart, the Julia Set evaluates a simple iterative equation for points in the complex plane. A point is *not* in the set if the process of iterating the equation diverges for that point. That is, if the sequence of values produced by iterating the equation grows toward infinity, a point is considered *outside* the set. Conversely, if the values taken by the equation remain bounded, the point *is* in the set.

Computationally, the iterative equation in question is remarkably simple, as shown in Equation 4.1.

Equation 4.1

$$Z_{n+1} = Z_n^2 + C$$

Computing an iteration of Equation 4.1 would therefore involve squaring the current value and adding a constant to get the next value of the equation.

CPU JULIA SET

We will examine a source listing now that will compute and visualize the Julia Set. Since this is a more complicated program than we have studied so far, we will split it into pieces here. Later in the chapter, you will see the entire source listing.

```
int main( void ) {
    CPUBitmap bitmap( DIM, DIM );
    unsigned char *ptr = bitmap.get_ptr();

    kernel( ptr );

    bitmap.display_and_exit();
}
```

Our main routine is remarkably simple. It creates the appropriate size bitmap image using a utility library provided. Next, it passes a pointer to the bitmap data to the kernel function.

```
void kernel( unsigned char *ptr ) {
    for (int y=0; y<DIM; y++) {
        for (int x=0; x<DIM; x++) {
            int offset = x + y * DIM;

            int juliaValue = julia( x, y );
            ptr[offset*4 + 0] = 255 * juliaValue;
            ptr[offset*4 + 1] = 0;
            ptr[offset*4 + 2] = 0;
            ptr[offset*4 + 3] = 255;
        }
    }
}
```

The computation kernel does nothing more than iterate through all points we care to render, calling `julia()` on each to determine membership in the Julia Set. The function `julia()` will return 1 if the point is in the set and 0 if it is not in the set. We set the point's color to be red if `julia()` returns 1 and black if it returns 0. These colors are arbitrary, and you should feel free to choose a color scheme that matches your personal aesthetics.

```
int julia( int x, int y ) {
    const float scale = 1.5;
    float jx = scale * (float)(DIM/2 - x)/(DIM/2);
    float jy = scale * (float)(DIM/2 - y)/(DIM/2);

    cuComplex c(-0.8, 0.156);
    cuComplex a(jx, jy);

    int i = 0;
    for (i=0; i<200; i++) {
        a = a * a + c;
        if (a.magnitude2() > 1000)
            return 0;
    }

    return 1;
}
```

This function is the meat of the example. We begin by translating our pixel coordinate to a coordinate in complex space. To center the complex plane at the image center, we shift by DIM/2. Then, to ensure that the image spans the range of -1.0 to 1.0, we scale the image coordinate by DIM/2. Thus, given an image point at (x,y), we get a point in complex space at ((DIM/2 - x)/(DIM/2), ((DIM/2 - y)/(DIM/2)).

Then, to potentially zoom in or out, we introduce a scale factor. Currently, the scale is hard-coded to be 1.5, but you should tweak this parameter to zoom in or out. If you are feeling really ambitious, you could make this a command-line parameter.

After obtaining the point in complex space, we then need to determine whether the point is in or out of the Julia Set. If you recall the previous section, we do this by computing the values of the iterative equation $Z_{n+1} = z_n^2 + C$. Since C is some arbitrary complex-valued constant, we have chosen -0.8 + 0.156i because it happens to yield an interesting picture. You should play with this constant if you want to see other versions of the Julia Set.

In the example, we compute 200 iterations of this function. After each iteration, we check whether the magnitude of the result exceeds some threshold (1,000 for our purposes). If so, the equation is diverging, and we can return 0 to indicate that the point is *not* in the set. On the other hand, if we finish all 200 iterations and the magnitude is still bounded under 1,000, we assume that the point is in the set, and we return 1 to the caller, kernel().

Since all the computations are being performed on complex numbers, we define a generic structure to store complex numbers.

```
struct cuComplex {
    float    r;
    float    i;
    cuComplex( float a, float b ) : r(a), i(b)  {}
    float magnitude2( void ) { return r * r + i * i; }
    cuComplex operator*(const cuComplex& a) {
        return cuComplex(r*a.r - i*a.i, i*a.r + r*a.i);
    }
    cuComplex operator+(const cuComplex& a) {
        return cuComplex(r+a.r, i+a.i);
    }
};
```

The class represents complex numbers with two data elements: a single-precision real component r and a single-precision imaginary component i. The class defines addition and multiplication operators that combine complex numbers as expected. (If you are completely unfamiliar with complex numbers, you can get a quick primer online.) Finally, we define a method that returns the magnitude of the complex number.

GPU JULIA SET

The device implementation is remarkably similar to the CPU version, continuing a trend you may have noticed.

```
int main( void ) {
    CPUBitmap bitmap( DIM, DIM );
    unsigned char   *dev_bitmap;

    HANDLE_ERROR( cudaMalloc( (void**)&dev_bitmap,
                              bitmap.image_size() ) );

    dim3    grid(DIM,DIM);
    kernel<<<grid,1>>>( dev_bitmap );

    HANDLE_ERROR( cudaMemcpy( bitmap.get_ptr(),
                              dev_bitmap,
                              bitmap.image_size(),
                              cudaMemcpyDeviceToHost ) );
    bitmap.display_and_exit();

    cudaFree( dev_bitmap );
}
```

This version of main() looks much more complicated than the CPU version, but the flow is actually identical. Like with the CPU version, we create a DIM x DIM bitmap image using our utility library. But because we will be doing computation on a GPU, we also declare a pointer called `dev_bitmap` to hold a copy of the data on the device. And to hold data, we need to allocate memory using `cudaMalloc()`.

We then run our `kernel()` function exactly like in the CPU version, although now it is a `__global__` function, meaning it will run on the GPU. As with the CPU example, we pass `kernel()` the pointer we allocated in the previous line to store the results. The only difference is that the memory resides on the GPU now, not on the host system.

The most significant difference is that we specify how many parallel blocks on which to execute the function `kernel()`. Because each point can be computed independently of every other point, we simply specify one copy of the function for each point we want to compute. We mentioned that for some problem domains, it helps to use two-dimensional indexing. Unsurprisingly, computing function values over a two-dimensional domain such as the complex plane is one of these problems. So, we specify a two-dimensional grid of blocks in this line:

```
dim3 grid(DIM,DIM);
```

The type `dim3` is not a standard C type, lest you feared you had forgotten some key pieces of information. Rather, the CUDA runtime header files define some convenience types to encapsulate multidimensional tuples. The type `dim3` represents a three-dimensional tuple that will be used to specify the size of our launch. But why do we use a three-dimensional value when we oh-so-clearly stated that our launch is a *two-dimensional* grid?

Frankly, we do this because a three-dimensional, `dim3` value is what the CUDA runtime expects. Although a three-dimensional launch grid is not currently supported, the CUDA runtime still expects a `dim3` variable where the last component equals 1. When we initialize it with only two values, as we do in the statement `dim3 grid(DIM,DIM)`, the CUDA runtime automatically fills the third dimension with the value 1, so everything here will work as expected. Although it's possible that NVIDIA will support a three-dimensional grid in the future, for now we'll just play nicely with the kernel launch API because when coders and APIs fight, the API always wins.

We then pass our `dim3` variable `grid` to the CUDA runtime in this line:

```
kernel<<<grid,1>>>( dev_bitmap );
```

Finally, a consequence of the results residing on the device is that after executing `kernel()`, we have to copy the results back to the host. As we learned in previous chapters, we accomplish this with a call to `cudaMemcpy()`, specifying the direction `cudaMemcpyDeviceToHost` as the last argument.

```
HANDLE_ERROR( cudaMemcpy( bitmap.get_ptr(),
                          dev_bitmap,
                          bitmap.image_size(),
                          cudaMemcpyDeviceToHost ) );
```

One of the last wrinkles in the difference of implementation comes in the implementation of `kernel()`.

```
__global__ void kernel( unsigned char *ptr ) {
    // map from threadIdx/BlockIdx to pixel position
    int x = blockIdx.x;
    int y = blockIdx.y;
    int offset = x + y * gridDim.x;

    // now calculate the value at that position
    int juliaValue = julia( x, y );
    ptr[offset*4 + 0] = 255 * juliaValue;
    ptr[offset*4 + 1] = 0;
    ptr[offset*4 + 2] = 0;
    ptr[offset*4 + 3] = 255;
}
```

First, we need `kernel()` to be declared as a `__global__` function so it runs on the device but can be called from the host. Unlike the CPU version, we no longer need nested `for()` loops to generate the pixel indices that get passed to `julia()`. As with the vector addition example, the CUDA runtime generates these indices for us in the variable `blockIdx`. This works because we declared our grid of blocks to have the same dimensions as our image, so we get one block for each pair of integers (x,y) between (0,0) and (DIM-1, DIM-1).

Next, the only additional information we need is a linear offset into our output buffer, `ptr`. This gets computed using another built-in variable, `gridDim`. This variable is a constant across all blocks and simply holds the dimensions of the grid that was launched. In this example, it will always be the value (DIM, DIM). So, multiplying the row index by the grid width and adding the column index will give us a unique index into `ptr` that ranges from 0 to (DIM*DIM-1).

```
int offset = x + y * gridDim.x;
```

Finally, we examine the actual code that determines whether a point is in or out of the Julia Set. This code should look identical to the CPU version, continuing a trend we have seen in many examples now.

```
__device__ int julia( int x, int y ) {
    const float scale = 1.5;
    float jx = scale * (float)(DIM/2 - x)/(DIM/2);
    float jy = scale * (float)(DIM/2 - y)/(DIM/2);

    cuComplex c(-0.8, 0.156);
    cuComplex a(jx, jy);

    int i = 0;
    for (i=0; i<200; i++) {
        a = a * a + c;
        if (a.magnitude2() > 1000)
            return 0;
    }

    return 1;
}
```

Again, we define a `cuComplex` structure that defines a method for storing a complex number with single-precision floating-point components. The structure also defines addition and multiplication operators as well as a function to return the magnitude of the complex value.

```
struct cuComplex {
    float   r;
    float   i;
    cuComplex( float a, float b ) : r(a), i(b)  {}
    __device__ float magnitude2( void ) {
        return r * r + i * i;
    }
    __device__ cuComplex operator*(const cuComplex& a) {
        return cuComplex(r*a.r - i*a.i, i*a.r + r*a.i);
    }
    __device__ cuComplex operator+(const cuComplex& a) {
        return cuComplex(r+a.r, i+a.i);
    }
};
```

Notice that we use the same language constructs in CUDA C that we use in our CPU version. The one difference is the qualifier __device__, which indicates that this code will run on a GPU and not on the host. Recall that because these functions are declared as __device__ functions, they will be callable only from other __device__ functions or from __global__ functions.

Since we've interrupted the code with commentary so frequently, here is the entire source listing from start to finish:

```
#include "../common/book.h"
#include "../common/cpu_bitmap.h"

#define DIM 1000
```

```
struct cuComplex {
    float    r;
    float    i;
    cuComplex( float a, float b ) : r(a), i(b)  {}
    __device__ float magnitude2( void ) {
        return r * r + i * i;
    }
    __device__ cuComplex operator*(const cuComplex& a) {
        return cuComplex(r*a.r - i*a.i, i*a.r + r*a.i);
    }
    __device__ cuComplex operator+(const cuComplex& a) {
        return cuComplex(r+a.r, i+a.i);
    }
};

__device__ int julia( int x, int y ) {
    const float scale = 1.5;
    float jx = scale * (float)(DIM/2 - x)/(DIM/2);
    float jy = scale * (float)(DIM/2 - y)/(DIM/2);

    cuComplex c(-0.8, 0.156);
    cuComplex a(jx, jy);

    int i = 0;
    for (i=0; i<200; i++) {
        a = a * a + c;
        if (a.magnitude2() > 1000)
            return 0;
    }

    return 1;
}
```

```
__global__ void kernel( unsigned char *ptr ) {
    // map from threadIdx/BlockIdx to pixel position
    int x = blockIdx.x;
    int y = blockIdx.y;
    int offset = x + y * gridDim.x;

    // now calculate the value at that position
    int juliaValue = julia( x, y );
    ptr[offset*4 + 0] = 255 * juliaValue;
    ptr[offset*4 + 1] = 0;
    ptr[offset*4 + 2] = 0;
    ptr[offset*4 + 3] = 255;
}

int main( void ) {
    CPUBitmap bitmap( DIM, DIM );
    unsigned char    *dev_bitmap;

    HANDLE_ERROR( cudaMalloc( (void**)&dev_bitmap,
                              bitmap.image_size() ) );

    dim3    grid(DIM,DIM);
    kernel<<<grid,1>>>( dev_bitmap );

    HANDLE_ERROR( cudaMemcpy( bitmap.get_ptr(), dev_bitmap,
                              bitmap.image_size(),
                              cudaMemcpyDeviceToHost ) );
    bitmap.display_and_exit();

    HANDLE_ERROR( cudaFree( dev_bitmap ) );
}
```

When you run the application, you should see an animating visualization of the Julia Set. To convince you that it has earned the title "A Fun Example," Figure 4.2 shows a screenshot taken from this application.

Figure 4.2 A screenshot from the GPU Julia Set application

4.3 Chapter Review

Congratulations, you can now write, compile, and run massively parallel code on a graphics processor! You should go brag to your friends. And if they are still under the misconception that GPU computing is exotic and difficult to master, they will be most impressed. The ease with which you accomplished it will be our secret. If they're people you trust with your secrets, suggest that they buy the book, too.

We have so far looked at how to instruct the CUDA runtime to execute multiple copies of our program in parallel on what we called *blocks*. We called the collection of blocks we launch on the GPU a *grid*. As the name might imply, a grid can be either a one- or two-dimensional collection of blocks. Each copy of the kernel can determine which block it is executing with the built-in variable `blockIdx`. Likewise, it can determine the size of the grid by using the built-in variable `gridDim`. Both of these built-in variables proved useful within our kernel to calculate the data index for which each block is responsible.

Chapter 5

Thread Cooperation

We have now written our first program using CUDA C as well as have seen how to write code that executes in parallel on a GPU. This is an excellent start! But arguably one of the most important components to parallel programming is the means by which the parallel processing elements cooperate on solving a problem. Rare are the problems where every processor can compute results and terminate execution without a passing thought as to what the other processors are doing. For even moderately sophisticated algorithms, we will need the parallel copies of our code to communicate and cooperate. So far, we have not seen any mechanisms for accomplishing this communication between sections of CUDA C code executing in parallel. Fortunately, there is a solution, one that we will begin to explore in this chapter.

5.1 Chapter Objectives

Through the course of this chapter, you will accomplish the following:

- You will learn about what CUDA C calls *threads*.

- You will learn a mechanism for different threads to communicate with each other.

- You will learn a mechanism to synchronize the parallel execution of different threads.

5.2 Splitting Parallel Blocks

In the previous chapter, we looked at how to launch parallel code on the GPU. We did this by instructing the CUDA runtime system on how many parallel copies of our kernel to launch. We call these parallel copies *blocks*.

The CUDA runtime allows these blocks to be split into *threads*. Recall that when we launched multiple parallel blocks, we changed the first argument in the angle brackets from 1 to the number of blocks we wanted to launch. For example, when we studied vector addition, we launched a block for each element in the vector of size N by calling this:

```
add<<<N,1>>>( dev_a, dev_b, dev_c );
```

Inside the angle brackets, the second parameter actually represents the number of threads per block we want the CUDA runtime to create on our behalf. To this point, we have only ever launched one thread per block. In the previous example, we launched the following:

N blocks x 1 thread/block = N parallel threads

So really, we could have launched N/2 blocks with two threads per block, N/4 blocks with four threads per block, and so on. Let's revisit our vector addition example armed with this new information about the capabilities of CUDA C.

5.2.1 VECTOR SUMS: REDUX

We endeavor to accomplish the same task as we did in the previous chapter. That is, we want to take two input vectors and store their sum in a third output vector. However, this time we will use threads instead of blocks to accomplish this.

You may be wondering, what is the advantage of using threads rather than blocks? Well, for now, there is no advantage worth discussing. But parallel threads within a block will have the ability to do things that parallel blocks cannot do. So for now, be patient and humor us while we walk through a parallel thread version of the parallel block example from the previous chapter.

GPU VECTOR SUMS USING THREADS

We will start by addressing the two changes of note when moving from parallel blocks to parallel threads. Our kernel invocation will change from one that launches N blocks of one thread apiece:

```
add<<<N,1>>>( dev_a, dev_b, dev_c );
```

to a version that launches N threads, all within one block:

```
add<<<1,N>>>( dev_a, dev_b, dev_c );
```

The only other change arises in the method by which we index our data. Previously, within our kernel we indexed the input and output data by block index.

```
int tid = blockIdx.x;
```

The punch line here should not be a surprise. Now that we have only a single block, we have to index the data by thread index.

```
int tid = threadIdx.x;
```

These are the only two changes required to move from a parallel block implementation to a parallel thread implementation. For completeness, here is the entire source listing with the changed lines in bold:

```
#include "../common/book.h"

#define N    10

__global__ void add( int *a, int *b, int *c ) {
    int tid = threadIdx.x;
    if (tid < N)
        c[tid] = a[tid] + b[tid];
}
```

```
int main( void ) {
    int a[N], b[N], c[N];
    int *dev_a, *dev_b, *dev_c;

    // allocate the memory on the GPU
    HANDLE_ERROR( cudaMalloc( (void**)&dev_a, N * sizeof(int) ) );
    HANDLE_ERROR( cudaMalloc( (void**)&dev_b, N * sizeof(int) ) );
    HANDLE_ERROR( cudaMalloc( (void**)&dev_c, N * sizeof(int) ) );

    // fill the arrays 'a' and 'b' on the CPU
    for (int i=0; i<N; i++) {
        a[i] = i;
        b[i] = i * i;
    }

    // copy the arrays 'a' and 'b' to the GPU
    HANDLE_ERROR( cudaMemcpy( dev_a,
                              a,
                              N * sizeof(int),
                              cudaMemcpyHostToDevice ) );
    HANDLE_ERROR( cudaMemcpy( dev_b,
                              b,
                              N * sizeof(int),
                              cudaMemcpyHostToDevice ) );

    add<<<1,N>>>( dev_a, dev_b, dev_c );

    // copy the array 'c' back from the GPU to the CPU
    HANDLE_ERROR( cudaMemcpy( c,
                              dev_c,
                              N * sizeof(int),
                              cudaMemcpyDeviceToHost ) );

    // display the results
    for (int i=0; i<N; i++) {
        printf( "%d + %d = %d\n", a[i], b[i], c[i] );
    }
```

```
    // free the memory allocated on the GPU
    cudaFree( dev_a );
    cudaFree( dev_b );
    cudaFree( dev_c );

    return 0;
}
```

Pretty simple stuff, right? In the next section, we'll see one of the limitations of this thread-only approach. And of course, later we'll see why we would even bother splitting blocks into other parallel components.

GPU SUMS OF A LONGER VECTOR

In the previous chapter, we noted that the hardware limits the number of blocks in a single launch to 65,535. Similarly, the hardware limits the number of threads per block with which we can launch a kernel. Specifically, this number cannot exceed the value specified by the maxThreadsPerBlock field of the device properties structure we looked at in Chapter 3. For many of the graphics processors currently available, this limit is 512 threads per block, so how would we use a thread-based approach to add two vectors of size greater than 512? We will have to use a combination of threads and blocks to accomplish this.

As before, this will require two changes: We will have to change the index computation within the kernel, and we will have to change the kernel launch itself.

Now that we have multiple blocks and threads, the indexing will start to look similar to the standard method for converting from a two-dimensional index space to a linear space.

```
    int tid = threadIdx.x + blockIdx.x * blockDim.x;
```

This assignment uses a new built-in variable, blockDim. This variable is a constant for all blocks and stores the number of threads along each dimension of the block. Since we are using a one-dimensional block, we refer only to blockDim.x. If you recall, gridDim stored a similar value, but it stored the number of blocks along each dimension of the entire grid. Moreover, gridDim is two-dimensional, whereas blockDim is actually three-dimensional. That is, the CUDA runtime allows you to launch a two-dimensional grid of blocks where each block is a three-dimensional array of threads. Yes, this is a lot of dimensions, and it is unlikely you will regularly need the five degrees of indexing freedom afforded you, but they are available if so desired.

Indexing the data in a linear array using the previous assignment actually is quite intuitive. If you disagree, it may help to think about your collection of blocks of threads spatially, similar to a two-dimensional array of pixels. We depict this arrangement in Figure 5.1.

If the threads represent columns and the blocks represent rows, we can get a unique index by taking the product of the block index with the number of threads in each block and adding the thread index within the block. This is identical to the method we used to linearize the two-dimensional image index in the Julia Set example.

```
int offset = x + y * DIM;
```

Here, `DIM` is the block dimension (measured in threads), `y` is the block index, and `x` is the thread index within the block. Hence, we arrive at the index:
`tid = threadIdx.x + blockIdx.x * blockDim.x`.

The other change is to the kernel launch itself. We still need `N` parallel threads to launch, but we want them to launch across multiple blocks so we do not hit the 512-thread limitation imposed upon us. One solution is to arbitrarily set the block size to some fixed number of threads; for this example, let's use 128 threads per block. Then we can just launch `N/128` blocks to get our total of `N` threads running.

The wrinkle here is that `N/128` is an integer division. This implies that if `N` were 127, `N/128` would be zero, and we will not actually compute anything if we launch

Block 0	Thread 0	Thread 1	Thread 2	Thread 3
Block 1	Thread 0	Thread 1	Thread 2	Thread 3
Block 2	Thread 0	Thread 1	Thread 2	Thread 3
Block 3	Thread 0	Thread 1	Thread 2	Thread 3

Figure 5.1 A two-dimensional arrangement of a collection of blocks and threads

zero threads. In fact, we will launch too few threads whenever N is not an exact multiple of 128. This is bad. We actually want this division to round up.

There is a common trick to accomplish this in integer division without calling ceil(). We actually compute (N+127)/128 instead of N/128. Either you can take our word that this will compute the smallest multiple of 128 greater than or equal to N or you can take a moment now to convince yourself of this fact.

We have chosen 128 threads per block and therefore use the following kernel launch:

```
add<<< (N+127)/128, 128 >>>( dev_a, dev_b, dev_c );
```

Because of our change to the division that ensures we launch enough threads, we will actually now launch *too many* threads when N is not an exact multiple of 128. But there is a simple remedy to this problem, and our kernel already takes care of it. We have to check whether a thread's offset is actually between 0 and N before we use it to access our input and output arrays:

```
if (tid < N)
    c[tid] = a[tid] + b[tid];
```

Thus, when our index overshoots the end of our array, as will always happen when we launch a nonmultiple of 128, we automatically refrain from performing the calculation. More important, we refrain from reading and writing memory off the end of our array.

GPU SUMS OF ARBITRARILY LONG VECTORS

We were not completely forthcoming when we first discussed launching parallel blocks on a GPU. In addition to the limitation on thread count, there is also a hardware limitation on the number of blocks (albeit much greater than the thread limitation). As we've mentioned previously, neither dimension of a grid of blocks may exceed 65,535.

So, this raises a problem with our current vector addition implementation. If we launch N/128 blocks to add our vectors, we will hit launch failures when our vectors exceed 65,535 * 128 = 8,388,480 elements. This seems like a large number, but with current memory capacities between 1GB and 4GB, the high-end graphics processors can hold orders of magnitude more data than vectors with 8 million elements.

Fortunately, the solution to this issue is extremely simple. We first make a change to our kernel.

```
__global__ void add( int *a, int *b, int *c ) {
    int tid = threadIdx.x + blockIdx.x * blockDim.x;
    while (tid < N) {
        c[tid] = a[tid] + b[tid];
        tid += blockDim.x * gridDim.x;
    }
}
```

This looks remarkably like our *original* version of vector addition! In fact, compare it to the following CPU implementation from the previous chapter:

```
void add( int *a, int *b, int *c ) {
    int tid = 0;      // this is CPU zero, so we start at zero
    while (tid < N) {
        c[tid] = a[tid] + b[tid];
        tid += 1;    // we have one CPU, so we increment by one
    }
}
```

Here we also used a `while()` loop to iterate through the data. Recall that we claimed that rather than incrementing the array index by 1, a multi-CPU or multi-core version could increment by the number of processors we wanted to use. We will now use that same principle in the GPU version.

In the GPU implementation, we consider the number of parallel threads launched to be the number of processors. Although the actual GPU may have fewer (or more) processing units than this, we think of each thread as logically executing in parallel and then allow the hardware to schedule the actual execution. Decoupling the parallelization from the actual method of hardware execution is one of burdens that CUDA C lifts off a software developer's shoulders. This should come as a relief, considering current NVIDIA hardware can ship with anywhere between 8 and 480 arithmetic units per chip!

Now that we understand the principle behind this implementation, we just need to understand how we determine the initial index value for each parallel thread and how we determine the increment. We want each parallel thread to start on a different data index, so we just need to take our thread and block indexes and linearize them as we saw in the "GPU Sums of a Longer Vector" section. Each thread will start at an index given by the following:

```
int tid = threadIdx.x + blockIdx.x * blockDim.x;
```

After each thread finishes its work at the current index, we need to increment each of them by the total number of threads running in the grid. This is simply the number of threads per block multiplied by the number of blocks in the grid, or `blockDim.x * gridDim.x`. Hence, the increment step is as follows:

```
tid += blockDim.x * gridDim.x;
```

We are almost there! The only remaining piece is to fix the launch itself. If you remember, we took this detour because the launch add<<< (N+127)/128,128>>>(dev_a, dev_b, dev_c) will fail when (N+127)/128 is greater than 65,535. To ensure we never launch too many blocks, we will just fix the number of blocks to some reasonably small value. Since we like copying and pasting so much, we will use 128 blocks, each with 128 threads.

```
add<<<128,128>>>( dev_a, dev_b, dev_c );
```

You should feel free to adjust these values however you see fit, provided that your values remain within the limits we've discussed. Later in the book, we will discuss the potential performance implications of these choices, but for now it suffices to choose 128 threads per block and 128 blocks. Now we can add vectors of arbitrary length, limited only by the amount of RAM we have on our GPU. Here is the entire source listing:

```
#include "../common/book.h"

#define N (33 * 1024)

__global__ void add( int *a, int *b, int *c ) {
    int tid = threadIdx.x + blockIdx.x * blockDim.x;
    while (tid < N) {
        c[tid] = a[tid] + b[tid];
        tid += blockDim.x * gridDim.x;
    }
}
```

```
int main( void ) {
    int a[N], b[N], c[N];
    int *dev_a, *dev_b, *dev_c;

    // allocate the memory on the GPU
    HANDLE_ERROR( cudaMalloc( (void**)&dev_a, N * sizeof(int) ) );
    HANDLE_ERROR( cudaMalloc( (void**)&dev_b, N * sizeof(int) ) );
    HANDLE_ERROR( cudaMalloc( (void**)&dev_c, N * sizeof(int) ) );

    // fill the arrays 'a' and 'b' on the CPU
    for (int i=0; i<N; i++) {
        a[i] = i;
        b[i] = i * i;
    }

    // copy the arrays 'a' and 'b' to the GPU
    HANDLE_ERROR( cudaMemcpy( dev_a,
                              a,
                              N * sizeof(int),
                              cudaMemcpyHostToDevice ) );
    HANDLE_ERROR( cudaMemcpy( dev_b,
                              b,
                              N * sizeof(int),
                              cudaMemcpyHostToDevice ) );

    add<<<128,128>>>( dev_a, dev_b, dev_c );

    // copy the array 'c' back from the GPU to the CPU
    HANDLE_ERROR( cudaMemcpy( c,
                              dev_c,
                              N * sizeof(int),
                              cudaMemcpyDeviceToHost ) );
    // verify that the GPU did the work we requested
    bool success = true;
    for (int i=0; i<N; i++) {
        if ((a[i] + b[i]) != c[i]) {
            printf( "Error:  %d + %d != %d\n", a[i], b[i], c[i] );
            success = false;
```

```
        }
    }
    if (success)    printf( "We did it!\n" );

    // free the memory allocated on the GPU
    cudaFree( dev_a );
    cudaFree( dev_b );
    cudaFree( dev_c );

    return 0;
}
```

5.2.2 GPU RIPPLE USING THREADS

As with the previous chapter, we will reward your patience with vector addition by presenting a more fun example that demonstrates some of the techniques we've been using. We will again use our GPU computing power to generate pictures procedurally. But to make things even more interesting, this time we will animate them. But don't worry, we've packaged all the unrelated animation code into helper functions so you won't have to master any graphics or animation.

```
struct DataBlock {
    unsigned char   *dev_bitmap;
    CPUAnimBitmap   *bitmap;
};

// clean up memory allocated on the GPU
void cleanup( DataBlock *d ) {
    cudaFree( d->dev_bitmap );
}

int main( void ) {
    DataBlock   data;
    CPUAnimBitmap  bitmap( DIM, DIM, &data );
    data.bitmap = &bitmap;
```

```
    HANDLE_ERROR( cudaMalloc( (void**)&data.dev_bitmap,
                              bitmap.image_size() ) );

    bitmap.anim_and_exit( (void (*)(void*,int))generate_frame,
                          (void (*)(void*))cleanup );
}
```

Most of the complexity of `main()` is hidden in the helper class
`CPUAnimBitmap`. You will notice that we again have a pattern of doing a
`cudaMalloc()`, executing device code that uses the allocated memory, and
then cleaning up with `cudaFree()`. This should be old hat to you by now.

In this example, we have slightly convoluted the means by which we accomplish
the middle step, "executing device code that uses the allocated memory." We
pass the `anim_and_exit()` method a function pointer to `generate_frame()`.
This function will be called by the class every time it wants to generate a new
frame of the animation.

```
void generate_frame( DataBlock *d, int ticks ) {
    dim3    blocks(DIM/16,DIM/16);
    dim3    threads(16,16);
    kernel<<<blocks,threads>>>( d->dev_bitmap, ticks );

    HANDLE_ERROR( cudaMemcpy( d->bitmap->get_ptr(),
                              d->dev_bitmap,
                              d->bitmap->image_size(),
                              cudaMemcpyDeviceToHost ) );
}
```

Although this function consists only of four lines, they all involve important
CUDA C concepts. First, we declare two two-dimensional variables, `blocks`
and `threads`. As our naming convention makes painfully obvious, the variable
`blocks` represents the number of parallel blocks we will launch in our grid. The
variable `threads` represents the number of threads we will launch per block.
Because we are generating an image, we use two-dimensional indexing so that
each thread will have a unique (x,y) index that we can easily put into correspon-
dence with a pixel in the output image. We have chosen to use blocks that consist

of a 16 x 16 array of threads. If the image has DIM x DIM pixels, we need to launch DIM/16 x DIM/16 blocks to get one thread per pixel. Figure 5.2 shows how this block and thread configuration would look in a (ridiculously) small, 48-pixel-wide, 32-pixel-high image.

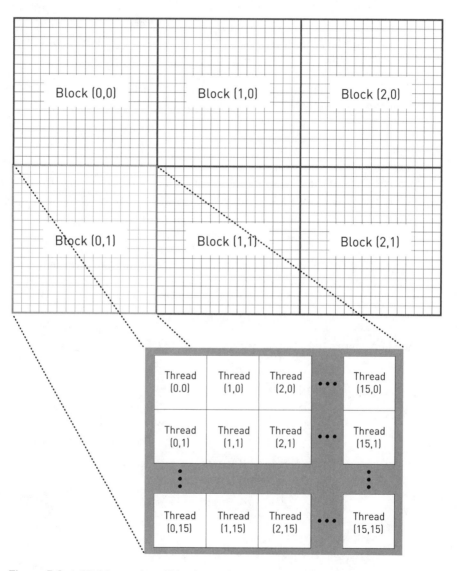

Figure 5.2 A 2D hierarchy of blocks and threads that could be used to process a 48 x 32 pixel image using one thread per pixel

If you have done any multithreaded CPU programming, you may be wondering why we would launch so many threads. For example, to render a full high-definition animation at 1920 x 1080, this method would create more than 2 million threads. Although we routinely create and schedule this many threads on a GPU, one would not dream of creating this many threads on a CPU. Because CPU thread management and scheduling must be done in software, it simply cannot scale to the number of threads that a GPU can. Because we can simply create a thread for each data element we want to process, parallel programming on a GPU can be far simpler than on a CPU.

After declaring the variables that hold the dimensions of our launch, we simply launch the kernel that will compute our pixel values.

```
kernel<<< blocks,threads>>>( d->dev _ bitmap, ticks );
```

The kernel will need two pieces of information that we pass as parameters. First, it needs a pointer to device memory that holds the output pixels. This is a global variable that had its memory allocated in main(). But the variable is "global" only for host code, so we need to pass it as a parameter to ensure that the CUDA runtime will make it available for our device code.

Second, our kernel will need to know the current animation time so it can generate the correct frame. The current time, ticks, is passed to the generate_frame() function from the infrastructure code in CPUAnimBitmap, so we can simply pass this on to our kernel.

And now, here's the kernel code itself:

```
__global__ void kernel( unsigned char *ptr, int ticks ) {
    // map from threadIdx/BlockIdx to pixel position
    int x = threadIdx.x + blockIdx.x * blockDim.x;
    int y = threadIdx.y + blockIdx.y * blockDim.y;
    int offset = x + y * blockDim.x * gridDim.x;

    // now calculate the value at that position
    float fx = x - DIM/2;
    float fy = y - DIM/2;
    float d = sqrtf( fx * fx + fy * fy );
```

```
    unsigned char grey = (unsigned char)(128.0f + 127.0f *
                                         cos(d/10.0f - ticks/7.0f) /
                                         (d/10.0f + 1.0f));
    ptr[offset*4 + 0] = grey;
    ptr[offset*4 + 1] = grey;
    ptr[offset*4 + 2] = grey;
    ptr[offset*4 + 3] = 255;
}
```

The first three are the most important lines in the kernel.

```
    int x = threadIdx.x + blockIdx.x * blockDim.x;
    int y = threadIdx.y + blockIdx.y * blockDim.y;
    int offset = x + y * blockDim.x * gridDim.x;
```

In these lines, each thread takes its index within its block as well as the index of its block within the grid, and it translates this into a unique (x, y) index within the image. So when the thread at index $(3, 5)$ in block $(12, 8)$ begins executing, it knows that there are 12 entire blocks to the left of it and 8 entire blocks above it. Within its block, the thread at $(3, 5)$ has three threads to the left and five above it. Because there are 16 threads per block, this means the thread in question has the following:

3 threads + 12 blocks * 16 threads/block = 195 threads to the left of it

5 threads + 8 blocks * 16 threads/block = 128 threads above it

This computation is identical to the computation of x and y in the first two lines and is how we map the thread and block indices to image coordinates. Then we simply linearize these x and y values to get an offset into the output buffer. Again, this is identical to what we did in the "GPU Sums of a Longer Vector" and "GPU Sums of Arbitrarily Long Vectors" sections.

```
    int offset = x + y * blockDim.x * gridDim.x;
```

Since we know which (x, y) pixel in the image the thread should compute and we know the time at which it needs to compute this value, we can compute any function of (x,y,t) and store this value in the output buffer. In this case, the function produces a time-varying sinusoidal "ripple."

```
float fx = x - DIM/2;
float fy = y - DIM/2;
float d = sqrtf( fx * fx + fy * fy );
unsigned char grey = (unsigned char)(128.0f + 127.0f *
                                     cos(d/10.0f - ticks/7.0f) /
                                     (d/10.0f + 1.0f));
```

We recommend that you not get too hung up on the computation of grey. It's essentially just a 2D function of time that makes a nice rippling effect when it's animated. A screenshot of one frame should look something like Figure 5.3.

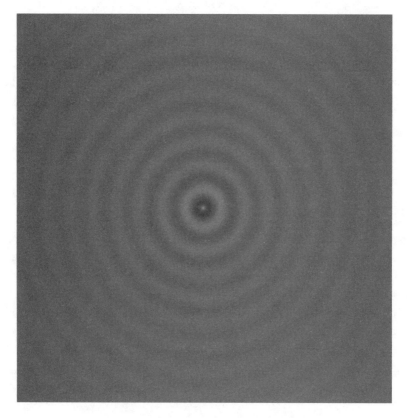

Figure 5.3 A screenshot from the GPU ripple example

5.3 Shared Memory and Synchronization

So far, the motivation for splitting blocks into threads was simply one of working around hardware limitations to the number of blocks we can have in flight. This is fairly weak motivation, because this could easily be done behind the scenes by the CUDA runtime. Fortunately, there are other reasons one might want to split a block into threads.

CUDA C makes available a region of memory that we call *shared memory*. This region of memory brings along with it another extension to the C language akin to __device__ and __global__. As a programmer, you can modify your variable declarations with the CUDA C keyword __shared__ to make this variable resident in shared memory. But what's the point?

We're glad you asked. The CUDA C compiler treats variables in shared memory differently than typical variables. It creates a copy of the variable for each block that you launch on the GPU. Every thread in that block shares the memory, but threads cannot see or modify the copy of this variable that is seen within other blocks. This provides an excellent means by which threads within a block can communicate and collaborate on computations. Furthermore, shared memory buffers reside physically on the GPU as opposed to residing in off-chip DRAM. Because of this, the latency to access shared memory tends to be far lower than typical buffers, making shared memory effective as a per-block, software-managed cache or scratchpad.

The prospect of communication between threads should excite you. It excites us, too. But nothing in life is free, and interthread communication is no exception. If we expect to communicate between threads, we also need a mechanism for synchronizing between threads. For example, if thread A writes a value to shared memory and we want thread B to do something with this value, we can't have thread B start its work until we know the write from thread A is complete. Without synchronization, we have created a race condition where the correctness of the execution results depends on the nondeterministic details of the hardware.

Let's take a look at an example that uses these features.

5.3.1 DOT PRODUCT

Congratulations! We have graduated from vector addition and will now take a look at vector dot products (sometimes called an *inner product*). We will quickly review what a dot product is, just in case you are unfamiliar with vector mathematics (or it has been a few years). The computation consists of two steps. First, we multiply corresponding elements of the two input vectors. This is very similar to vector addition but utilizes multiplication instead of addition. However, instead of then storing these values to a third, output vector, we sum them all to produce a single scalar output.

For example, if we take the dot product of two four-element vectors, we would get Equation 5.1.

Equation 5.1

$$(x_1, x_2, x_3, x_4) \cdot (y_1, y_2, y_3, y_4) = x_1 y_1 + x_2 y_2 + x_3 y_3 + x_4 y_4$$

Perhaps the algorithm we tend to use is becoming obvious. We can do the first step exactly how we did vector addition. Each thread multiplies a pair of corresponding entries, and then every thread moves on to its next pair. Because the result needs to be the sum of all these pairwise products, each thread keeps a running sum of the pairs it has added. Just like in the addition example, the threads increment their indices by the total number of threads to ensure we don't miss any elements and don't multiply a pair twice. Here is the first step of the dot product routine:

```
#include "../common/book.h"


#define imin(a,b) (a<b?a:b)


const int N = 33 * 1024;
const int threadsPerBlock = 256;


__global__ void dot( float *a, float *b, float *c ) {
    __shared__ float cache[threadsPerBlock];
    int tid = threadIdx.x + blockIdx.x * blockDim.x;
    int cacheIndex = threadIdx.x;
```

```
float   temp = 0;
while (tid < N) {
    temp += a[tid] * b[tid];
    tid += blockDim.x * gridDim.x;
}


// set the cache values
cache[cacheIndex] = temp;
```

As you can see, we have declared a buffer of shared memory named cache. This buffer will be used to store each thread's running sum. Soon we will see *why* we do this, but for now we will simply examine the mechanics by which we accomplish it. It is trivial to declare a variable to reside in shared memory, and it is identical to the means by which you declare a variable as static or volatile in standard C:

```
__shared__ float cache[threadsPerBlock];
```

We declare the array of size threadsPerBlock so each thread in the block has a place to store its temporary result. Recall that when we have allocated memory globally, we allocated enough for every thread that runs the kernel, or threadsPerBlock times the total number of blocks. But since the compiler will create a copy of the shared variables for each block, we need to allocate only enough memory such that each thread in the block has an entry.

After allocating the shared memory, we compute our data indices much like we have in the past:

```
int tid = threadIdx.x + blockIdx.x * blockDim.x;
int cacheIndex = threadIdx.x;
```

The computation for the variable tid should look familiar by now; we are just combining the block and thread indices to get a global offset into our input arrays. The offset into our shared memory cache is simply our thread index. Again, we don't need to incorporate our block index into this offset because each block has its own private copy of this shared memory.

Finally, we clear our shared memory buffer so that later we will be able to blindly sum the entire array without worrying whether a particular entry has valid data stored there:

```
// set the cache values
cache[cacheIndex] = temp;
```

It will be possible that not every entry will be used if the size of the input vectors is not a multiple of the number of threads per block. In this case, the last block will have some threads that do nothing and therefore do not write values.

Each thread computes a running sum of the product of corresponding entries in a and b. After reaching the end of the array, each thread stores its temporary sum into the shared buffer.

```
float   temp = 0;
while (tid < N) {
    temp += a[tid] * b[tid];
    tid += blockDim.x * gridDim.x;
}

// set the cache values
cache[cacheIndex] = temp;
```

At this point in the algorithm, we need to sum all the temporary values we've placed in the cache. To do this, we will need some of the threads to read the values that have been stored there. However, as we mentioned, this is a potentially dangerous operation. We need a method to guarantee that all of these writes to the shared array cache[] complete before anyone tries to read from this buffer. Fortunately, such a method exists:

```
// synchronize threads in this block
__syncthreads();
```

This call guarantees that every thread in the block has completed instructions prior to the __syncthreads() before the hardware will execute the next instruction on any thread. This is exactly what we need! We now know that when the first thread executes the first instruction after our `__syncthreads()`, every other thread in the block has also finished executing up to the `__syncthreads()`.

Now that we have guaranteed that our temporary cache has been filled, we can sum the values in it. We call the general process of taking an input array and performing some computations that produce a smaller array of results a *reduction*. Reductions arise often in parallel computing, which leads to the desire to give them a name.

The naïve way to accomplish this reduction would be having one thread iterate over the shared memory and calculate a running sum. This will take us time proportional to the length of the array. However, since we have hundreds of threads available to do our work, we can do this reduction in parallel and take time that is proportional to the logarithm of the length of the array. At first, the following code will look convoluted; we'll break it down in a moment.

The general idea is that each thread will add two of the values in `cache[]` and store the result back to `cache[]`. Since each thread combines two entries into one, we complete this step with half as many entries as we started with. In the next step, we do the same thing on the remaining half. We continue in this fashion for `log2(threadsPerBlock)` steps until we have the sum of every entry in `cache[]`. For our example, we're using 256 threads per block, so it takes 8 iterations of this process to reduce the 256 entries in `cache[]` to a single sum.

The code for this follows:

```
// for reductions, threadsPerBlock must be a power of 2
// because of the following code
int i = blockDim.x/2;
while (i != 0) {
    if (cacheIndex < i)
        cache[cacheIndex] += cache[cacheIndex + i];
    __syncthreads();
    i /= 2;
}
```

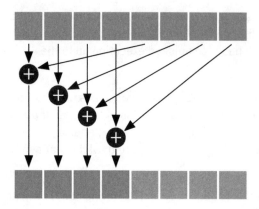

Figure 5.4 One step of a summation reduction

For the first step, we start with `i` as half the number of `threadsPerBlock`. We only want the threads with indices less than this value to do any work, so we conditionally add two entries of `cache[]` if the thread's index is less than `i`. We protect our addition within an `if(cacheIndex < i)` block. Each thread will take the entry at its index in `cache[]`, add it to the entry at its index offset by `i`, and store this sum back to `cache[]`.

Suppose there were eight entries in `cache[]` and, as a result, `i` had the value 4. One step of the reduction would look like Figure 5.4.

After we have completed a step, we have the same restriction we did after computing all the pairwise products. Before we can read the values we just stored in `cache[]`, we need to ensure that every thread that needs to write to `cache[]` has already done so. The `__syncthreads()` after the assignment ensures this condition is met.

After termination of this `while()` loop, each block has but a single number remaining. This number is sitting in the first entry of `cache[]` and is the sum of every pairwise product the threads in that block computed. We then store this single value to global memory and end our kernel:

```
    if (cacheIndex == 0)
        c[blockIdx.x] = cache[0];
}
```

Why do we do this global store only for the thread with `cacheIndex == 0`? Well, since there is only one number that needs writing to global memory, only a single thread needs to perform this operation. Conceivably, every thread could perform this write and the program would still work, but doing so would create an unnecessarily large amount of memory traffic to write a single value. For simplicity, we chose the thread with index 0, though you could conceivably have chosen any `cacheIndex` to write `cache[0]` to global memory. Finally, since each block will write exactly one value to the global array `c[]`, we can simply index it by `blockIdx`.

We are left with an array `c[]`, each entry of which contains the sum produced by one of the parallel blocks. The last step of the dot product is to sum the entries of `c[]`. Even though the dot product is not fully computed, we exit the kernel and return control to the host at this point. But why do we return to the host before the computation is complete?

Previously, we referred to an operation like a dot product as a *reduction*. Roughly speaking, this is because we produce fewer output data elements than we input. In the case of a dot product, we always produce exactly one output, regardless of the size of our input. It turns out that a massively parallel machine like a GPU tends to waste its resources when performing the last steps of a reduction, since the size of the data set is so small at that point; it is hard to utilize 480 arithmetic units to add 32 numbers!

For this reason, we return control to the host and let the CPU finish the final step of the addition, summing the array `c[]`. In a larger application, the GPU would now be free to start another dot product or work on another large computation. However, in this example, we are done with the GPU.

In explaining this example, we broke with tradition and jumped right into the actual kernel computation. We hope you will have no trouble understanding the body of `main()` up to the kernel call, since it is overwhelmingly similar to what we have shown before.

```
const int blocksPerGrid =
            imin( 32, (N+threadsPerBlock-1) / threadsPerBlock );

int main( void ) {
    float    *a, *b, c, *partial_c;
    float    *dev_a, *dev_b, *dev_partial_c;
```

```
// allocate memory on the CPU side
a = new float[N];
b = new float[N];
partial_c = new float[blocksPerGrid];

// allocate the memory on the GPU
HANDLE_ERROR( cudaMalloc( (void**)&dev_a,
                          N*sizeof(float) ) );
HANDLE_ERROR( cudaMalloc( (void**)&dev_b,
                          N*sizeof(float) ) );
HANDLE_ERROR( cudaMalloc( (void**)&dev_partial_c,
                          blocksPerGrid*sizeof(float) ) );

// fill in the host memory with data
for (int i=0; i<N; i++) {
    a[i] = i;
    b[i] = i*2;
}

// copy the arrays 'a' and 'b' to the GPU
HANDLE_ERROR( cudaMemcpy( dev_a, a, N*sizeof(float),
                          cudaMemcpyHostToDevice ) );
HANDLE_ERROR( cudaMemcpy( dev_b, b, N*sizeof(float),
                          cudaMemcpyHostToDevice ) );

dot<<<blocksPerGrid,threadsPerBlock>>>( dev_a,
                                        dev_b,
                                        dev_partial_c );
```

To avoid you passing out from boredom, we will quickly summarize this code:

1. Allocate host and device memory for input and output arrays.

2. Fill input arrays a[] and b[], and then copy these to the device using cudaMemcpy().

3. Call our dot product kernel using some predetermined number of threads per block and blocks per grid.

Despite most of this being commonplace to you now, it is worth examining the computation for the number of blocks we launch. We discussed how the dot product is a reduction and how each block launched will compute a partial sum. The length of this list of partial sums should be something manageably small for the CPU yet large enough such that we have enough blocks in flight to keep even the fastest GPUs busy. We have chosen 32 blocks, although this is a case where you may notice better or worse performance for other choices, especially depending on the relative speeds of your CPU and GPU.

But what if we are given a very short list and 32 blocks of 256 threads apiece is too many? If we have N data elements, we need only N threads in order to compute our dot product. So in this case, we need the smallest multiple of threadsPerBlock that is greater than or equal to N. We have seen this once before when we were adding vectors. In this case, we get the smallest multiple of threadsPerBlock that is greater than or equal to N by computing (N+(threadsPerBlock-1)) / threadsPerBlock. As you may be able to tell, this is actually a fairly common trick in integer math, so it is worth digesting this even if you spend most of your time working outside the CUDA C realm.

Therefore, the number of blocks we launch should be either 32 or (N+(threadsPerBlock-1)) / threadsPerBlock, whichever value is smaller.

```
const int blocksPerGrid =
            imin( 32, (N+threadsPerBlock-1) / threadsPerBlock );
```

Now it should be clear how we arrive at the code in main(). After the kernel finishes, we still have to sum the result. But like the way we copy our input to the GPU before we launch a kernel, we need to copy our output back to the CPU before we continue working with it. So after the kernel finishes, we copy back the list of partial sums and complete the sum on the CPU.

```
// copy the array 'c' back from the GPU to the CPU
HANDLE_ERROR( cudaMemcpy( partial_c, dev_partial_c,
                          blocksPerGrid*sizeof(float),
                          cudaMemcpyDeviceToHost ) );
```

```
// finish up on the CPU side
c = 0;
for (int i=0; i<blocksPerGrid; i++) {
    c += partial_c[i];
}
```

Finally, we check our results and clean up the memory we've allocated on both the CPU and GPU. Checking the results is made easier because we've filled the inputs with predictable data. If you recall, a [] is filled with the integers from 0 to N-1 and b [] is just 2*a [] .

```
// fill in the host memory with data
for (int i=0; i<N; i++) {
    a[i] = i;
    b[i] = i*2;
}
```

Our dot product should be two times the sum of the squares of the integers from 0 to N-1. For the reader who loves discrete mathematics (and what's not to love?!), it will be an amusing diversion to derive the closed-form solution for this summation. For those with less patience or interest, we present the closed-form here, as well as the rest of the body of main () :

```
#define sum_squares(x)   (x*(x+1)*(2*x+1)/6)
printf( "Does GPU value %.6g = %.6g?\n", c,
        2 * sum_squares( (float)(N - 1) ) );

// free memory on the GPU side
cudaFree( dev_a );
cudaFree( dev_b );
cudaFree( dev_partial_c );

// free memory on the CPU side
delete [] a;
delete [] b;
delete [] partial_c;
}
```

If you found all our explanatory interruptions bothersome, here is the entire source listing, sans commentary:

```c
#include "../common/book.h"

#define imin(a,b) (a<b?a:b)

const int N = 33 * 1024;
const int threadsPerBlock = 256;
const int blocksPerGrid =
            imin( 32, (N+threadsPerBlock-1) / threadsPerBlock );

__global__ void dot( float *a, float *b, float *c ) {
    __shared__ float cache[threadsPerBlock];
    int tid = threadIdx.x + blockIdx.x * blockDim.x;
    int cacheIndex = threadIdx.x;

    float   temp = 0;
    while (tid < N) {
        temp += a[tid] * b[tid];
        tid += blockDim.x * gridDim.x;
    }

    // set the cache values
    cache[cacheIndex] = temp;

    // synchronize threads in this block
    __syncthreads();

    // for reductions, threadsPerBlock must be a power of 2
    // because of the following code
    int i = blockDim.x/2;
    while (i != 0) {
        if (cacheIndex < i)
            cache[cacheIndex] += cache[cacheIndex + i];
        __syncthreads();
        i /= 2;
    }
```

```
    if (cacheIndex == 0)
        c[blockIdx.x] = cache[0];
}


int main( void ) {
    float   *a, *b, c, *partial_c;
    float   *dev_a, *dev_b, *dev_partial_c;

    // allocate memory on the CPU side
    a = (float*)malloc( N*sizeof(float) );
    b = (float*)malloc( N*sizeof(float) );
    partial_c = (float*)malloc( blocksPerGrid*sizeof(float) );

    // allocate the memory on the GPU
    HANDLE_ERROR( cudaMalloc( (void**)&dev_a,
                              N*sizeof(float) ) );
    HANDLE_ERROR( cudaMalloc( (void**)&dev_b,
                              N*sizeof(float) ) );
    HANDLE_ERROR( cudaMalloc( (void**)&dev_partial_c,
                              blocksPerGrid*sizeof(float) ) );

    // fill in the host memory with data
    for (int i=0; i<N; i++) {
        a[i] = i;
        b[i] = i*2;
    }

    // copy the arrays 'a' and 'b' to the GPU
    HANDLE_ERROR( cudaMemcpy( dev_a, a, N*sizeof(float),
                              cudaMemcpyHostToDevice ) );
    HANDLE_ERROR( cudaMemcpy( dev_b, b, N*sizeof(float),
                              cudaMemcpyHostToDevice ) );
```

```
    dot<<<blocksPerGrid,threadsPerBlock>>>( dev_a, dev_b,
                                        dev_partial_c );

    // copy the array 'c' back from the GPU to the CPU
    HANDLE_ERROR( cudaMemcpy( partial_c, dev_partial_c,
                        blocksPerGrid*sizeof(float),
                        cudaMemcpyDeviceToHost ) );

    // finish up on the CPU side
    c = 0;
    for (int i=0; i<blocksPerGrid; i++) {
        c += partial_c[i];
    }

    #define sum_squares(x)   (x*(x+1)*(2*x+1)/6)
    printf( "Does GPU value %.6g = %.6g?\n", c,
            2 * sum_squares( (float)(N - 1) ) );

    // free memory on the GPU side
    cudaFree( dev_a );
    cudaFree( dev_b );
    cudaFree( dev_partial_c );

    // free memory on the CPU side
    free( a );
    free( b );
    free( partial_c );
}
```

5.3.1 DOT PRODUCT OPTIMIZED (INCORRECTLY)

We quickly glossed over the second __syncthreads() in the dot product example. Now we will take a closer look at it as well as examining an attempt to improve it. If you recall, we needed the second __syncthreads() because we update our shared memory variable `cache[]` and need these updates to be visible to every thread on the next iteration through the loop.

```
int i = blockDim.x/2;
while (i != 0) {
    if (cacheIndex < i)
        cache[cacheIndex] += cache[cacheIndex + i];
    __syncthreads();
    i /= 2;
}
```

Observe that we update our shared memory buffer `cache[]` only if `cacheIndex` is less than `i`. Since `cacheIndex` is really just `threadIdx.x`, this means that only *some* of the threads are updating entries in the shared memory cache. Since we are using `__syncthreads` only to ensure that these updates have taken place before proceeding, it stands to reason that we might see a speed improvement only if we wait for the threads that are actually writing to shared memory. We do this by moving the synchronization call inside the `if()` block:

```
int i = blockDim.x/2;
while (i != 0) {
    if (cacheIndex < i) {
        cache[cacheIndex] += cache[cacheIndex + i];
        __syncthreads();
    }
    i /= 2;
}
```

Although this was a valiant effort at optimization, it will not actually work. In fact, the situation is worse than that. This change to the kernel will actually cause the GPU to stop responding, forcing you to kill your program. But what could have gone so catastrophically wrong with such a seemingly innocuous change?

To answer this question, it helps to imagine every thread in the block marching through the code one line at a time. At each instruction in the program, every thread executes the same instruction, but each can operate on different data. But what happens when the instruction that every thread is supposed to execute is inside a conditional block like an `if()`? Obviously not every thread should execute that instruction, right? For example, consider a kernel that contains the following fragment of code that intends for odd-indexed threads to update the value of some variable:

```
int myVar = 0;
if( threadIdx.x % 2 )
    myVar = threadIdx.x;
```

In the previous example, when the threads arrive at the line in bold, only the threads with odd indices will execute it since the threads with even indices do not satisfy the condition `if( threadIdx.x % 2 )`. The even-numbered threads simply do nothing while the odd threads execute this instruction. When some of the threads need to execute an instruction while others don't, this situation is known as *thread divergence*. Under normal circumstances, divergent branches simply result in some threads remaining idle, while the other threads actually execute the instructions in the branch.

But in the case of `__syncthreads()`, the result is somewhat tragic. The CUDA Architecture guarantees that *no thread* will advance to an instruction beyond the `__syncthreads()` until *every* thread in the block has executed the `__syncthreads()`. Unfortunately, if the `__syncthreads()` sits in a divergent branch, some of the threads will *never* reach the `__syncthreads()`. Therefore, because of the guarantee that no instruction after a `__syncthreads()` can be executed before every thread has executed it, the hardware simply continues to wait for these threads. And waits. And waits. Forever.

This is the situation in the dot product example when we move the `__syncthreads()` call inside the `if()` block. Any thread with `cacheIndex` greater than or equal to `i` will *never* execute the `__syncthreads()`. This effectively hangs the processor because it results in the GPU waiting for something that will never happen.

```
if (cacheIndex < i) {
    cache[cacheIndex] += cache[cacheIndex + i];
    __syncthreads();
}
```

The moral of this story is that __syncthreads() is a powerful mechanism for ensuring that your massively parallel application still computes the correct results. But because of this potential for unintended consequences, we still need to take care when using it.

5.3.2 SHARED MEMORY BITMAP

We have looked at examples that use shared memory and employed __syncthreads() to ensure that data is ready before we continue. In the name of speed, you may be tempted to live dangerously and omit the __syncthreads(). We will now look at a graphical example that requires __syncthreads() for correctness. We will show you screenshots of the intended output and of the output when run without __syncthreads(). It won't be pretty.

The body of main() is identical to the GPU Julia Set example, although this time we launch multiple threads per block:

```
#include "cuda.h"
#include "../common/book.h"
#include "../common/cpu_bitmap.h"

#define DIM 1024
#define PI 3.1415926535897932f

int main( void ) {
    CPUBitmap bitmap( DIM, DIM );
    unsigned char    *dev_bitmap;

    HANDLE_ERROR( cudaMalloc( (void**)&dev_bitmap,
                              bitmap.image_size() ) );

    dim3    grids(DIM/16,DIM/16);
    dim3    threads(16,16);
    kernel<<<grids,threads>>>( dev_bitmap );
```

```
HANDLE_ERROR( cudaMemcpy( bitmap.get_ptr(), dev_bitmap,
                          bitmap.image_size(),
                          cudaMemcpyDeviceToHost ) );
bitmap.display_and_exit();

cudaFree( dev_bitmap );
}
```

As with the Julia Set example, each thread will be computing a pixel value for a single output location. The first thing that each thread does is compute its x and y location in the output image. This computation is identical to the tid computation in the vector addition example, although we compute it in two dimensions this time:

```
__global__ void kernel( unsigned char *ptr ) {
    // map from threadIdx/blockIdx to pixel position
    int x = threadIdx.x + blockIdx.x * blockDim.x;
    int y = threadIdx.y + blockIdx.y * blockDim.y;
    int offset = x + y * blockDim.x * gridDim.x;
```

Since we will be using a shared memory buffer to cache our computations, we declare one such that each thread in our 16 x 16 block has an entry.

```
__shared__ float    shared[16][16];
```

Then, each thread computes a value to be stored into this buffer.

```
    // now calculate the value at that position
    const float period = 128.0f;

    shared[threadIdx.x][threadIdx.y] =
            255 * (sinf(x*2.0f*PI/ period) + 1.0f) *
                (sinf(y*2.0f*PI/ period) + 1.0f) / 4.0f;
```

And lastly, we store these values back out to the pixel, reversing the order of x and y:

```
    ptr[offset*4 + 0] = 0;
    ptr[offset*4 + 1] = shared[15-threadIdx.x][15-threadIdx.y];
    ptr[offset*4 + 2] = 0;
    ptr[offset*4 + 3] = 255;
}
```

Granted, these computations are somewhat arbitrary. We've simply come up with something that will draw a grid of green spherical blobs. So after compiling and running this kernel, we output an image like the one in Figure 5.5.

What happened here? As you may have guessed from the way we set up this example, we're missing an important synchronization point. When a thread stores the computed value in shared[][] to the pixel, it is possible that the thread responsible for writing that value to shared[][] has not finished writing it yet. The only way to guarantee that this does not happen is by using __syncthreads(). Thus, the result is a corrupted picture of green blobs.

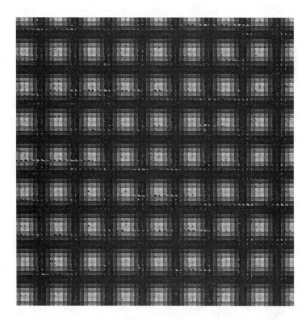

Figure 5.5 A screenshot rendered without proper synchronization

Although this may not be the end of the world, your application might be computing more important values.

Instead, we need to add a synchronization point between the write to shared memory and the subsequent read from it.

```
        shared[threadIdx.x][threadIdx.y] =
               255 * (sinf(x*2.0f*PI/ period) + 1.0f) *
                     (sinf(y*2.0f*PI/ period) + 1.0f) / 4.0f;


        __syncthreads();


        ptr[offset*4 + 0] = 0;
        ptr[offset*4 + 1] = shared[15-threadIdx.x][15-threadIdx.y];
        ptr[offset*4 + 2] = 0;
        ptr[offset*4 + 3] = 255;

    }
```

With this __syncthreads() in place, we then get a far more predictable (and aesthetically pleasing) result, as shown in Figure 5.6.

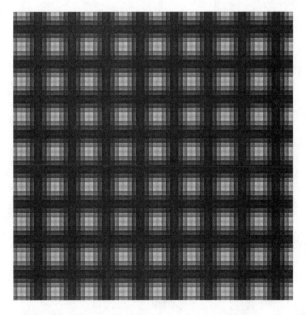

Figure 5.6 A screenshot after adding the correct synchronization

5.4 Chapter Review

We know how blocks can be subdivided into smaller parallel execution units known as *threads*. We revisited the vector addition example of the previous chapter to see how to perform addition of arbitrarily long vectors. We also showed an example of *reduction* and how we use shared memory and synchronization to accomplish this. In fact, this example showed how the GPU and CPU can collaborate on computing results. Finally, we showed how perilous it can be to an application when we neglect the need for synchronization.

You have learned most of the basics of CUDA C as well as some of the ways it resembles standard C and a lot of the important ways it differs from standard C. This would be an excellent time to consider some of the problems you have encountered and which ones might lend themselves to parallel implementations with CUDA C. As we progress, we will look at some of the other features we can use to accomplish tasks on the GPU, as well as some of the more advanced API features that CUDA provides to us.

Chapter 6

Constant Memory and Events

We hope you have learned much about writing code that executes on the GPU. You should know how to spawn parallel blocks to execute your kernels, and you should know how to further split these blocks into parallel threads. You have also seen ways to enable communication and synchronization between these threads. But since the book is not over yet, you may have guessed that CUDA C has even more features that might be useful to you.

This chapter will introduce you to a couple of these more advanced features. Specifically, there exist ways in which you can exploit special regions of memory on your GPU in order to accelerate your applications. In this chapter, we will discuss one of these regions of memory: *constant memory*. In addition, because we are looking at our first method for enhancing the performance of your CUDA C applications, you will also learn how to measure the performance of your applications using CUDA *events*. From these measurements, you will be able to quantify the gain (or loss!) from any enhancements you make.

6.1 Chapter Objectives

Through the course of this chapter, you will accomplish the following:

- You will learn about using constant memory with CUDA C.

- You will learn about the performance characteristics of constant memory.

- You will learn how to use CUDA events to measure application performance.

6.2 Constant Memory

Previously, we discussed how modern GPUs are equipped with enormous amounts of arithmetic processing power. In fact, the computational advantage graphics processors have over CPUs helped precipitate the initial interest in using graphics processors for general-purpose computing. With hundreds of arithmetic units on the GPU, often the bottleneck is not the arithmetic throughput of the chip but rather the memory bandwidth of the chip. There are so many ALUs on graphics processors that sometimes we just can't keep the input coming to them fast enough to sustain such high rates of computation. So, it is worth investigating means by which we can reduce the amount of memory traffic required for a given problem.

We have seen CUDA C programs that have used both global and shared memory so far. However, the language makes available another kind of memory known as *constant memory*. As the name may indicate, we use constant memory for data that will not change over the course of a kernel execution. NVIDIA hardware provides 64KB of constant memory that it treats differently than it treats standard global memory. In some situations, using constant memory rather than global memory will reduce the required memory bandwidth.

6.2.1 RAY TRACING INTRODUCTION

We will look at one way of exploiting constant memory in the context of a simple *ray tracing* application. First, we will give you some background in the major concepts behind ray tracing. If you are already comfortable with the concepts behind ray tracing, you can skip to the "Ray Tracing on the GPU" section.

Simply put, ray tracing is one way of producing a two-dimensional image of a scene consisting of three-dimensional objects. But isn't this what GPUs were originally designed for? How is this different from what OpenGL or DirectX do when you play your favorite game? Well, GPUs do indeed solve this same problem, but they use a technique known as *rasterization*. There are many excellent books on rasterization, so we will not endeavor to explain the differences here. It suffices to say that they are completely different methods that solve the same problem.

So, how does ray tracing produce an image of a three-dimensional scene? The idea is simple: We choose a spot in our scene to place an imaginary camera. This simplified digital camera contains a light sensor, so to produce an image, we need to determine what light would hit that sensor. Each pixel of the resulting image should be the same color and intensity of the ray of light that hits that spot sensor.

Since light incident at any point on the sensor can come from any place in our scene, it turns out it's easier to work backward. That is, rather than trying to figure out what light ray hits the pixel in question, what if we imagine shooting a ray *from* the pixel and into the scene? In this way, each pixel behaves something like an eye that is "looking" into the scene. Figure 6.1 illustrates these rays being cast out of each pixel and into the scene.

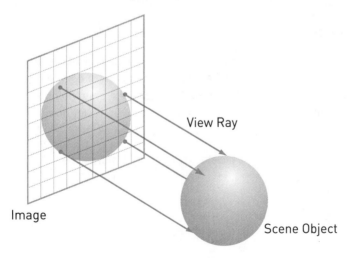

Figure 6.1 A simple ray tracing scheme

We figure out what color is seen by each pixel by tracing a ray from the pixel in question through the scene until it hits one of our objects. We then say that the pixel would "see" this object and can assign its color based on the color of the object it sees. Most of the computation required by ray tracing is in the computation of these intersections of the ray with the objects in the scene.

Moreover, in more complex ray tracing models, shiny objects in the scene can reflect rays, and translucent objects can refract the rays of light. This creates secondary rays, tertiary rays, and so on. In fact, this is one of the attractive features of ray tracing; it is very simple to get a basic ray tracer working, but we can build models of more complex phenomenon into the ray tracer in order to produce more realistic images.

6.2.2 RAY TRACING ON THE GPU

Since APIs such as OpenGL and DirectX are not designed to allow ray-traced rendering, we will have to use CUDA C to implement our basic ray tracer. Our ray tracer will be extraordinarily simple so that we can concentrate on the use of constant memory, so if you were expecting code that could form the basis of a full-blown production renderer, you will be disappointed. Our basic ray tracer will only support scenes of spheres, and the camera is restricted to the z-axis, facing the origin. Moreover, we will not support any lighting of the scene to avoid the complications of secondary rays. Instead of computing lighting effects, we will simply assign each sphere a color and then shade them with some precomputed function if they are visible.

So, what *will* the ray tracer do? It will fire a ray from each pixel and keep track of which rays hit which spheres. It will also track the depth of each of these hits. In the case where a ray passes through multiple spheres, only the sphere closest to the camera can be seen. In essence, our "ray tracer" is not doing much more than hiding surfaces that cannot be seen by the camera.

We will model our spheres with a data structure that stores the sphere's center coordinate of (x, y, z), its radius, and its color of (r, b, g).

```
#define INF     2e10f

struct Sphere {
    float   r,b,g;
    float   radius;
    float   x,y,z;
    __device__ float hit( float ox, float oy, float *n ) {
        float dx = ox - x;
        float dy = oy - y;
        if (dx*dx + dy*dy < radius*radius) {
            float dz = sqrtf( radius*radius - dx*dx - dy*dy );
            *n = dz / sqrtf( radius * radius );
            return dz + z;
        }
        return -INF;
    }
};
```

You will also notice that the structure has a method called `hit( float ox, float oy, float *n )`. Given a ray shot from the pixel at (`ox, oy`), this method computes whether the ray intersects the sphere. If the ray *does* intersect the sphere, the method computes the distance from the camera where the ray hits the sphere. We need this information for the reason mentioned before: In the event that the ray hits more than one sphere, only the closest sphere can actually be seen.

Our `main()` routine follows roughly the same sequence as our previous image-generating examples.

```
#include "cuda.h"
#include "../common/book.h"
#include "../common/cpu_bitmap.h"


#define rnd( x ) (x * rand() / RAND_MAX)
#define SPHERES 20


Sphere  *s;
```

```
int main( void ) {
    // capture the start time
    cudaEvent_t     start, stop;
    HANDLE_ERROR( cudaEventCreate( &start ) );
    HANDLE_ERROR( cudaEventCreate( &stop ) );
    HANDLE_ERROR( cudaEventRecord( start, 0 ) );

    CPUBitmap bitmap( DIM, DIM );
    unsigned char   *dev_bitmap;

    // allocate memory on the GPU for the output bitmap
    HANDLE_ERROR( cudaMalloc( (void**)&dev_bitmap,
                              bitmap.image_size() ) );
    // allocate memory for the Sphere dataset
    HANDLE_ERROR( cudaMalloc( (void**)&s,
                              sizeof(Sphere) * SPHERES ) );
```

We allocate memory for our input data, which is an array of spheres that compose our scene. Since we need this data on the GPU but are generating it with the CPU, we have to do both a cudaMalloc() *and* a malloc() to allocate memory on both the GPU and the CPU. We also allocate a bitmap image that we will fill with output pixel data as we ray trace our spheres on the GPU.

After allocating memory for input and output, we randomly generate the center coordinate, color, and radius for our spheres:

```
    // allocate temp memory, initialize it, copy to
    // memory on the GPU, and then free our temp memory
    Sphere *temp_s = (Sphere*)malloc( sizeof(Sphere) * SPHERES );
    for (int i=0; i<SPHERES; i++) {
        temp_s[i].r = rnd( 1.0f );
        temp_s[i].g = rnd( 1.0f );
        temp_s[i].b = rnd( 1.0f );
        temp_s[i].x = rnd( 1000.0f ) - 500;
        temp_s[i].y = rnd( 1000.0f ) - 500;
        temp_s[i].z = rnd( 1000.0f ) - 500;
        temp_s[i].radius = rnd( 100.0f ) + 20;
    }
```

The program currently generates a random array of 20 spheres, but this quantity is specified in a #define and can be adjusted accordingly.

We copy this array of spheres to the GPU using cudaMemcpy() and then free the temporary buffer.

```
HANDLE_ERROR( cudaMemcpy( s, temp_s,
                                 sizeof(Sphere) * SPHERES,
                                 cudaMemcpyHostToDevice ) );
free( temp_s );
```

Now that our input is on the GPU and we have allocated space for the output, we are ready to launch our kernel.

```
// generate a bitmap from our sphere data
dim3    grids(DIM/16,DIM/16);
dim3    threads(16,16);
kernel<<<grids,threads>>>( dev_bitmap );
```

We will examine the kernel itself in a moment, but for now you should take it on faith that it ray traces the scene and generates pixel data for the input scene of spheres. Finally, we copy the output image back from the GPU and display it. It should go without saying that we free all allocated memory that hasn't already been freed.

```
// copy our bitmap back from the GPU for display
HANDLE_ERROR( cudaMemcpy( bitmap.get_ptr(), dev_bitmap,
                             bitmap.image_size(),
                             cudaMemcpyDeviceToHost ) );
bitmap.display_and_exit();

// free our memory
cudaFree( dev_bitmap );
cudaFree( s );
}
```

All of this should be commonplace to you now. So, how do we do the actual ray tracing? Because we have settled on a very simple ray tracing model, our kernel will be very easy to understand. Each thread is generating one pixel for our output image, so we start in the usual manner by computing the x- and y-coordinates for the thread as well as the linearized offset into our output buffer. We will also shift our (x, y) image coordinates by DIM/2 so that the z-axis runs through the center of the image.

```
__global__ void kernel( unsigned char *ptr ) {
    // map from threadIdx/BlockIdx to pixel position
    int x = threadIdx.x + blockIdx.x * blockDim.x;
    int y = threadIdx.y + blockIdx.y * blockDim.y;
    int offset = x + y * blockDim.x * gridDim.x;
    float    ox = (x - DIM/2);
    float    oy = (y - DIM/2);
```

Since each ray needs to check each sphere for intersection, we will now iterate through the array of spheres, checking each for a hit.

```
    float    r=0, g=0, b=0;
    float    maxz = -INF;
    for(int i=0; i<SPHERES; i++) {
        float    n;
        float    t = s[i].hit( ox, oy, &n );
        if (t > maxz) {
            float fscale = n;
            r = s[i].r * fscale;
            g = s[i].g * fscale;
            b = s[i].b * fscale;
        }
    }
```

Clearly, the majority of the interesting computation lies in the for() loop. We iterate through each of the input spheres and call its hit() method to determine whether the ray from our pixel "sees" the sphere. If the ray hits the current sphere, we determine whether the hit is closer to the camera than the last sphere we hit. If it is closer, we store this depth as our new closest sphere. In addition, we store the color associated with this sphere so that when the loop has terminated, the thread knows the color of the sphere that is closest to the camera. Since this is the color that the ray from our pixel "sees," we conclude that this is the color of the pixel and store this value in our output image buffer.

After every sphere has been checked for intersection, we can store the current color into the output image.

```
    ptr[offset*4 + 0] = (int)(r * 255);
    ptr[offset*4 + 1] = (int)(g * 255);
    ptr[offset*4 + 2] = (int)(b * 255);
    ptr[offset*4 + 3] = 255;
}
```

Note that if no spheres have been hit, the color that we store will be whatever color we initialized the variables r, b, and g to. In this case, we set r, b, and g to zero so the background will be black. You can change these values to render a different color background. Figure 6.2 shows an example of what the output should look like when rendered with 20 spheres and a black background.

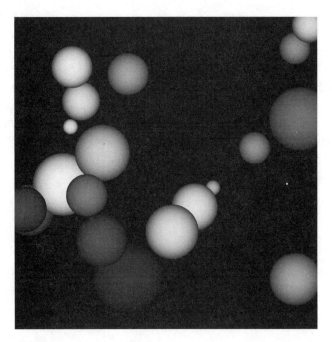

Figure 6.2 A screenshot from the ray tracing example

Since we randomly generated the sphere positions, colors, and sizes, we advise you not to panic if your output doesn't match this image identically.

6.2.3 RAY TRACING WITH CONSTANT MEMORY

You may have noticed that we never mentioned constant memory in the ray tracing example. Now it's time to improve this example using the benefits of constant memory. Since we cannot modify constant memory, we clearly can't use it for the output image data. And this example has only one input, the array of spheres, so it should be pretty obvious what data we will store in constant memory.

The mechanism for declaring memory constant is identical to the one we used for declaring a buffer as shared memory. Instead of declaring our array like this:

```
Sphere   *s;
```

we add the modifier __constant__ before it:

```
__constant__   Sphere s[SPHERES];
```

Notice that in the original example, we declared a pointer and then used cudaMalloc() to allocate GPU memory for it. When we changed it to constant memory, we also changed the declaration to statically allocate the space in constant memory. We no longer need to worry about calling cudaMalloc() or cudaFree() for our array of spheres, but we do need to commit to a size for this array at compile-time. For many applications, this is an acceptable trade-off for the performance benefits of constant memory. We will talk about these benefits momentarily, but first we will look at how the use of constant memory changes our main() routine:

```
int main( void ) {
    CPUBitmap bitmap( DIM, DIM );
    unsigned char    *dev_bitmap;

    // allocate memory on the GPU for the output bitmap
    HANDLE_ERROR( cudaMalloc( (void**)&dev_bitmap,
                             bitmap.image_size() ) );
```

```
    // allocate temp memory, initialize it, copy to constant
    // memory on the GPU, and then free our temp memory
    Sphere *temp_s = (Sphere*)malloc( sizeof(Sphere) * SPHERES );
    for (int i=0; i<SPHERES; i++) {
        temp_s[i].r = rnd( 1.0f );
        temp_s[i].g = rnd( 1.0f );
        temp_s[i].b = rnd( 1.0f );
        temp_s[i].x = rnd( 1000.0f ) - 500;
        temp_s[i].y = rnd( 1000.0f ) - 500;
        temp_s[i].z = rnd( 1000.0f ) - 500;
        temp_s[i].radius = rnd( 100.0f ) + 20;
    }
    HANDLE_ERROR( cudaMemcpyToSymbol( s, temp_s,
                                      sizeof(Sphere) * SPHERES) );
    free( temp_s );

    // generate a bitmap from our sphere data
    dim3    grids(DIM/16,DIM/16);
    dim3    threads(16,16);
    kernel<<<grids,threads>>>( dev_bitmap );

    // copy our bitmap back from the GPU for display
    HANDLE_ERROR( cudaMemcpy( bitmap.get_ptr(), dev_bitmap,
                              bitmap.image_size(),
                              cudaMemcpyDeviceToHost ) );
    bitmap.display_and_exit();

    // free our memory
    cudaFree( dev_bitmap );
}
```

Largely, this is identical to the previous implementation of main(). As we mentioned previously, we no longer need the call to cudaMalloc() to allocate space for our array of spheres. The other change has been highlighted in the listing:

```
HANDLE_ERROR( cudaMemcpyToSymbol( s, temp_s,
                            sizeof(Sphere) * SPHERES ) );
```

We use this special version of cudaMemcpy() when we copy from host memory to constant memory on the GPU. The only differences between cudaMemcpyToSymbol() and cudaMemcpy() using cudaMemcpyHostToDevice are that cudaMemcpyToSymbol() copies to constant memory and cudaMemcpy() copies to global memory.

Outside the __constant__ modifier and the two changes to main(), the versions with and without constant memory are identical.

6.2.4 PERFORMANCE WITH CONSTANT MEMORY

Declaring memory as __constant__ constrains our usage to be read-only. In taking on this constraint, we expect to get something in return. As we previously mentioned, reading from constant memory can conserve memory bandwidth when compared to reading the same data from global memory. There are two reasons why reading from the 64KB of constant memory can save bandwidth over standard reads of global memory:

- A single read from constant memory can be broadcast to other "nearby" threads, effectively saving up to 15 reads.

- Constant memory is cached, so consecutive reads of the same address will not incur any additional memory traffic.

What do we mean by the word *nearby*? To answer this question, we will need to explain the concept of a *warp*. For those readers who are more familiar with *Star Trek* than with weaving, a warp in this context has nothing to do with the speed of travel through space. In the world of weaving, a warp refers to the group of *threads* being woven together into fabric. In the CUDA Architecture, a *warp* refers to a collection of 32 threads that are "woven together" and get executed in lockstep. At every line in your program, each thread in a warp executes the same instruction on different data.

When it comes to handling constant memory, NVIDIA hardware can broadcast a single memory read to each half-warp. A half-warp—not nearly as creatively named as a warp—is a group of 16 threads: half of a 32-thread warp. If every thread in a half-warp requests data from the same address in constant memory, your GPU will generate only a single read request and subsequently broadcast the data to every thread. If you are reading a lot of data from constant memory, you will generate only 1/16 (roughly 6 percent) of the memory traffic as you would when using global memory.

But the savings don't stop at a 94 percent reduction in bandwidth when reading constant memory! Because we have committed to leaving the memory unchanged, the hardware can aggressively cache the constant data on the GPU. So after the first read from an address in constant memory, other half-warps requesting the same address, and therefore hitting the constant cache, will generate no additional memory traffic.

In the case of our ray tracer, every thread in the launch reads the data corresponding to the first sphere so the thread can test its ray for intersection. After we modify our application to store the spheres in constant memory, the hardware needs to make only a single request for this data. After caching the data, every other thread avoids generating memory traffic as a result of one of the two constant memory benefits:

- It receives the data in a half-warp broadcast.

- It retrieves the data from the constant memory cache.

Unfortunately, there can potentially be a downside to performance when using constant memory. The half-warp broadcast feature is in actuality a double-edged sword. Although it can dramatically accelerate performance when all 16 threads are reading the same address, it actually slows performance to a crawl when all 16 threads read different addresses.

The trade-off to allowing the broadcast of a single read to 16 threads is that the 16 threads are allowed to place only a single read request at a time. For example, if all 16 threads in a half-warp need different data from constant memory, the 16 different reads get serialized, effectively taking 16 times the amount of time to place the request. If they were reading from conventional global memory, the request could be issued at the same time. In this case, reading from constant memory would probably be slower than using global memory.

6.3 Measuring Performance with Events

Fully aware that there may be either positive or negative implications, you have changed your ray tracer to use constant memory. How do you determine how this has impacted the performance of your program? One of the simplest metrics involves answering this simple question: Which version takes less time to finish? We could use one of the CPU or operating system timers, but this will include latency and variation from any number of sources (operating system thread scheduling, availability of high-precision CPU timers, and so on). Furthermore, while the GPU kernel runs, we may be asynchronously performing computation on the host. The only way to time these host computations is using the CPU or operating system timing mechanism. So to measure the time a GPU spends on a task, we will use the CUDA event API.

An *event* in CUDA is essentially a GPU time stamp that is recorded at a user-specified point in time. Since the GPU itself is recording the time stamp, it eliminates a lot of the problems we might encounter when trying to time GPU execution with CPU timers. The API is relatively easy to use, since taking a time stamp consists of just two steps: creating an event and subsequently recording an event. For example, at the beginning of some sequence of code, we instruct the CUDA runtime to make a record of the current time. We do so by creating and then recording the event:

```
cudaEvent_t start;
cudaEventCreate(&start);
cudaEventRecord( start, 0 );
```

You will notice that when we instruct the runtime to record the event `start`, we also pass it a second argument. In the previous example, this argument is 0. The exact nature of this argument is unimportant for our purposes right now, so we intend to leave it mysteriously unexplained rather than open a new can of worms. If your curiosity is killing you, we intend to discuss this when we talk about *streams*.

To time a block of code, we will want to create both a start event and a stop event. We will have the CUDA runtime record when we start tell it to do some other work on the GPU and then tell it to record when we've stopped:

```
cudaEvent_t start, stop;
cudaEventCreate(&start);
cudaEventCreate(&stop);
cudaEventRecord( start, 0 );

// do some work on the GPU

cudaEventRecord( stop, 0 );
```

Unfortunately, there is still a problem with timing GPU code in this way. The fix will require only one line of code but will require some explanation. The trickiest part of using events arises as a consequence of the fact that some of the calls we make in CUDA C are actually *asynchronous*. For example, when we launched the kernel in our ray tracer, the GPU begins executing our code, but the CPU continues executing the next line of our program before the GPU finishes. This is excellent from a performance standpoint because it means we can be computing something on the GPU and CPU at the same time, but conceptually it makes timing tricky.

You should imagine calls to cudaEventRecord() as an instruction to record the current time being placed into the GPU's pending queue of work. As a result, our event won't actually be recorded until the GPU finishes everything prior to the call to cudaEventRecord(). In terms of having our stop event measure the correct time, this is precisely what we want. But we cannot safely *read* the value of the stop event until the GPU has completed its prior work and recorded the stop event. Fortunately, we have a way to instruct the CPU to synchronize on an event, the event API function cudaEventSynchronize():

```
cudaEvent_t start, stop;
cudaEventCreate(&start);
cudaEventCreate(&stop);
cudaEventRecord( start, 0 );

// do some work on the GPU

cudaEventRecord( stop, 0 );
cudaEventSynchronize( stop );
```

Now, we have instructed the runtime to block further instruction until the GPU has reached the stop event. When the call to cudaEventSynchronize()

returns, we know that all GPU work before the stop event has completed, so it is safe to read the time stamp recorded in stop. It is worth noting that because CUDA events get implemented directly on the GPU, they are unsuitable for timing mixtures of device and host code. That is, you will get unreliable results if you attempt to use CUDA events to time more than kernel executions and memory copies involving the device.

6.3.1 MEASURING RAY TRACER PERFORMANCE

To time our ray tracer, we will need to create a start and stop event, just as we did when learning about events. The following is a timing-enabled version of the ray tracer that does *not* use constant memory:

```
int main( void ) {
    // capture the start time
    cudaEvent_t     start, stop;
    HANDLE_ERROR( cudaEventCreate( &start ) );
    HANDLE_ERROR( cudaEventCreate( &stop ) );
    HANDLE_ERROR( cudaEventRecord( start, 0 ) );

    CPUBitmap bitmap( DIM, DIM );
    unsigned char    *dev_bitmap;

    // allocate memory on the GPU for the output bitmap
    HANDLE_ERROR( cudaMalloc( (void**)&dev_bitmap,
                              bitmap.image_size() ) );
    // allocate memory for the Sphere dataset
    HANDLE_ERROR( cudaMalloc( (void**)&s,
                              sizeof(Sphere) * SPHERES ) );

    // allocate temp memory, initialize it, copy to
    // memory on the GPU, and then free our temp memory
    Sphere *temp_s = (Sphere*)malloc( sizeof(Sphere) * SPHERES );
    for (int i=0; i<SPHERES; i++) {
        temp_s[i].r = rnd( 1.0f );
        temp_s[i].g = rnd( 1.0f );
        temp_s[i].b = rnd( 1.0f );
        temp_s[i].x = rnd( 1000.0f ) - 500;
```

```
        temp_s[i].y = rnd( 1000.0f ) - 500;
        temp_s[i].z = rnd( 1000.0f ) - 500;
        temp_s[i].radius = rnd( 100.0f ) + 20;
    }
    HANDLE_ERROR( cudaMemcpy( s, temp_s,
                             sizeof(Sphere) * SPHERES,
                             cudaMemcpyHostToDevice ) );
    free( temp_s );

    // generate a bitmap from our sphere data
    dim3    grids(DIM/16,DIM/16);
    dim3    threads(16,16);
    kernel<<<grids,threads>>>( s, dev_bitmap );

    // copy our bitmap back from the GPU for display
    HANDLE_ERROR( cudaMemcpy( bitmap.get_ptr(), dev_bitmap,
                             bitmap.image_size(),
                             cudaMemcpyDeviceToHost ) );

    // get stop time, and display the timing results
    HANDLE_ERROR( cudaEventRecord( stop, 0 ) );
    HANDLE_ERROR( cudaEventSynchronize( stop ) );

    float   elapsedTime;
    HANDLE_ERROR( cudaEventElapsedTime( &elapsedTime,
                                       start, stop ) );
    printf( "Time to generate:  %3.1f ms\n", elapsedTime );

    HANDLE_ERROR( cudaEventDestroy( start ) );
    HANDLE_ERROR( cudaEventDestroy( stop ) );

    // display
    bitmap.display_and_exit();

    // free our memory
    cudaFree( dev_bitmap );
    cudaFree( s );
}
```

Notice that we have thrown two additional functions into the mix, the calls to `cudaEventElapsedTime()` and `cudaEventDestroy()`. The function `cudaEventElapsedTime()` is a utility that computes the elapsed time between two previously recorded events. The time in milliseconds elapsed between the two events is returned in the first argument, the address of a floating-point variable.

The call to `cudaEventDestroy()` needs to be made when we're finished using an event created with `cudaEventCreate()`. This is identical to calling `free()` on memory previously allocated with `malloc()`, so we needn't stress how important it is to match every `cudaEventCreate()` with a `cudaEventDestroy()`.

We can instrument the ray tracer that does use constant memory in the same fashion:

```
int main( void ) {
    // capture the start time
    cudaEvent_t     start, stop;
    HANDLE_ERROR( cudaEventCreate( &start ) );
    HANDLE_ERROR( cudaEventCreate( &stop ) );
    HANDLE_ERROR( cudaEventRecord( start, 0 ) );

    CPUBitmap bitmap( DIM, DIM );
    unsigned char   *dev_bitmap;

    // allocate memory on the GPU for the output bitmap
    HANDLE_ERROR( cudaMalloc( (void**)&dev_bitmap,
                              bitmap.image_size() ) );

    // allocate temp memory, initialize it, copy to constant
    // memory on the GPU, and then free our temp memory
    Sphere *temp_s = (Sphere*)malloc( sizeof(Sphere) * SPHERES );
    for (int i=0; i<SPHERES; i++) {
        temp_s[i].r = rnd( 1.0f );
        temp_s[i].g = rnd( 1.0f );
        temp_s[i].b = rnd( 1.0f );
        temp_s[i].x = rnd( 1000.0f ) - 500;
```

```
        temp_s[i].y = rnd( 1000.0f ) - 500;
        temp_s[i].z = rnd( 1000.0f ) - 500;
        temp_s[i].radius = rnd( 100.0f ) + 20;
    }
    HANDLE_ERROR( cudaMemcpyToSymbol( s, temp_s,
                                    sizeof(Sphere) * SPHERES) );
    free( temp_s );

    // generate a bitmap from our sphere data
    dim3     grids(DIM/16,DIM/16);
    dim3     threads(16,16);
    kernel<<<grids,threads>>>( dev_bitmap );

    // copy our bitmap back from the GPU for display
    HANDLE_ERROR( cudaMemcpy( bitmap.get_ptr(), dev_bitmap,
                            bitmap.image_size(),
                            cudaMemcpyDeviceToHost ) );


    // get stop time, and display the timing results
    HANDLE_ERROR( cudaEventRecord( stop, 0 ) );
    HANDLE_ERROR( cudaEventSynchronize( stop ) );
    float    elapsedTime;
    HANDLE_ERROR( cudaEventElapsedTime( &elapsedTime,
                                        start, stop ) );
    printf( "Time to generate:  %3.1f ms\n", elapsedTime );

    HANDLE_ERROR( cudaEventDestroy( start ) );
    HANDLE_ERROR( cudaEventDestroy( stop ) );

    // display
    bitmap.display_and_exit();

    // free our memory
    cudaFree( dev_bitmap );
}
```

Now when we run our two versions of the ray tracer, we can compare the time it takes to complete the GPU work. This will tell us at a high level whether introducing constant memory has improved the performance of our application or worsened it. Fortunately, in this case, performance is improved dramatically by using constant memory. Our experiments on a GeForce GTX 280 show the constant memory ray tracer performing up to 50 percent faster than the version that uses global memory. On a different GPU, your mileage might vary, although the ray tracer that uses constant memory should always be at least as fast as the version without it.

6.4 Chapter Review

In addition to the global and shared memory we explored in previous chapters, NVIDIA hardware makes other types of memory available for our use. Constant memory comes with additional constraints over standard global memory, but in some cases, subjecting ourselves to these constraints can yield additional performance. Specifically, we can see additional performance when threads in a warp need access to the same read-only data. Using constant memory for data with this access pattern can conserve bandwidth both because of the capacity to broadcast reads across a half-warp and because of the presence of a constant memory cache on chip. Memory bandwidth bottlenecks a wide class of algorithms, so having mechanisms to ameliorate this situation can prove incredibly useful.

We also learned how to use CUDA events to request the runtime to record time stamps at specific points during GPU execution. We saw how to synchronize the CPU with the GPU on one of these events and then how to compute the time elapsed between two events. In doing so, we built up a method to compare the running time between two different methods for ray tracing spheres, concluding that, for the application at hand, using constant memory gained us a significant amount of performance.

Chapter 7

Texture Memory

When we looked at constant memory, we saw how exploiting special memory spaces under the right circumstances can dramatically accelerate applications. We also learned how to measure these performance gains in order to make informed decisions about performance choices. In this chapter, we will learn about how to allocate and use *texture memory*. Like constant memory, texture memory is another variety of read-only memory that can improve performance and reduce memory traffic when reads have certain access patterns. Although texture memory was originally designed for traditional graphics applications, it can also be used quite effectively in some GPU computing applications.

7.1 Chapter Objectives

Through the course of this chapter, you will accomplish the following:

- You will learn about the performance characteristics of texture memory.

- You will learn how to use one-dimensional texture memory with CUDA C.

- You will learn how to use two-dimensional texture memory with CUDA C.

7.2 Texture Memory Overview

If you read the introduction to this chapter, the secret is already out: There is yet another type of read-only memory that is available for use in your programs written in CUDA C. Readers familiar with the workings of graphics hardware will not be surprised, but the GPU's sophisticated *texture memory* may also be used for general-purpose computing. Although NVIDIA designed the texture units for the classical OpenGL and DirectX rendering pipelines, texture memory has some properties that make it extremely useful for computing.

Like constant memory, texture memory is cached on chip, so in some situations it will provide higher effective bandwidth by reducing memory requests to off-chip DRAM. Specifically, texture caches are designed for graphics applications where memory access patterns exhibit a great deal of *spatial locality*. In a computing application, this roughly implies that a thread is likely to read from an address "near" the address that nearby threads read, as shown in Figure 7.1.

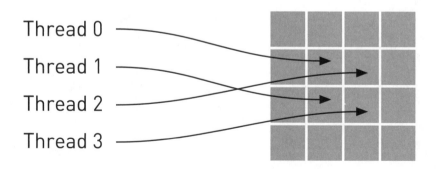

Figure 7.1 A mapping of threads into a two-dimensional region of memory

Arithmetically, the four addresses shown are not consecutive, so they would not be cached together in a typical CPU caching scheme. But since GPU texture caches are designed to accelerate access patterns such as this one, you will see an increase in performance in this case when using texture memory instead of global memory. In fact, this sort of access pattern is not incredibly uncommon in general-purpose computing, as we shall see.

7.3 Simulating Heat Transfer

Physical simulations can be among the most computationally challenging problems to solve. Fundamentally, there is often a trade-off between accuracy and computational complexity. As a result, computer simulations have become more and more important in recent years, thanks in large part to the increased accuracy possible as a consequence of the parallel computing revolution. Since many physical simulations can be parallelized quite easily, we will look at a very simple simulation model in this example.

7.3.1 SIMPLE HEATING MODEL

To demonstrate a situation where you can effectively employ texture memory, we will construct a simple two-dimensional heat transfer simulation. We start by assuming that we have some rectangular room that we divide into a grid. Inside the grid, we will randomly scatter a handful of "heaters" with various fixed temperatures. Figure 7.2 shows an example of what this room might look like.

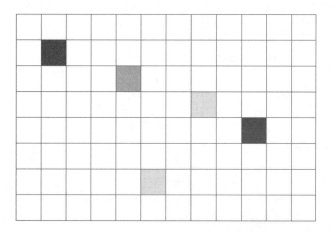

Figure 7.2 A room with "heaters" of various temperature

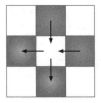

Figure 7.3 Heat dissipating from warm cells into cold cells

Given a rectangular grid and configuration of heaters, we are looking to simulate what happens to the temperature in every grid cell as time progresses. For simplicity, cells with heaters in them always remain a constant temperature. At every step in time, we will assume that heat "flows" between a cell and its neighbors. If a cell's neighbor is warmer than it is, the warmer neighbor will tend to warm it up. Conversely, if a cell has a neighbor cooler than it is, it will cool off. Qualitatively, Figure 7.3 represents this flow of heat.

In our heat transfer model, we will compute the new temperature in a grid cell as a sum of the differences between its temperature and the temperatures of its neighbor, or, essentially, an update equation as shown in Equation 7.1.

Equation 7.1

$$T_{NEW} = T_{OLD} + \sum_{NEIGHBORS} k \cdot (T_{NEIGHBOR} - T_{OLD})$$

In the equation for updating a cell's temperature, the constant k simply represents the rate at which heat flows through the simulation. A large value of k will drive the system to a constant temperature quickly, while a small value will allow the solution to retain large temperature gradients longer. Since we consider only four neighbors (top, bottom, left, right) and k and T_{OLD} remain constant in the equation, this update becomes like the one shown in Equation 7.2.

Equation 7.2

$$T_{NEW} = T_{OLD} + k \cdot (T_{TOP} + T_{BOTTOM} + T_{LEFT} + T_{RIGHT} - 4 \cdot T_{OLD})$$

Like with the ray tracing example in the previous chapter, this model is not intended to be close to what might be used in industry (in fact, it is not really even an approximation of something physically accurate). We have simplified this model immensely in order to draw attention to the techniques at hand. With this in mind, let's take a look at how the update given by Equation 7.2 can be computed on the GPU.

7.3.2 COMPUTING TEMPERATURE UPDATES

We will cover the specifics of each step in a moment, but at a high level, our update process proceeds as follows:

1. Given some grid of input temperatures, copy the temperature of cells with heaters to this grid. This will overwrite any previously computed temperatures in these cells, thereby enforcing our restriction that "heating cells" remain at a constant temperature. This copy gets performed in `copy_const_kernel()`.

2. Given the input temperature grid, compute the output temperatures based on the update in Equation 7.2. This update gets performed in `blend_kernel()`.

3. Swap the input and output buffers in preparation of the next time step. The output temperature grid computed in step 2 will become the input temperature grid that we start with in step 1 when simulating the next time step.

Before beginning the simulation, we assume we have generated a grid of constants. Most of the entries in this grid are zero, but some entries contain nonzero temperatures that represent heaters at fixed temperatures. This buffer of constants will not change over the course of the simulation and gets read at each time step.

Because of the way we are modeling our heat transfer, we start with the output grid from the previous time step. Then, according to step 1, we copy the temperatures of the cells with heaters into this output grid, overwriting any previously computed temperatures. We do this because we have assumed that the temperature of these heater cells remains constant. We perform this copy of the constant grid onto the input grid with the following kernel:

```
__global__ void copy_const_kernel( float *iptr,
                                    const float *cptr ) {
    // map from threadIdx/BlockIdx to pixel position
    int x = threadIdx.x + blockIdx.x * blockDim.x;
    int y = threadIdx.y + blockIdx.y * blockDim.y;
    int offset = x + y * blockDim.x * gridDim.x;

    if (cptr[offset] != 0)  iptr[offset] = cptr[offset];
}
```

The first three lines should look familiar. The first two lines convert a thread's `threadIdx` and `blockIdx` into an x- and a y-coordinate. The third line computes a linear `offset` into our constant and input buffers. The highlighted line performs the copy of the heater temperature in `cptr[]` to the input grid in `iptr[]`. Notice that the copy is performed only if the cell in the constant grid is nonzero. We do this to preserve any values that were computed in the previous time step within cells that do not contain heaters. Cells with heaters will have nonzero entries in `cptr[]` and will therefore have their temperatures preserved from step to step thanks to this copy kernel.

Step 2 of the algorithm is the most computationally involved. To perform the updates, we can have each thread take responsibility for a single cell in our simulation. Each thread will read its cell's temperature and the temperatures of its neighboring cells, perform the previous update computation, and then update its temperature with the new value. Much of this kernel resembles techniques you've used before.

```
__global__ void blend_kernel( float *outSrc,
                              const float *inSrc ) {
    // map from threadIdx/BlockIdx to pixel position
    int x = threadIdx.x + blockIdx.x * blockDim.x;
    int y = threadIdx.y + blockIdx.y * blockDim.y;
    int offset = x + y * blockDim.x * gridDim.x;

    int left = offset - 1;
    int right = offset + 1;
    if (x == 0)    left++;
    if (x == DIM-1) right--;

    int top = offset - DIM;
    int bottom = offset + DIM;
    if (y == 0)    top += DIM;
    if (y == DIM-1) bottom -= DIM;

    outSrc[offset] = inSrc[offset] + SPEED * ( inSrc[top] +
                     inSrc[bottom] + inSrc[left] + inSrc[right] -
                     inSrc[offset]*4);
}
```

Notice that we start exactly as we did for the examples that produced images as their output. However, instead of computing the color of a pixel, the threads are computing temperatures of simulation grid cells. Nevertheless, they start by converting their `threadIdx` and `blockIdx` into an `x`, `y`, and `offset`. You might be able to recite these lines in your sleep by now (although for your sake, we hope you aren't actually reciting them in your sleep).

Next, we determine the offsets of our left, right, top, and bottom neighbors so that we can read the temperatures of those cells. We will need those values to compute the updated temperature in the current cell. The only complication here is that we need to adjust indices on the border so that cells around the edges do not wrap around. Finally, in the highlighted line, we perform the update from Equation 7.2, adding the old temperature and the scaled differences of that temperature and the cell's neighbors' temperatures.

7.3.3 ANIMATING THE SIMULATION

The remainder of the code primarily sets up the grid and then displays an animated output of the heat map. We will walk through that code now:

```
#include "cuda.h"
#include "../common/book.h"
#include "../common/cpu_anim.h"


#define DIM 1024
#define PI 3.1415926535897932f
#define MAX_TEMP 1.0f
#define MIN_TEMP 0.0001f
#define SPEED   0.25f


// globals needed by the update routine
struct DataBlock {
    unsigned char   *output_bitmap;
    float           *dev_inSrc;
    float           *dev_outSrc;
    float           *dev_constSrc;
    CPUAnimBitmap   *bitmap;
```

```
        cudaEvent_t      start, stop;
        float            totalTime;
        float            frames;
    };

    void anim_gpu( DataBlock *d, int ticks ) {
        HANDLE_ERROR( cudaEventRecord( d->start, 0 ) );
        dim3    blocks(DIM/16,DIM/16);
        dim3    threads(16,16);
        CPUAnimBitmap  *bitmap = d->bitmap;

        for (int i=0; i<90; i++) {
            copy_const_kernel<<<blocks,threads>>>( d->dev_inSrc,
                                                   d->dev_constSrc );
            blend_kernel<<<blocks,threads>>>( d->dev_outSrc,
                                              d->dev_inSrc );
            swap( d->dev_inSrc, d->dev_outSrc );
        }
        float_to_color<<<blocks,threads>>>( d->output_bitmap,
                                            d->dev_inSrc );

        HANDLE_ERROR( cudaMemcpy( bitmap->get_ptr(),
                                  d->output_bitmap,
                                  bitmap->image_size(),
                                  cudaMemcpyDeviceToHost ) );

        HANDLE_ERROR( cudaEventRecord( d->stop, 0 ) );
        HANDLE_ERROR( cudaEventSynchronize( d->stop ) );
        float   elapsedTime;
        HANDLE_ERROR( cudaEventElapsedTime( &elapsedTime,
                                            d->start, d->stop ) );
        d->totalTime += elapsedTime;
        ++d->frames;
        printf( "Average Time per frame:  %3.1f ms\n",
                d->totalTime/d->frames  );
    }
```

```
void anim_exit( DataBlock *d ) {
    cudaFree( d->dev_inSrc );
    cudaFree( d->dev_outSrc );
    cudaFree( d->dev_constSrc );

    HANDLE_ERROR( cudaEventDestroy( d->start ) );
    HANDLE_ERROR( cudaEventDestroy( d->stop ) );
}
```

We have equipped the code with event-based timing as we did in previous chapter's ray tracing example. The timing code serves the same purpose as it did previously. Since we will endeavor to accelerate the initial implementation, we have put in place a mechanism by which we can measure performance and convince ourselves that we have succeeded.

The function `anim_gpu()` gets called by the animation framework on every frame. The arguments to this function are a pointer to a `DataBlock` and the number of `ticks` of the animation that have elapsed. As with the animation examples, we use blocks of 256 threads that we organize into a two-dimensional grid of 16 x 16. Each iteration of the `for()` loop in `anim_gpu()` computes a single time step of the simulation as described by the three-step algorithm at the beginning of Section 7.2.2: Computing Temperature Updates. Since the `DataBlock` contains the constant buffer of heaters as well as the output of the last time step, it encapsulates the entire state of the animation, and consequently, `anim_gpu()` does not actually need to use the value of `ticks` anywhere.

You will notice that we have chosen to do 90 time steps per frame. This number is not magical but was determined somewhat experimentally as a reasonable trade-off between having to download a bitmap image for every time step and computing too many time steps per frame, resulting in a jerky animation. If you were more concerned with getting the output of each simulation step than you were with animating the results in real time, you could change this such that you computed only a single step on each frame.

After computing the 90 time steps since the previous frame, `anim_gpu()` is ready to copy a bitmap frame of the current animation back to the CPU. Since the `for()` loop leaves the input and output swapped, we first swap the input and output buffers so that the output actually contains the output of the 90th time step. We convert the temperatures to colors using the kernel `float_to_color()` and then copy the resultant image back to the CPU with a `cudaMemcpy()` that specifies the direction of copy as `cudaMemcpyDeviceToHost`. Finally, to prepare for the next sequence of time steps, we swap the output buffer back to the input buffer since it will serve as input to the next time step.

```
int main( void ) {
    DataBlock    data;
    CPUAnimBitmap bitmap( DIM, DIM, &data );
    data.bitmap = &bitmap;
    data.totalTime = 0;
    data.frames = 0;
    HANDLE_ERROR( cudaEventCreate( &data.start ) );
    HANDLE_ERROR( cudaEventCreate( &data.stop ) );

    HANDLE_ERROR( cudaMalloc( (void**)&data.output_bitmap,
                               bitmap.image_size() ) );

    // assume float == 4 chars in size (i.e., rgba)
    HANDLE_ERROR( cudaMalloc( (void**)&data.dev_inSrc,
                               bitmap.image_size() ) );
    HANDLE_ERROR( cudaMalloc( (void**)&data.dev_outSrc,
                               bitmap.image_size() ) );
    HANDLE_ERROR( cudaMalloc( (void**)&data.dev_constSrc,
                               bitmap.image_size() ) );

    float *temp = (float*)malloc( bitmap.image_size() );
    for (int i=0; i<DIM*DIM; i++) {
        temp[i] = 0;
        int x = i % DIM;
        int y = i / DIM;
        if ((x>300) && (x<600) && (y>310) && (y<601))
            temp[i] = MAX_TEMP;
    }
```

```
temp[DIM*100+100] = (MAX_TEMP + MIN_TEMP)/2;
temp[DIM*700+100] = MIN_TEMP;
temp[DIM*300+300] = MIN_TEMP;
temp[DIM*200+700] = MIN_TEMP;
for (int y=800; y<900; y++) {
    for (int x=400; x<500; x++) {
        temp[x+y*DIM] = MIN_TEMP;
    }
}
HANDLE_ERROR( cudaMemcpy( data.dev_constSrc, temp,
                         bitmap.image_size(),
                         cudaMemcpyHostToDevice ) );

for (int y=800; y<DIM; y++) {
    for (int x=0; x<200; x++) {
        temp[x+y*DIM] = MAX_TEMP;
    }
}
HANDLE_ERROR( cudaMemcpy( data.dev_inSrc, temp,
                         bitmap.image_size(),
                         cudaMemcpyHostToDevice ) );

free( temp );

bitmap.anim_and_exit( (void (*)(void*,int))anim_gpu,
                      (void (*)(void*))anim_exit );
}
```

Figure 7.4 shows an example of what the output might look like. You will notice in the image some of the "heaters" that appear to be pixel-sized islands that disrupt the continuity of the temperature distribution.

7.3.4 USING TEXTURE MEMORY

There is a considerable amount of *spatial locality* in the memory access pattern required to perform the temperature update in each step. As we explained previously, this is exactly the type of access pattern that GPU texture memory is

Figure 7.4 A screenshot from the animated heat transfer simulation

designed to accelerate. Given that we want to use texture memory, we need to learn the mechanics of doing so.

First, we will need to declare our inputs as texture references. We will use references to floating-point textures, since our temperature data is floating-point.

```
// these exist on the GPU side
texture<float>  texConstSrc;
texture<float>  texIn;
texture<float>  texOut;
```

The next major difference is that after allocating GPU memory for these three buffers, we need to *bind* the references to the memory buffer using `cudaBindTexture()`. This basically tells the CUDA runtime two things:

- We intend to use the specified buffer as a texture.

- We intend to use the specified texture reference as the texture's "name."

After the three allocations in our heat transfer simulation, we bind the three allocations to the texture references declared earlier (texConstSrc, texIn, and texOut).

```
HANDLE_ERROR( cudaMalloc( (void**)&data.dev_inSrc,
                          imageSize ) );
HANDLE_ERROR( cudaMalloc( (void**)&data.dev_outSrc,
                          imageSize ) );
HANDLE_ERROR( cudaMalloc( (void**)&data.dev_constSrc,
                          imageSize ) );


HANDLE_ERROR( cudaBindTexture( NULL, texConstSrc,
                               data.dev_constSrc,
                               imageSize ) );
HANDLE_ERROR( cudaBindTexture( NULL, texIn,
                               data.dev_inSrc,
                               imageSize ) );
HANDLE_ERROR( cudaBindTexture( NULL, texOut,
                               data.dev_outSrc,
                               imageSize ) );
```

At this point, our textures are completely set up, and we're ready to launch our kernel. However, when we're reading from textures in the kernel, we need to use special functions to instruct the GPU to route our requests through the texture unit and not through standard global memory. As a result, we can no longer simply use square brackets to read from buffers; we need to modify blend_kernel() to use tex1Dfetch() when reading from memory.

Additionally, there is another difference between using global and texture memory that requires us to make another change. Although it looks like a function, tex1Dfetch() is a compiler intrinsic. And since texture references must be declared globally at file scope, we can no longer pass the input and output buffers as parameters to blend_kernel() because the compiler needs to know at compile time which textures tex1Dfetch() should be sampling. Rather than passing pointers to input and output buffers as we previously did, we will pass to blend_kernel() a boolean flag dstOut that indicates which buffer to use as input and which to use as output. The changes to `blend_kernel()` are highlighted here:

```
__global__ void blend_kernel( float *dst,
                              bool dstOut ) {
    // map from threadIdx/BlockIdx to pixel position
    int x = threadIdx.x + blockIdx.x * blockDim.x;
    int y = threadIdx.y + blockIdx.y * blockDim.y;
    int offset = x + y * blockDim.x * gridDim.x;

    int left = offset - 1;
    int right = offset + 1;
    if (x == 0)   left++;
    if (x == DIM-1) right--;

    int top = offset - DIM;
    int bottom = offset + DIM;
    if (y == 0)   top += DIM;
    if (y == DIM-1) bottom -= DIM;

    float  t, l, c, r, b;
    if (dstOut) {
        t = tex1Dfetch(texIn,top);
        l = tex1Dfetch(texIn,left);
        c = tex1Dfetch(texIn,offset);
        r = tex1Dfetch(texIn,right);
        b = tex1Dfetch(texIn,bottom);

    } else {
        t = tex1Dfetch(texOut,top);
        l = tex1Dfetch(texOut,left);
        c = tex1Dfetch(texOut,offset);
        r = tex1Dfetch(texOut,right);
        b = tex1Dfetch(texOut,bottom);
    }
    dst[offset] = c + SPEED * (t + b + r + l - 4 * c);
}
```

Since the `copy_const_kernel()` kernel reads from our buffer that holds the heater positions and temperatures, we will need to make a similar modification there in order to read through texture memory instead of global memory:

```
__global__ void copy_const_kernel( float *iptr ) {
    // map from threadIdx/BlockIdx to pixel position
    int x = threadIdx.x + blockIdx.x * blockDim.x;
    int y = threadIdx.y + blockIdx.y * blockDim.y;
    int offset = x + y * blockDim.x * gridDim.x;

    float c = tex1Dfetch(texConstSrc,offset);
    if (c != 0)
        iptr[offset] = c;
}
```

Since the signature of `blend_kernel()` changed to accept a flag that switches the buffers between input and output, we need a corresponding change to the `anim_gpu()` routine. Rather than swapping buffers, we set `dstOut = !dstOut` to toggle the flag after each series of calls:

```
void anim_gpu( DataBlock *d, int ticks ) {
    HANDLE_ERROR( cudaEventRecord( d->start, 0 ) );
    dim3    blocks(DIM/16,DIM/16);
    dim3    threads(16,16);
    CPUAnimBitmap  *bitmap = d->bitmap;

    // since tex is global and bound, we have to use a flag to
    // select which is in/out per iteration
    volatile bool dstOut = true;
    for (int i=0; i<90; i++) {
        float   *in, *out;
        if (dstOut) {
            in  = d->dev_inSrc;
            out = d->dev_outSrc;
```

```
            } else {
                out = d->dev_inSrc;
                in  = d->dev_outSrc;
            }
            copy_const_kernel<<<blocks,threads>>>( in );
            blend_kernel<<<blocks,threads>>>( out, dstOut );
            dstOut = !dstOut;
        }
        float_to_color<<<blocks,threads>>>( d->output_bitmap,
                                            d->dev_inSrc );

        HANDLE_ERROR( cudaMemcpy( bitmap->get_ptr(),
                                  d->output_bitmap,
                                  bitmap->image_size(),
                                  cudaMemcpyDeviceToHost ) );

        HANDLE_ERROR( cudaEventRecord( d->stop, 0 ) );
        HANDLE_ERROR( cudaEventSynchronize( d->stop ) );
        float    elapsedTime;
        HANDLE_ERROR( cudaEventElapsedTime( &elapsedTime,
                                            d->start, d->stop ) );
        d->totalTime += elapsedTime;
        ++d->frames;
        printf( "Average Time per frame:  %3.1f ms\n",
                d->totalTime/d->frames  );
    }
```

The final change to our heat transfer routine involves cleaning up at the end of the application's run. Rather than just freeing the global buffers, we also need to unbind textures:

```
// clean up memory allocated on the GPU
void anim_exit( DataBlock *d ) {
    cudaUnbindTexture( texIn );
    cudaUnbindTexture( texOut );
    cudaUnbindTexture( texConstSrc );
    cudaFree( d->dev_inSrc );
    cudaFree( d->dev_outSrc );
    cudaFree( d->dev_constSrc );

    HANDLE_ERROR( cudaEventDestroy( d->start ) );
    HANDLE_ERROR( cudaEventDestroy( d->stop ) );
}
```

7.3.5 USING TWO-DIMENSIONAL TEXTURE MEMORY

Toward the beginning of this book, we mentioned how some problems have two-dimensional domains, and therefore it can be convenient to use two-dimensional blocks and grids at times. The same is true for texture memory. There are many cases when having a two-dimensional memory region can be useful, a claim that should come as no surprise to anyone familiar with multidimensional arrays in standard C. Let's look at how we can modify our heat transfer application to use two-dimensional textures.

First, our texture reference declarations change. If unspecified, texture references are one-dimensional by default, so we add a dimensionality argument of 2 in order to declare two-dimensional textures.

```
texture<float,2>  texConstSrc;
texture<float,2>  texIn;
texture<float,2>  texOut;
```

The simplification promised by converting to two-dimensional textures comes in the blend_kernel() method. Although we need to change our tex1Dfetch()

calls to tex2D() calls, we no longer need to use the linearized offset variable to compute the set of offsets top, left, right, and bottom. When we switch to a two-dimensional texture, we can use x and y directly to address the texture.

Furthermore, we no longer have to worry about bounds overflow when we switch to using tex2D(). If one of x or y is less than zero, tex2D() will return the value at zero. Likewise, if one of these values is greater than the width, tex2D() will return the value at width 1. Note that in our application, this behavior is ideal, but it's possible that other applications would desire other behavior.

As a result of these simplifications, our kernel cleans up nicely.

```
__global__ void blend_kernel( float *dst,
                              bool dstOut ) {
    // map from threadIdx/BlockIdx to pixel position
    int x = threadIdx.x + blockIdx.x * blockDim.x;
    int y = threadIdx.y + blockIdx.y * blockDim.y;
    int offset = x + y * blockDim.x * gridDim.x;

    float   t, l, c, r, b;
    if (dstOut) {
        t = tex2D(texIn,x,y-1);
        l = tex2D(texIn,x-1,y);
        c = tex2D(texIn,x,y);
        r = tex2D(texIn,x+1,y);
        b = tex2D(texIn,x,y+1);
    } else {
        t = tex2D(texOut,x,y-1);
        l = tex2D(texOut,x-1,y);
        c = tex2D(texOut,x,y);
        r = tex2D(texOut,x+1,y);
        b = tex2D(texOut,x,y+1);
    }
    dst[offset] = c + SPEED * (t + b + r + l - 4 * c);
}
```

Since all of our previous calls to tex1Dfetch() need to be changed to tex2D() calls, we make the corresponding change in copy_const_kernel(). Similarly to the kernel blend_kernel(), we no longer need to use offset to address the texture; we simply use x and y to address the constant source:

```
__global__ void copy_const_kernel( float *iptr ) {
    // map from threadIdx/BlockIdx to pixel position
    int x = threadIdx.x + blockIdx.x * blockDim.x;
    int y = threadIdx.y + blockIdx.y * blockDim.y;
    int offset = x + y * blockDim.x * gridDim.x;

    float c = tex2D(texConstSrc,x,y);
    if (c != 0)
        iptr[offset] = c;
}
```

The final change to the one-dimensional texture version of our heat transfer simulation is along the same lines as our previous changes. Specifically, in main(), we need to change our texture binding calls to instruct the runtime that the buffer we plan to use will be treated as a two-dimensional texture, not a one-dimensional one:

```
HANDLE_ERROR( cudaMalloc( (void**)&data.dev_inSrc,
                          imageSize ) );
HANDLE_ERROR( cudaMalloc( (void**)&data.dev_outSrc,
                          imageSize ) );
HANDLE_ERROR( cudaMalloc( (void**)&data.dev_constSrc,
                          imageSize ) );

cudaChannelFormatDesc desc = cudaCreateChannelDesc<float>();
HANDLE_ERROR( cudaBindTexture2D( NULL, texConstSrc,
                                 data.dev_constSrc,
                                 desc, DIM, DIM,
                                 sizeof(float) * DIM ) );
```

```
        HANDLE_ERROR( cudaBindTexture2D( NULL, texIn,
                                          data.dev_inSrc,
                                          desc, DIM, DIM,
                                          sizeof(float) * DIM ) );

        HANDLE_ERROR( cudaBindTexture2D( NULL, texOut,
                                          data.dev_outSrc,
                                          desc, DIM, DIM,
                                          sizeof(float) * DIM ) );
```

As with the nontexture and one-dimensional texture versions, we begin
by allocating storage for our input arrays. We deviate from the one-
dimensional example because the CUDA runtime requires that we provide a
cudaChannelFormatDesc when we bind two-dimensional textures. The
previous listing includes a declaration of a channel format descriptor. In our
case, we can accept the default parameters and simply need to specify that
we require a floating-point descriptor. We then bind the three input buffers as
two-dimensional textures using cudaBindTexture2D(), the dimensions of
the texture (DIM x DIM), and the channel format descriptor (desc). The rest of
main() remains the same.

```
int main( void ) {
    DataBlock     data;
    CPUAnimBitmap bitmap( DIM, DIM, &data );
    data.bitmap = &bitmap;
    data.totalTime = 0;
    data.frames = 0;
    HANDLE_ERROR( cudaEventCreate( &data.start ) );
    HANDLE_ERROR( cudaEventCreate( &data.stop ) );

    int imageSize = bitmap.image_size();

    HANDLE_ERROR( cudaMalloc( (void**)&data.output_bitmap,
                              imageSize ) );
```

```
// assume float == 4 chars in size (i.e., rgba)
HANDLE_ERROR( cudaMalloc( (void**)&data.dev_inSrc,
                          imageSize ) );
HANDLE_ERROR( cudaMalloc( (void**)&data.dev_outSrc,
                          imageSize ) );
HANDLE_ERROR( cudaMalloc( (void**)&data.dev_constSrc,
                          imageSize ) );

cudaChannelFormatDesc desc = cudaCreateChannelDesc<float>();
HANDLE_ERROR( cudaBindTexture2D( NULL, texConstSrc,
                                 data.dev_constSrc,
                                 desc, DIM, DIM,
                                 sizeof(float) * DIM ) );

HANDLE_ERROR( cudaBindTexture2D( NULL, texIn,
                                 data.dev_inSrc,
                                 desc, DIM, DIM,
                                 sizeof(float) * DIM ) );

HANDLE_ERROR( cudaBindTexture2D( NULL, texOut,
                                 data.dev_outSrc,
                                 desc, DIM, DIM,
                                 sizeof(float) * DIM ) );

// initialize the constant data
float *temp = (float*)malloc( imageSize );
for (int i=0; i<DIM*DIM; i++) {
    temp[i] = 0;
    int x = i % DIM;
    int y = i / DIM;
    if ((x>300) && (x<600) && (y>310) && (y<601))
        temp[i] = MAX_TEMP;
}
```

```
        temp[DIM*100+100] = (MAX_TEMP + MIN_TEMP)/2;
        temp[DIM*700+100] = MIN_TEMP;
        temp[DIM*300+300] = MIN_TEMP;
        temp[DIM*200+700] = MIN_TEMP;
        for (int y=800; y<900; y++) {
            for (int x=400; x<500; x++) {
                temp[x+y*DIM] = MIN_TEMP;
            }
        }
        HANDLE_ERROR( cudaMemcpy( data.dev_constSrc, temp,
                                  imageSize,
                                  cudaMemcpyHostToDevice ) );


        // initialize the input data
        for (int y=800; y<DIM; y++) {
            for (int x=0; x<200; x++) {
                temp[x+y*DIM] = MAX_TEMP;
            }
        }
        HANDLE_ERROR( cudaMemcpy( data.dev_inSrc, temp,
                                  imageSize,
                                  cudaMemcpyHostToDevice ) );
        free( temp );

        bitmap.anim_and_exit( (void (*)(void*,int))anim_gpu,
                              (void (*)(void*))anim_exit );
    }
```

Although we needed different functions to instruct the runtime to bind one-dimensional or two-dimensional textures, we use the same routine to unbind the texture, cudaUnbindTexture(). Because of this, our cleanup routine can remain unchanged.

```
    // clean up memory allocated on the GPU
    void anim_exit( DataBlock *d ) {
        cudaUnbindTexture( texIn );
        cudaUnbindTexture( texOut );
```

```
        cudaUnbindTexture( texConstSrc );
        cudaFree( d->dev_inSrc );
        cudaFree( d->dev_outSrc );
        cudaFree( d->dev_constSrc );

        HANDLE_ERROR( cudaEventDestroy( d->start ) );
        HANDLE_ERROR( cudaEventDestroy( d->stop ) );
    }
```

The version of our heat transfer simulation that uses two-dimensional textures has essentially identical performance characteristics as the version that uses one-dimensional textures. So from a performance standpoint, the decision between one- and two-dimensional textures is likely to be inconsequential. For our particular application, the code is a little simpler when using two-dimensional textures because we happen to be simulating a two-dimensional domain. But in general, since this is not always the case, we suggest you make the decision between one- and two-dimensional textures on a case-by-case basis.

7.4 Chapter Review

As we saw in the previous chapter with constant memory, some of the benefit of texture memory comes as the result of on-chip caching. This is especially notice-able in applications such as our heat transfer simulation: applications that have some spatial coherence to their data access patterns. We saw how either one- or two-dimensional textures can be used, both having similar performance char-acteristics. As with a block or grid shape, the choice of one- or two-dimensional texture is largely one of convenience. Since the code became somewhat cleaner when we switched to two-dimensional textures and the borders are handled auto-matically, we would probably advocate the use of a 2D texture in our heat transfer application. But as you saw, it will work fine either way.

Texture memory can provide additional speedups if we utilize some of the conver-sions that texture samplers can perform automatically, such as unpacking packed data into separate variables or converting 8- and 16-bit integers to normalized floating-point numbers. We didn't explore either of these capabilities in the heat transfer application, but they might be useful to you!

Chapter 8

Graphics Interoperability

Since this book has focused on general-purpose computation, for the most part we've ignored that GPUs contain some special-purpose components as well. The GPU owes its success to its ability to perform complex rendering tasks in real time, freeing the rest of the system to concentrate on other work. This leads us to the obvious question: Can we use the GPU for both rendering *and* general-purpose computation in the same application? What if the images we want to render rely on the results of our computations? Or what if we want to take the frame we've rendered and perform some image-processing or statistics computations on it?

Fortunately, not only is this interaction between general-purpose computation and rendering modes possible, but it's fairly easy to accomplish given what you already know. CUDA C applications can seamlessly interoperate with either of the two most popular real-time rendering APIs, OpenGL and DirectX. This chapter will look at the mechanics by which you can enable this functionality.

The examples in this chapter deviate some from the precedents we've set in previous chapters. In particular, this chapter assumes a significant amount about your background with other technologies. Specifically, we have included a considerable amount of OpenGL and GLUT code in these examples, almost none of which will we explain in great depth. There are many superb resources to learn graphics APIs, both online and in bookstores, but these topics are well beyond the intended scope of this book. Rather, this chapter intends to focus on CUDA C and the facilities it offers to incorporate it into your graphics applications. If you are unfamiliar with OpenGL or DirectX, you are unlikely to derive much benefit from this chapter and may want to skip to the next.

8.1 Chapter Objectives

Through the course of this chapter, you will accomplish the following:

- You will learn what *graphics interoperability* is and why you might use it.

- You will learn how to set up a CUDA device for graphics interoperability.

- You will learn how to share data between your CUDA C kernels and OpenGL rendering.

8.2 Graphics Interoperation

To demonstrate the mechanics of interoperation between graphics and CUDA C, we'll write an application that works in two steps. The first step uses a CUDA C kernel to generate image data. In the second step, the application passes this data to the OpenGL driver to render. To accomplish this, we will use much of the CUDA C we have seen in previous chapters along with some OpenGL and GLUT calls.

To start our application, we include the relevant GLUT and CUDA headers in order to ensure the correct functions and enumerations are defined. We also define the size of the window into which our application plans to render. At 512 x 512 pixels, we will do relatively small drawings.

```
#define GL_GLEXT_PROTOTYPES
#include "GL/glut.h"
#include "cuda.h"
#include "cuda_gl_interop.h"
#include "../common/book.h"
#include "../common/cpu_bitmap.h"


#define    DIM    512
```

Additionally, we declare two global variables that will store handles to the data we intend to share between OpenGL and data. We will see momentarily how we use these two variables, but they will store different handles to the *same* buffer. We need two separate variables because OpenGL and CUDA will both have different "names" for the buffer. The variable `bufferObj` will be OpenGL's name for the data, and the variable `resource` will be the CUDA C name for it.

```
GLuint  bufferObj;
cudaGraphicsResource *resource;
```

Now let's take a look at the actual application. The first thing we do is select a CUDA device on which to run our application. On many systems, this is not a complicated process, since they will often contain only a single CUDA-enabled GPU. However, an increasing number of systems contain more than one CUDA-enabled GPU, so we need a method to choose one. Fortunately, the CUDA runtime provides such a facility to us.

```
int main( int argc, char **argv ) {
    cudaDeviceProp  prop;
    int dev;

    memset( &prop, 0, sizeof( cudaDeviceProp ) );
    prop.major = 1;
    prop.minor = 0;
    HANDLE_ERROR( cudaChooseDevice( &dev, &prop ) );
```

You may recall that we saw `cudaChooseDevice()` in Chapter 3, but since it was something of an ancillary point, we'll review it again now. Essentially, this code tells the runtime to select any GPU that has a *compute capability* of version 1.0 or better. It accomplishes this by first creating and clearing a `cudaDeviceProp` structure and then by setting its `major` version to 1 and `minor` version to 0. It passes this information to `cudaChooseDevice()`, which instructs the runtime to select a GPU in the system that satisfies the constraints specified by the `cudaDeviceProp` structure. In the next chapter, we will look more at what is meant by a GPU's *compute capability*, but for now it suffices to say that it roughly indicates the features a GPU supports. All CUDA-capable GPUs have at least compute capability 1.0, so the net effect of this call is that the runtime will select any CUDA-capable device and return an identifier for this device in the variable `dev`. There is no guarantee that this device is the best or fastest GPU, nor is there a guarantee that the device will be the same GPU from version to version of the CUDA runtime.

If the result of device selection is so seemingly underwhelming, why do we bother with all this effort to fill a `cudaDeviceProp` structure and call `cudaChooseDevice()` to get a valid device ID? Furthermore, we never hassled with this tomfoolery before, so why now? These are good questions. It turns out that we need to know the CUDA device ID so that we can tell the CUDA runtime that we intend to use the device for CUDA *and* OpenGL. We achieve this with a call to `cudaGLSetGLDevice()`, passing the device ID `dev` we obtained from `cudaChooseDevice()`:

```
HANDLE _ ERROR( cudaGLSetGLDevice( dev ) );
```

After the CUDA runtime initialization, we can proceed to initialize the OpenGL driver by calling our GL Utility Toolkit (GLUT) setup functions. This sequence of calls should look relatively familiar if you've used GLUT before:

```
// these GLUT calls need to be made before the other GL calls
glutInit( &argc, argv );
glutInitDisplayMode( GLUT_DOUBLE | GLUT_RGBA );
glutInitWindowSize( DIM, DIM );
glutCreateWindow( "bitmap" );
```

At this point in `main()`, we've prepared our CUDA runtime to play nicely with the OpenGL driver by calling `cudaGLSetGLDevice()`. Then we initialized GLUT and created a window named "bitmap" in which to draw our results. Now we can get on to the actual OpenGL interoperation!

Shared data buffers are the key component to interoperation between CUDA C kernels and OpenGL rendering. To pass data between OpenGL and CUDA, we will first need to create a buffer that can be used with both APIs. We start this process by creating a pixel buffer object in OpenGL and storing the handle in our global variable `GLuint bufferObj`:

```
glGenBuffers( 1, &bufferObj );
glBindBuffer( GL_PIXEL_UNPACK_BUFFER_ARB, bufferObj );
glBufferData( GL_PIXEL_UNPACK_BUFFER_ARB, DIM * DIM * 4,
              NULL, GL_DYNAMIC_DRAW_ARB );
```

If you have never used a pixel buffer object (PBO) in OpenGL, you will typically create one with these three steps: First, we generate a buffer handle
with `glGenBuffers()`. Then, we bind the handle to a pixel buffer with
`glBindBuffer()`. Finally, we request the OpenGL driver to allocate a buffer for
us with `glBufferData()`. In this example, we request a buffer to hold DIM x DIM
32-bit values and use the enumerant `GL_DYNAMIC_DRAW_ARB` to indicate that the
buffer will be modified repeatedly by the application. Since we have no data to preload
the buffer with, we pass `NULL` as the penultimate argument to `glBufferData()`.

All that remains in our quest to set up graphics interoperability is notifying the
CUDA runtime that we intend to share the OpenGL buffer named `bufferObj`
with CUDA. We do this by registering `bufferObj` with the CUDA runtime as a
graphics resource.

```
    HANDLE_ERROR(
        cudaGraphicsGLRegisterBuffer( &resource,
                                       bufferObj,
                                       cudaGraphicsMapFlagsNone )
    );
```

We specify to the CUDA runtime that we intend to use the
OpenGL PBO `bufferObj` with both OpenGL and CUDA by calling
`cudaGraphicsGLRegisterBuffer()`. The CUDA runtime returns a CUDA-
friendly handle to the buffer in the variable `resource`. This handle will be used to
refer to `bufferObj` in subsequent calls to the CUDA runtime.

The flag `cudaGraphicsMapFlagsNone` specifies that there is no particular
behavior of this buffer that we want to specify, although we have the option to
specify with `cudaGraphicsMapFlagsReadOnly` that the buffer will be read-
only. We could also use `cudaGraphicsMapFlagsWriteDiscard` to specify
that the previous contents will be discarded, making the buffer essentially
write-only. These flags allow the CUDA and OpenGL drivers to optimize the hardware settings for buffers with restricted access patterns, although they are not
required to be set.

Effectively, the call to `glBufferData()` requests the OpenGL driver to allocate a
buffer large enough to hold DIM x DIM 32-bit values. In subsequent OpenGL calls,
we'll refer to this buffer with the handle `bufferObj`, while in CUDA runtime calls,
we'll refer to this buffer with the pointer `resource`. Since we would like to read
from and write to this buffer from our CUDA C kernels, we will need more than just
a handle to the object. We will need an actual address in device memory that can be

passed to our kernel. We achieve this by instructing the CUDA runtime to map the shared resource and then by requesting a pointer to the mapped resource.

```
uchar4* devPtr;
size_t  size;
HANDLE_ERROR( cudaGraphicsMapResources( 1, &resource, NULL ) );
HANDLE_ERROR(
    cudaGraphicsResourceGetMappedPointer( (void**)&devPtr,
                                          &size,
                                          resource )
            );
```

We can then use `devPtr` as we would use any device pointer, except that the data can also be used by OpenGL as a pixel source. After all these setup shenanigans, the rest of `main()` proceeds as follows: First, we launch our kernel, passing it the pointer to our shared buffer. This kernel, the code of which we have not seen yet, generates image data to be rendered. Next, we unmap our shared resource. This call is important to make prior to performing rendering tasks because it provides synchronization between the CUDA and graphics portions of the application. Specifically, it implies that all CUDA operations performed prior to the call to `cudaGraphicsUnmapResources()` will complete before ensuing graphics calls begin.

Lastly, we register our keyboard and display callback functions with GLUT (`key_func` and `draw_func`), and we relinquish control to the GLUT rendering loop with `glutMainLoop()`.

```
dim3    grids(DIM/16,DIM/16);
dim3    threads(16,16);
kernel<<<grids,threads>>>( devPtr );

HANDLE_ERROR( cudaGraphicsUnmapResources( 1, &resource, NULL ) );

// set up GLUT and kick off main loop
glutKeyboardFunc( key_func );
glutDisplayFunc( draw_func );
glutMainLoop();
}
```

The remainder of the application consists of the three functions we just high-lighted, `kernel()`, `key_func()`, and `draw_func()`. So, let's take a look at those.

The kernel function takes a device pointer and generates image data. In the following example, we're using a kernel inspired by the ripple example in Chapter 5:

```
// based on ripple code, but uses uchar4, which is the
// type of data graphic interop uses
__global__ void kernel( uchar4 *ptr ) {
    // map from threadIdx/BlockIdx to pixel position
    int x = threadIdx.x + blockIdx.x * blockDim.x;
    int y = threadIdx.y + blockIdx.y * blockDim.y;
    int offset = x + y * blockDim.x * gridDim.x;

    // now calculate the value at that position
    float fx = x/(float)DIM - 0.5f;
    float fy = y/(float)DIM - 0.5f;
    unsigned char   green = 128 + 127 *
                            sin( abs(fx*100) - abs(fy*100) );

    // accessing uchar4 vs. unsigned char*
    ptr[offset].x = 0;
    ptr[offset].y = green;
    ptr[offset].z = 0;
    ptr[offset].w = 255;
}
```

Many familiar concepts are at work here. The method for turning thread and block indices into x- and y-coordinates and a linear offset has been examined several times. We then perform some reasonably arbitrary computations to determine the color for the pixel at that (x, y) location, and we store those values to memory. We're again using CUDA C to procedurally generate an image on the GPU. The important thing to realize is that this image will then be handed *directly* to OpenGL for rendering without the CPU ever getting involved. On the other hand, in the ripple example of Chapter 5, we generated image data on the GPU very much like this, but our application then copied the buffer back to the CPU for display.

So, how do we draw the CUDA-generated buffer using OpenGL? Well, if you recall the setup we performed in `main()`, you'll remember the following:

```
glBindBuffer( GL_PIXEL_UNPACK_BUFFER_ARB, bufferObj );
```

This call bound the shared buffer as a pixel source for the OpenGL driver to use in all subsequent calls to `glDrawPixels()`. Essentially, this means that a call to `glDrawPixels()` is all that we need in order to render the image data our CUDA C kernel generated. Consequently, the following is all that our `draw_func()` needs to do:

```
static void draw_func( void ) {
    glDrawPixels( DIM, DIM, GL_RGBA, GL_UNSIGNED_BYTE, 0 );
    glutSwapBuffers();
}
```

It's possible you've seen `glDrawPixels()` with a buffer pointer as the last argument. The OpenGL driver will copy from this buffer if no buffer is bound as a GL_PIXEL_UNPACK_BUFFER_ARB source. However, since our data is already on the GPU and we *have* bound our shared buffer as the GL_PIXEL_UNPACK_BUFFER_ARB source, this last parameter instead becomes an offset into the bound buffer. Because we want to render the entire buffer, this offset is zero for our application.

The last component to this example seems somewhat anticlimactic, but we've decided to give our users a method to exit the application. In this vein, our `key_func()` callback responds only to the Esc key and uses this as a signal to clean up and exit:

```
static void key_func( unsigned char key, int x, int y ) {
    switch (key) {
        case 27:
        // clean up OpenGL and CUDA
        HANDLE_ERROR( cudaGraphicsUnregisterResource( resource ) );
        glBindBuffer( GL_PIXEL_UNPACK_BUFFER_ARB, 0 );
        glDeleteBuffers( 1, &bufferObj );
        exit(0);
    }
}
```

Figure 8.1 A screenshot of the hypnotic graphics interoperation example

When run, this example draws a mesmerizing picture in "NVIDIA Green" and black, shown in Figure 8.1. Try using it to hypnotize your friends (or enemies).

8.3 GPU Ripple with Graphics Interoperability

In "Section 8.1: Graphics Interoperation," we referred to Chapter 5's GPU ripple example a few times. If you recall, that application created a CPUAnimBitmap and passed it a function to be called whenever a frame needed to be generated.

```
int main( void ) {
    DataBlock   data;
    CPUAnimBitmap  bitmap( DIM, DIM, &data );
    data.bitmap = &bitmap;

    HANDLE_ERROR( cudaMalloc( (void**)&data.dev_bitmap,
                              bitmap.image_size() ) );
```

```
        bitmap.anim_and_exit( (void (*)(void*,int))generate_frame,
                              (void (*)(void*))cleanup );
}
```

With the techniques we've learned in the previous section, we intend to create a GPUAnimBitmap structure. This structure will serve the same purpose as the CPUAnimBitmap, but in this improved version, the CUDA and OpenGL components will cooperate without CPU intervention. When we're done, the application will use a GPUAnimBitmap so that main() will become simply as follows:

```
int main( void ) {
    GPUAnimBitmap  bitmap( DIM, DIM, NULL );

    bitmap.anim_and_exit(
        (void (*)(uchar4*,void*,int))generate_frame, NULL );
}
```

The GPUAnimBitmap structure uses the same calls we just examined in Section 8.1: Graphics Interoperation. However, now these calls will be abstracted away in a GPUAnimBitmap structure so that future examples (and potentially your own applications) will be cleaner.

8.3.1 THE GPUANIMBITMAP STRUCTURE

Several of the data members for our GPUAnimBitmap will look familiar to you from Section 8.1: Graphics Interoperation.

```
struct GPUAnimBitmap {
    GLuint  bufferObj;
    cudaGraphicsResource *resource;
    int     width, height;
    void    *dataBlock;
    void    (*fAnim)(uchar4*,void*,int);
    void    (*animExit)(void*);
    void    (*clickDrag)(void*,int,int,int,int);
    int     dragStartX, dragStartY;
```

We know that OpenGL and the CUDA runtime will have different names for our GPU buffer, and we know that we will need to refer to both of these names, depending on whether we are making OpenGL or CUDA C calls. Therefore, our structure will store both OpenGL's bufferObj name and the CUDA runtime's resource name. Since we are dealing with a bitmap image that we intend to display, we know that the image will have a width and height to it.

To allow users of our GPUAnimBitmap to register for certain callback events, we will also store a void* pointer to arbitrary user data in dataBlock. Our class will never look at this data but will simply pass it back to any registered callback functions. The callbacks that a user may register are stored in fAnim, animExit, and clickDrag. The function fAnim() gets called in every call to glutIdleFunc(), and this function is responsible for producing the image data that will be rendered in the animation. The function animExit() will be called once, when the animation exits. This is where the user should implement cleanup code that needs to be executed when the animation ends. Finally, clickDrag(), an optional function, implements the user's response to mouse click/drag events. If the user registers this function, it gets called after every sequence of mouse button press, drag, and release events. The location of the initial mouse click in this sequence is stored in (dragStartX, dragStartY) so that the start and endpoints of the click/drag event can be passed to the user when the mouse button is released. This can be used to implement interactive animations that will impress your friends.

Initializing a GPUAnimBitmap follows the same sequence of code that we saw in our previous example. After stashing away arguments in the appropriate structure members, we start by querying the CUDA runtime for a suitable CUDA device:

```
GPUAnimBitmap( int w, int h, void *d ) {
    width = w;
    height = h;
    dataBlock = d;
    clickDrag = NULL;
```

```
// first, find a CUDA device and set it to graphic interop
cudaDeviceProp  prop;
int dev;
memset( &prop, 0, sizeof( cudaDeviceProp ) );
prop.major = 1;
prop.minor = 0;
HANDLE_ERROR( cudaChooseDevice( &dev, &prop ) );
```

After finding a compatible CUDA device, we make the important
`cudaGLSetGLDevice()` call to the CUDA runtime in order to notify it that we
intend to use `dev` as a device for interoperation with OpenGL:

```
cudaGLSetGLDevice( dev );
```

Since our framework uses GLUT to create a windowed rendering environment, we
need to initialize GLUT. This is unfortunately a bit awkward, since `glutInit()`
wants command-line arguments to pass to the windowing system. Since we have
none we want to pass, we would like to simply specify zero command-line arguments. Unfortunately, some versions of GLUT have a bug that cause applications
to crash when zero arguments are given. So, we trick GLUT into thinking that
we're passing an argument, and as a result, life is good.

```
int     c=1;
char    *foo = "name";
glutInit( &c, &foo );
```

We continue initializing GLUT exactly as we did in the previous example. We
create a window in which to render, specifying a title with the string "bitmap." If
you'd like to name your window something more interesting, be our guest.

```
glutInitDisplayMode( GLUT_DOUBLE | GLUT_RGBA );
glutInitWindowSize( width, height );
glutCreateWindow( "bitmap" );
```

Next, we request for the OpenGL driver to allocate a buffer handle that we imme-diately bind to the GL_PIXEL_UNPACK_BUFFER_ARB target to ensure that future calls to glDrawPixels() will draw to our interop buffer:

```
glGenBuffers( 1, &bufferObj );
glBindBuffer( GL_PIXEL_UNPACK_BUFFER_ARB, bufferObj );
```

Last, but most certainly not least, we request that the OpenGL driver allocate a region of GPU memory for us. Once this is done, we inform the CUDA runtime of this buffer and request a CUDA C name for this buffer by registering bufferObj with cudaGraphicsGLRegisterBuffer().

```
glBufferData( GL_PIXEL_UNPACK_BUFFER_ARB, width * height * 4,
              NULL, GL_DYNAMIC_DRAW_ARB );

    HANDLE_ERROR(
      cudaGraphicsGLRegisterBuffer( &resource,
                                    bufferObj,
                                    cudaGraphicsMapFlagsNone ) );
}
```

With the GPUAnimBitmap set up, the only remaining concern is exactly how we perform the rendering. The meat of the rendering will be done in our glutIdleFunction(). This function will essentially do three things. First, it maps our shared buffer and retrieves a GPU pointer for this buffer.

```
// static method used for GLUT callbacks
static void idle_func( void ) {
    static int ticks = 1;
    GPUAnimBitmap*  bitmap = *(get_bitmap_ptr());
    uchar4*         devPtr;
    size_t  size;
```

```
HANDLE_ERROR(
    cudaGraphicsMapResources( 1, &(bitmap->resource), NULL )
            );
HANDLE_ERROR(
    cudaGraphicsResourceGetMappedPointer( (void**)&devPtr,
                                          &size,
                                          bitmap->resource )
            );
```

Second, it calls the user-specified function fAnim() that presumably will launch a CUDA C kernel to fill the buffer at devPtr with image data.

```
bitmap->fAnim( devPtr, bitmap->dataBlock, ticks++ );
```

And lastly, it unmaps the GPU pointer that will release the buffer for use by the OpenGL driver in rendering. This rendering will be triggered by a call to glutPostRedisplay().

```
HANDLE_ERROR(
    cudaGraphicsUnmapResources( 1,
                                &(bitmap->resource),
                                NULL ) );

    glutPostRedisplay();
}
```

The remainder of the GPUAnimBitmap structure consists of important but somewhat tangential infrastructure code. If you have an interest in it, you should by all means examine it. But we feel that you'll be able to proceed successfully, even if you lack the time or interest to digest the rest of the code in GPUAnimBitmap.

8.3.2 GPU RIPPLE REDUX

Now that we have a GPU version of CPUAnimBitmap, we can proceed to retrofit our GPU ripple application to perform its animation entirely on the GPU. To begin, we will include gpu_anim.h, the home of our implementation of

GPUAnimBitmap. We also include nearly the same kernel as we examined in Chapter 5.

```
#include "../common/book.h"
#include "../common/gpu_anim.h"


#define DIM 1024


__global__ void kernel( uchar4 *ptr, int ticks ) {
    // map from threadIdx/BlockIdx to pixel position
    int x = threadIdx.x + blockIdx.x * blockDim.x;
    int y = threadIdx.y + blockIdx.y * blockDim.y;
    int offset = x + y * blockDim.x * gridDim.x;


    // now calculate the value at that position
    float fx = x - DIM/2;
    float fy = y - DIM/2;
    float d = sqrtf( fx * fx + fy * fy );
    unsigned char grey = (unsigned char)(128.0f + 127.0f *
                                          cos(d/10.0f -
                                          ticks/7.0f) /
                                          (d/10.0f + 1.0f));
    ptr[offset].x = grey;
    ptr[offset].y = grey;
    ptr[offset].z = grey;
    ptr[offset].w = 255;
}
```

The one and only change we've made is highlighted. The reason for this change is because OpenGL interoperation requires that our shared surfaces be "graphics friendly." Because real-time rendering typically uses arrays of four-component (red/green/blue/alpha) data elements, our target buffer is no longer simply an array of unsigned char as it previously was. It's now required to be an array of type uchar4. In reality, we treated our buffer in Chapter 5 as a four-component buffer, so we always indexed it with ptr[offset*4+k], where k indicates the component from 0 to 3. But now, the four-component nature of the data is made explicit with the switch to a uchar4 type.

Since kernel() is a CUDA C function that generates image data, all that remains is writing a host function that will be used as a callback in the idle_func() member of GPUAnimBitmap. For our current application, all this function does is launch the CUDA C kernel:

```
void generate_frame( uchar4 *pixels, void*, int ticks ) {
    dim3    grids(DIM/16,DIM/16);
    dim3    threads(16,16);
    kernel<<<grids,threads>>>( pixels, ticks );
}
```

That's basically everything we need, since all of the heavy lifting was done in the GPUAnimBitmap structure. To get this party started, we just create a GPUAnimBitmap and register our animation callback function, generate_frame().

```
int main( void ) {
    GPUAnimBitmap  bitmap( DIM, DIM, NULL );

    bitmap.anim_and_exit(
        (void (*)(uchar4*,void*,int))generate_frame, NULL );
}
```

8.4 Heat Transfer with Graphics Interop

So, what has been the point of doing all of this? If you look at the internals of the CPUAnimBitmap, the structure we used for previous animation examples, we would see that it works almost exactly like the rendering code in Section 8.1: Graphics Interoperation.

Almost.

The key difference between the CPUAnimBitmap and the previous example is buried in the call to glDrawPixels().

```
glDrawPixels( bitmap->x,
              bitmap->y,
              GL_RGBA,
              GL_UNSIGNED_BYTE,
              bitmap->pixels );
```

We remarked in the first example of this chapter that you may have previously seen calls to `glDrawPixels()` with a buffer pointer as the last argument. Well, if you hadn't before, you have now. This call in the `Draw()` routine of `CPUAnimBitmap` triggers a copy of the CPU buffer in `bitmap->pixels` to the GPU for rendering. To do this, the CPU needs to stop what it's doing and initiate a copy onto the GPU for every frame. This requires synchronization between the CPU and GPU and additional latency to initiate and complete a transfer over the PCI Express bus. Since the call to `glDrawPixels()` expects a host pointer in the last argument, this also means that after generating a frame of image data with a CUDA C kernel, our Chapter 5 ripple application needed to copy the frame from the GPU to the CPU with a `cudaMemcpy()`.

```
void generate_frame( DataBlock *d, int ticks ) {
    dim3    grids(DIM/16,DIM/16);
    dim3    threads(16,16);
    kernel<<<grids,threads>>>( d->dev_bitmap, ticks );

    HANDLE_ERROR( cudaMemcpy( d->bitmap->get_ptr(),
                              d->dev_bitmap,
                              d->bitmap->image_size(),
                              cudaMemcpyDeviceToHost ) );
}
```

Taken together, these facts mean that our original GPU ripple application was more than a little silly. We used CUDA C to compute image values for our rendering in each frame, but after the computations were done, we copied the buffer to the CPU, which then copied the buffer *back* to the GPU for display. This means that we introduced unnecessary data transfers between the host and the device that stood between us and maximum performance. Let's revisit a compute-intensive animation application that might see its performance improve by migrating it to use graphics interoperation for its rendering.

If you recall the previous chapter's heat simulation application, you will remember that it also used `CPUAnimBitmap` in order to display the output of its simulation computations. We will modify this application to use our newly implemented `GPUAnimBitmap` structure and look at how the resulting performance changes. As with the ripple example, our `GPUAnimBitmap` is almost a perfect drop-in replacement for `CPUAnimBitmap`, with the exception of the `unsigned char` to `uchar4` change. So, the signature of our animation routine changes in order to accommodate this shift in data types.

```
void anim_gpu( uchar4* outputBitmap, DataBlock *d, int ticks ) {
    HANDLE_ERROR( cudaEventRecord( d->start, 0 ) );
    dim3    blocks(DIM/16,DIM/16);
    dim3    threads(16,16);

    // since tex is global and bound, we have to use a flag to
    // select which is in/out per iteration
    volatile bool dstOut = true;
    for (int i=0; i<90; i++) {
        float    *in, *out;
        if (dstOut) {
            in  = d->dev_inSrc;
            out = d->dev_outSrc;
        } else {
            out = d->dev_inSrc;
            in  = d->dev_outSrc;
        }
        copy_const_kernel<<<blocks,threads>>>( in );
        blend_kernel<<<blocks,threads>>>( out, dstOut );
        dstOut = !dstOut;
    }
    float_to_color<<<blocks,threads>>>( outputBitmap,
                                        d->dev_inSrc );
```

```
        HANDLE_ERROR( cudaEventRecord( d->stop, 0 ) );
        HANDLE_ERROR( cudaEventSynchronize( d->stop ) );
        float    elapsedTime;
        HANDLE_ERROR( cudaEventElapsedTime( &elapsedTime,
                                        d->start, d->stop ) );
        d->totalTime += elapsedTime;
        ++d->frames;
        printf( "Average Time per frame:  %3.1f ms\n",
                d->totalTime/d->frames  );
    }
```

Since the float_to_color() kernel is the only function that actually uses the outputBitmap, it's the only other function that needs modification as a result of our shift to uchar4. This function was simply considered utility code in the previous chapter, and we will continue to consider it utility code. However, we have overloaded this function and included both unsigned char and uchar4 versions in book.h. You will notice that the differences between these functions are identical to the differences between kernel() in the CPU-animated and GPU-animated versions of GPU ripple. Most of the code for the float_to_ color() kernels has been omitted for clarity, but we encourage you to consult book.h if you're dying to see the details.

```
    __global__  void float_to_color( unsigned char *optr,
                                      const float *outSrc ) {

        // convert floating-point value to 4-component color

        optr[offset*4 + 0] = value( m1, m2, h+120 );
        optr[offset*4 + 1] = value( m1, m2, h );
        optr[offset*4 + 2] = value( m1, m2, h -120 );
        optr[offset*4 + 3] = 255;
    }
```

```
__global__ void float_to_color( uchar4 *optr,
                                const float *outSrc ) {


    // convert floating-point value to 4-component color

    optr[offset].x = value( m1, m2, h+120 );
    optr[offset].y = value( m1, m2, h );
    optr[offset].z = value( m1, m2, h -120 );
    optr[offset].w = 255;
}
```

Outside of these changes, the only major difference is in the change from CPUAnimBitmap to GPUAnimBitmap to perform animation.

```
int main( void ) {
    DataBlock    data;
    GPUAnimBitmap bitmap( DIM, DIM, &data );
    data.totalTime = 0;
    data.frames = 0;
    HANDLE_ERROR( cudaEventCreate( &data.start ) );
    HANDLE_ERROR( cudaEventCreate( &data.stop ) );

    int imageSize = bitmap.image_size();

    // assume float == 4 chars in size (i.e., rgba)
    HANDLE_ERROR( cudaMalloc( (void**)&data.dev_inSrc,
                            imageSize ) );
    HANDLE_ERROR( cudaMalloc( (void**)&data.dev_outSrc,
                            imageSize ) );
    HANDLE_ERROR( cudaMalloc( (void**)&data.dev_constSrc,
                            imageSize ) );

    HANDLE_ERROR( cudaBindTexture( NULL, texConstSrc,
                                 data.dev_constSrc,
                                 imageSize ) );
```

```
HANDLE_ERROR( cudaBindTexture( NULL, texIn,
                               data.dev_inSrc,
                               imageSize ) );

HANDLE_ERROR( cudaBindTexture( NULL, texOut,
                               data.dev_outSrc,
                               imageSize ) );

// initialize the constant data
float *temp = (float*)malloc( imageSize );
for (int i=0; i<DIM*DIM; i++) {
    temp[i] = 0;
    int x = i % DIM;
    int y = i / DIM;
    if ((x>300) && (x<600) && (y>310) && (y<601))
        temp[i] = MAX_TEMP;
}
temp[DIM*100+100] = (MAX_TEMP + MIN_TEMP)/2;
temp[DIM*700+100] = MIN_TEMP;
temp[DIM*300+300] = MIN_TEMP;
temp[DIM*200+700] = MIN_TEMP;
for (int y=800; y<900; y++) {
    for (int x=400; x<500; x++) {
        temp[x+y*DIM] = MIN_TEMP;
    }
}
HANDLE_ERROR( cudaMemcpy( data.dev_constSrc, temp,
                          imageSize,
                          cudaMemcpyHostToDevice ) );

// initialize the input data
for (int y=800; y<DIM; y++) {
    for (int x=0; x<200; x++) {
        temp[x+y*DIM] = MAX_TEMP;
    }
}
```

```
        HANDLE_ERROR( cudaMemcpy( data.dev_inSrc, temp,
                                  imageSize,
                                  cudaMemcpyHostToDevice ) );
        free( temp );

        bitmap.anim_and_exit( (void (*)(uchar4*,void*,int))anim_gpu,
                              (void (*)(void*))anim_exit );
    }
```

Although it might be instructive to take a glance at the rest of this enhanced heat simulation application, it is not sufficiently different from the previous chapter's version to warrant more description. The important component is answering the question, how does performance change now that we've completely migrated the application to the GPU? Without having to copy every frame back to the host for display, the situation should be much happier than it was previously.

So, exactly how much better is it to use the graphics interoperability to perform the rendering? Previously, the heat transfer example consumed about 25.3ms per frame on our GeForce GTX 285–based test machine. After converting the application to use graphics interoperability, this drops by 15 percent to 21.6ms per frame. The net result is that our rendering loop is 15 percent faster and no longer requires intervention from the host every time we want to display a frame. That's not bad for a day's work!

8.5 DirectX Interoperability

Although we've looked only at examples that use interoperation with the OpenGL rendering system, DirectX interoperation is nearly identical. You will still use a `cudaGraphicsResource` to refer to buffers that you share between DirectX and CUDA, and you will still use calls to `cudaGraphicsMapResources()` and `cudaGraphicsResourceGetMappedPointer()` to retrieve CUDA-friendly pointers to these shared resources.

For the most part, the calls that differ between OpenGL and DirectX interoperability have embarrassingly simple translations to DirectX. For example, rather than calling `cudaGLSetGLDevice()`, we call `cudaD3D9SetDirect3DDevice()` to specify that a CUDA device should be enabled for Direct3D 9.0 interoperability.

Likewise, `cudaD3D10SetDirect3DDevice()` enables a device for Direct3D 10 interoperation and `cudaD3D11SetDirect3DDevice()` for Direct3D 11.

The details of DirectX interoperability probably will not surprise you if you've worked through this chapter's OpenGL examples. But if you want to use DirectX interoperation and want a small project to get started, we suggest that you migrate this chapter's examples to use DirectX. To get started, we recommend consulting the *NVIDIA CUDA Programming Guide* for a reference on the API and taking a look at the GPU Computing SDK code samples on DirectX interoperability.

8.6 Chapter Review

Although much of this book has been devoted to using the GPU for parallel, general-purpose computing, we can't forget the GPU's successful day job as a rendering engine. Many applications require or would benefit from the use of standard computer graphics rendering. Since the GPU is master of the rendering domain, all that stood between us and the exploitation of these resources was a lack of understanding of the mechanics in convincing the CUDA runtime and graphics drivers to cooperate. Now that we have seen how this is done, we no longer need the host to intervene in displaying the graphical results of our computations. This simultaneously accelerates the application's rendering loop and frees the host to perform other computations in the meantime. Otherwise, if there are no other computations to be performed, it leaves our system more responsive to other events or applications.

There are many other ways to use graphics interoperability that we left unexplored. We looked primarily at using a CUDA C kernel to write into a pixel buffer object for display in a window. This image data can also be used as a texture that can be applied to any surface in the scene. In addition to modifying pixel buffer objects, you can also share vertex buffer objects between CUDA and the graphics engine. Among other things, this allows you to write CUDA C kernels that perform collision detection between objects or compute vertex displacement maps to be used to render objects or surfaces that interact with the user or their surroundings. If you're interested in computer graphics, CUDA C's graphics interoperability API enables a slew of new possibilities for your applications!

Chapter 9

Atomics

In the first half of the book, we saw many occasions where something complicated to accomplish with a single-threaded application becomes quite easy when implemented using CUDA C. For example, thanks to the behind-the-scenes work of the CUDA runtime, we no longer needed `for()` loops in order to do per-pixel updates in our animations or heat simulations. Likewise, thousands of parallel blocks and threads get created and automatically enumerated with thread and block indices simply by calling a `__global__` function from host code.

On the other hand, there are some situations where something incredibly simple in single-threaded applications actually presents a serious problem when we try to implement the same algorithm on a massively parallel architecture. In this chapter, we'll take a look at some of the situations where we need to use special primitives in order to safely accomplish things that can be quite trivial to do in a traditional, single-threaded application.

9.1 Chapter Objectives

Through the course of this chapter, you will accomplish the following:

- You will learn about the *compute capability* of various NVIDIA GPUs.

- You will learn about what atomic operations are and why you might need them.

- You will learn how to perform arithmetic with atomic operations in your CUDA C kernels.

9.2 Compute Capability

All of the topics we have covered to this point involve capabilities that every CUDA-enabled GPU possesses. For example, every GPU built on the CUDA Architecture can launch kernels, access global memory, and read from constant and texture memories. But just like different models of CPUs have varying capabilities and instruction sets (for example, MMX, SSE, or SSE2), so too do CUDA-enabled graphics processors. NVIDIA refers to the supported features of a GPU as its *compute capability*.

9.2.1 THE COMPUTE CAPABILITY OF NVIDIA GPUS

As of press time, NVIDIA GPUs could potentially support compute capabilities 1.0, 1.1, 1.2, 1.3, or 2.0. Higher-capability versions represent supersets of the versions below them, implementing a "layered onion" or "Russian nesting doll" hierarchy (depending on your metaphorical preference). For example, a GPU with compute capability 1.2 supports all the features of compute capabilities 1.0 and 1.1. The *NVIDIA CUDA Programming Guide* contains an up-to-date list of all CUDA-capable GPUs and their corresponding compute capability. Table 9.1 lists the NVIDIA GPUs available at press time. The compute capability supported by each GPU is listed next to the device's name.

Table 9.1 Selected CUDA-Enabled GPUs and Their Corresponding Compute Capabilities

GPU	COMPUTE CAPABILITY
GeForce GTX 480, GTX 470	2.0
GeForce GTX 295	1.3
GeForce GTX 285, GTX 280	1.3
GeForce GTX 260	1.3
GeForce 9800 GX2	1.1
GeForce GTS 250, GTS 150, 9800 GTX, 9800 GTX+, 8800 GTS 512	1.1
GeForce 8800 Ultra, 8800 GTX	1.0
GeForce 9800 GT, 8800 GT, GTX 280M, 9800M GTX	1.1
GeForce GT 130, 9600 GSO, 8800 GS, 8800M GTX, GTX 260M, 9800M GT	1.1
GeForce 8800 GTS	1.0
GeForce 9600 GT, 8800M GTS, 9800M GTS	1.1
GeForce 9700M GT	1.1
GeForce GT 120, 9500 GT, 8600 GTS, 8600 GT, 9700M GT, 9650M GS, 9600M GT, 9600M GS, 9500M GS, 8700M GT, 8600M GT, 8600M GS	1.1
GeForce G100, 8500 GT, 8400 GS, 8400M GT, 9500M G, 9300M G, 8400M GS, 9400 mGPU, 9300 mGPU, 8300 mGPU, 8200 mGPU, 8100 mGPU	1.1
GeForce 9300M GS, 9200M GS, 9100M G, 8400M G	1.1
Tesla S2070, S2050, C2070, C2050	2.0
Tesla S1070, C1060	1.3

Continued

Table 9.1 Selected CUDA-Enabled GPUs and Their Corresponding Compute Capabilities (Continued)

GPU	COMPUTE CAPABILITY
Tesla S870 , D870, C870	1.0
Quadro Plex 2200 D2	1.3
Quadro Plex 2100 D4	1.1
Quadro Plex 2100 Model S4	1.0
Quadro Plex 1000 Model IV	1.0
Quadro FX 5800	1.3
Quadro FX 4800	1.3
Quadro FX 4700 X2	1.1
Quadro FX 3700M	1.1
Quadro FX 5600	1.0
Quadro FX 3700	1.1
Quadro FX 3600M	1.1
Quadro FX 4600	1.0
Quadro FX 2700M	1.1
Quadro FX 1700, FX 570, NVS 320M, FX 1700M, FX 1600M, FX 770M, FX 570M	1.1
Quadro FX 370, NVS 290, NVS 140M, NVS 135M, FX 360M	1.1
Quadro FX 370M, NVS 130M	1.1

Of course, since NVIDIA releases new graphics processors all the time, this table will undoubtedly be out-of-date the moment this book is published. Fortunately, NVIDIA has a website, and on this website you will find the CUDA Zone. Among other things, the CUDA Zone is home to the most up-to-date list of supported CUDA devices. We recommend that you consult this list before doing anything drastic as a result of being unable to find your new GPU in Table 9.1. Or you can simply run the example from Chapter 3 that prints the compute capability of each CUDA device in the system.

Because this is the chapter on atomics, of particular relevance is the hardware capability to perform atomic operations on memory. Before we look at what atomic operations are and why you care, you should know that atomic operations on global memory are supported only on GPUs of compute capability 1.1 or higher. Furthermore, atomic operations on *shared* memory require a GPU of compute capability 1.2 or higher. Because of the superset nature of compute capability versions, GPUs of compute capability 1.2 therefore support both shared memory atomics and global memory atomics. Similarly, GPUs of compute capability 1.3 support both of these as well.

If it turns out that your GPU is of compute capability 1.0 and it doesn't support atomic operations on global memory, well maybe we've just given you the perfect excuse to upgrade! If you decide you're not ready to splurge on a new atomics-enabled graphics processor, you can continue to read about atomic operations and the situations in which you might want to use them. But if you find it too heartbreaking that you won't be able to run the examples, feel free to skip to the next chapter.

9.2.2 COMPILING FOR A MINIMUM COMPUTE CAPABILITY

Suppose that we have written code that requires a certain minimum compute capability. For example, imagine that you've finished this chapter and go off to write an application that relies heavily on global memory atomics. Having studied this text extensively, you know that global memory atomics require a compute capability of 1.1. To compile your code, you need to inform the compiler that the kernel cannot run on hardware with a capability less than 1.1. Moreover, in telling the compiler this, you're also giving it the freedom to make other optimizations that may be available only on GPUs of compute capability 1.1 or greater. Informing the compiler of this is as simple as adding a command-line option to your invocation of nvcc:

```
nvcc -arch=sm_11
```

Similarly, to build a kernel that relies on shared memory atomics, you need to inform the compiler that the code requires compute capability 1.2 or greater:

```
nvcc -arch=sm_12
```

9.3 Atomic Operations Overview

Programmers typically never need to use atomic operations when writing traditional single-threaded applications. If this is the situation with you, don't worry; we plan to explain what they are and why we might need them in a multithreaded application. To clarify atomic operations, we'll look at one of the first things you learned when learning C or C++, the increment operator:

```
x++;
```

This is a single expression in standard C, and after executing this expression, the value in x should be one greater than it was prior to executing the increment. But what sequence of operations does this imply? To add one to the value of x, we first need to know what value is currently in x. After reading the value of x, we can modify it. And finally, we need to write this value back to x.

So the three steps in this operation are as follows:

1. Read the value in x.

2. Add 1 to the value read in step 1.

3. Write the result back to x.

Sometimes, this process is generally called a *read-modify-write* operation, since step 2 can consist of any operation that changes the value that was read from x.

Now consider a situation where two threads need to perform this increment on the value in x. Let's call these threads A and B. For A and B to both increment the value in x, both threads need to perform the three operations we've described. Let's suppose x starts with the value 7. Ideally we would like thread A and thread B to do the steps shown in Table 9.2.

Table 9.2 Two threads incrementing the value in x

STEP	EXAMPLE
1. Thread A reads the value in x.	A reads 7 from x.
2. Thread A adds 1 to the value it read.	A computes 8.
3. Thread A writes the result back to x.	x <- 8.
4. Thread B reads the value in x.	B reads 8 from x.
5. Thread B adds 1 to the value it read.	B computes 9.
6. Thread B writes the result back to x.	x <- 9.

Since x starts with the value 7 and gets incremented by two threads, we would expect it to hold the value 9 after they've completed. In the previous sequence of operations, this is indeed the result we obtain. Unfortunately, there are many other orderings of these steps that produce the wrong value. For example, consider the ordering shown in Table 9.3 where thread A and thread B's operations become interleaved with each other.

Table 9.3 Two threads incrementing the value in x with interleaved operations

STEP	EXAMPLE
Thread A reads the value in x.	A reads 7 from x.
Thread B reads the value in x.	B reads 7 from x.
Thread A adds 1 to the value it read.	A computes 8.
Thread B adds 1 to the value it read.	B computes 8.
Thread A writes the result back to x.	x <- 8.
Thread B writes the result back to x.	x <- 8.

Therefore, if our threads get scheduled unfavorably, we end up computing the wrong result. There are many other orderings for these six operations, some of which produce correct results and some of which do not. When moving from a single-threaded to a multithreaded version of this application, we suddenly have potential for unpredictable results if multiple threads need to read or write shared values.

In the previous example, we need a way to perform the *read-modify-write* without being interrupted by another thread. Or more specifically, no other thread can read or write the value of x until we have completed our operation. Because the execution of these operations cannot be broken into smaller parts by other threads, we call operations that satisfy this constraint as *atomic*. CUDA C supports several atomic operations that allow you to operate safely on memory, even when thousands of threads are potentially competing for access.

Now we'll take a look at an example that requires the use of atomic operations to compute correct results.

9.4 Computing Histograms

Oftentimes, algorithms require the computation of a *histogram* of some set of data. If you haven't had any experience with histograms in the past, that's not a big deal. Essentially, given a data set that consists of some set of elements, a histogram represents a count of the frequency of each element. For example, if we created a histogram of the letters in the phrase *Programming with CUDA C*, we would end up with the result shown in Figure 9.1.

Although simple to describe and understand, computing histograms of data arises surprisingly often in computer science. It's used in algorithms for image processing, data compression, computer vision, machine learning, audio encoding, and many others. We will use histogram computation as the algorithm for the following code examples.

2	2	1	2	1	2	2	1	1	1	2	1	1	1
A	C	D	G	H	I	M	N	O	P	R	T	U	W

Figure 9.1 Letter frequency histogram built from the string *Programming with CUDA C*

9.4.1 CPU HISTOGRAM COMPUTATION

Because the computation of a histogram may not be familiar to all readers, we'll start with an example of how to compute a histogram on the CPU. This example will also serve to illustrate how computing a histogram is relatively simple in a single-threaded CPU application. The application will be given some large stream of data. In an actual application, the data might signify anything from pixel colors to audio samples, but in our sample application, it will be a stream of randomly generated bytes. We can create this random stream of bytes using a utility function we have provided called `big_random_block()`. In our application, we create 100MB of random data.

```
#include "../common/book.h"

#define SIZE    (100*1024*1024)

int main( void ) {
    unsigned char *buffer = (unsigned char*)big_random_block( SIZE );
```

Since each random 8-bit byte can be any of 256 different values (from 0x00 to 0xFF), our histogram needs to contain 256 *bins* in order to keep track of the number of times each value has been seen in the data. We create a 256-bin array and initialize all the bin counts to zero.

```
    unsigned int    histo[256];
    for (int i=0; i<256; i++)
        histo[i] = 0;
```

Once our histogram has been created and all the bins are initialized to zero, we need to tabulate the frequency with which each value appears in the data contained in `buffer[]`. The idea here is that whenever we see some value z in the array `buffer[]`, we want to increment the value in bin z of our histogram. This way, we're counting the number of times we have seen an occurrence of the value z.

If buffer[i] is the current value we are looking at, we want to increment the count we have in the bin numbered buffer[i]. Since bin buffer[i] is located at histo[buffer[i]], we can increment the appropriate counter in a single line of code.

```
histo[buffer[i]]++;
```

We do this for each element in buffer[] with a simple for() loop:

```
for (int i=0; i<SIZE; i++)
    histo[buffer[i]]++;
```

At this point, we've completed our histogram of the input data. In a full application, this histogram might be the input to the next step of computation. In our simple example, however, this is all we care to compute, so we end the application by verifying that all the bins of our histogram sum to the expected value.

```
long histoCount = 0;
for (int i=0; i<256; i++) {
    histoCount += histo[i];
}
printf( "Histogram Sum:  %ld\n", histoCount );
```

If you've followed closely, you will realize that this sum will always be the same, regardless of the random input array. Each bin counts the number of times we have seen the corresponding data element, so the sum of all of these bins should be the total number of data elements we've examined. In our case, this will be the value SIZE.

And needless to say (but we will anyway), we clean up after ourselves and return.

```
    free( buffer );
    return 0;
}
```

On our benchmark machine, a Core 2 Duo, the histogram of this 100MB array of data can be constructed in 0 .416 seconds. This will provide a baseline performance for the GPU version we intend to write.

9.4.2 GPU HISTOGRAM COMPUTATION

We would like to adapt the histogram computation example to run on the GPU. If our input array is large enough, it might save a considerable amount of time to have different threads examining different parts of the buffer. Having different threads read different parts of the input should be easy enough. After all, it's very similar to things we have seen so far. The problem with computing a histogram from the input data arises from the fact that multiple threads may want to increment the same bin of the output histogram at the same time. In this situation, we will need to use atomic increments to avoid a situation like the one described in Section 9.2: Atomic Operations Overview.

Our `main()` routine looks very similar to the CPU version, although we will need to add some of the CUDA C plumbing in order to get input to the GPU and results from the GPU. However, we start exactly as we did on the CPU:

```
int main( void ) {
    unsigned char *buffer = (unsigned char*)big_random_block( SIZE );
```

We will be interested in measuring how our code performs, so we initialize events for timing exactly like we always have.

```
cudaEvent_t     start, stop;
HANDLE_ERROR( cudaEventCreate( &start ) );
HANDLE_ERROR( cudaEventCreate( &stop ) );
HANDLE_ERROR( cudaEventRecord( start, 0 ) );
```

After setting up our input data and events, we look to GPU memory. We will need to allocate space for our random input data and our output histogram. After allocating the input buffer, we copy the array we generated with `big_random_block()` to the GPU. Likewise, after allocating the histogram, we initialize it to zero just like we did in the CPU version.

```
// allocate memory on the GPU for the file's data
unsigned char *dev_buffer;
unsigned int *dev_histo;
HANDLE_ERROR( cudaMalloc( (void**)&dev_buffer, SIZE ) );
HANDLE_ERROR( cudaMemcpy( dev_buffer, buffer, SIZE,
                          cudaMemcpyHostToDevice ) );

HANDLE_ERROR( cudaMalloc( (void**)&dev_histo,
                          256 * sizeof( long ) ) );
HANDLE_ERROR( cudaMemset( dev_histo, 0,
                          256 * sizeof( int ) ) );
```

You may notice that we slipped in a new CUDA runtime function, `cudaMemset()`. This function has a similar signature to the standard C function `memset()`, and the two functions behave nearly identically. The difference in signature is between these functions is that `cudaMemset()` returns an error code while the C library function `memset()` does not. This error code will inform the caller whether anything bad happened while attempting to set GPU memory. Aside from the error code return, the only difference is that `cudaMemset()` operates on GPU memory while `memset()` operates on host memory.

After initializing the input and output buffers, we are ready to compute our histogram. You will see how we prepare and launch the histogram kernel momentarily. For the time being, assume that we have computed the histogram on the GPU. After finishing, we need to copy the histogram back to the CPU, so we allocate a 256-entry array and perform a copy from device to host.

```
unsigned int    histo[256];
HANDLE_ERROR( cudaMemcpy( histo, dev_histo,
                          256 * sizeof( int ),
                          cudaMemcpyDeviceToHost ) );
```

At this point, we are done with the histogram computation so we can stop our timers and display the elapsed time. Just like the previous event code, this is identical to the timing code we've used for several chapters.

```
// get stop time, and display the timing results
HANDLE_ERROR( cudaEventRecord( stop, 0 ) );
HANDLE_ERROR( cudaEventSynchronize( stop ) );
float    elapsedTime;
HANDLE_ERROR( cudaEventElapsedTime( &elapsedTime,
                                    start, stop ) );
printf( "Time to generate:  %3.1f ms\n", elapsedTime );
```

At this point, we could pass the histogram as input to another stage in the algorithm, but since we are not using the histogram for anything else, we will simply verify that the computed GPU histogram matches what we get on the CPU. First, we verify that the histogram sum matches what we expect. This is identical to the CPU code shown here:

```
long histoCount = 0;
for (int i=0; i<256; i++) {
    histoCount += histo[i];
}
printf( "Histogram Sum:  %ld\n", histoCount );
```

To fully verify the GPU histogram, though, we will use the CPU to compute the same histogram. The obvious way to do this would be to allocate a new histogram array, compute a histogram from the input using the code from Section 9.3.1: CPU Histogram Computation, and, finally, ensure that each bin in the GPU and CPU version match. But rather than allocate a new histogram array, we'll opt to start with the GPU histogram and compute the CPU histogram "in reverse."

By computing the histogram "in reverse," we mean that rather than starting at zero and incrementing bin values when we see data elements, we will start with the GPU histogram and *decrement* the bin's value when the CPU sees data elements. Therefore, the CPU has computed the same histogram as the GPU if and only if every bin has the value zero when we are finished. In some sense, we are computing the difference between these two histograms. The code will look remarkably like the CPU histogram computation but with a decrement operator instead of an increment operator.

```
// verify that we have the same counts via CPU
for (int i=0; i<SIZE; i++)
    histo[buffer[i]]--;
for (int i=0; i<256; i++) {
    if (histo[i] != 0)
        printf( "Failure at %d!\n", i );
}
```

As usual, the finale involves cleaning up our allocated CUDA events, GPU memory, and host memory.

```
HANDLE_ERROR( cudaEventDestroy( start ) );
HANDLE_ERROR( cudaEventDestroy( stop ) );
cudaFree( dev_histo );
cudaFree( dev_buffer );
free( buffer );
return 0;
}
```

Before, we assumed that we had launched a kernel that computed our histogram and then pressed on to discuss the aftermath. Our kernel launch is slightly more complicated than usual because of performance concerns. Because the histogram contains 256 bins, using 256 threads per block proves convenient as well as results in high performance. But we have a lot of flexibility in terms of the number of blocks we launch. For example, with 100MB of data, we have 104,857,600 bytes of data. We could launch a single block and have each thread examine 409,600 data elements. Likewise, we could launch 409,600 blocks and have each thread examine a single data element.

As you might have guessed, the optimal solution is at a point between these two extremes. By running some performance experiments, optimal performance is achieved when the number of blocks we launch is exactly twice the number of multiprocessors our GPU contains. For example, a GeForce GTX 280 has 30 multiprocessors, so our histogram kernel happens to run fastest on a GeForce GTX 280 when launched with 60 parallel blocks.

In Chapter 3, we discussed a method for querying various properties of the hardware on which our program is running. We will need to use one of these device properties if we intend to dynamically size our launch based on our current hardware platform. To accomplish this, we will use the following code segment. Although you haven't yet seen the kernel implementation, you should still be able to follow what is going on.

```
cudaDeviceProp  prop;
HANDLE_ERROR( cudaGetDeviceProperties( &prop, 0 ) );
int blocks = prop.multiProcessorCount;
histo_kernel<<<blocks*2,256>>>( dev_buffer, SIZE, dev_histo );
```

Since our walk-through of `main()` has been somewhat fragmented, here is the entire routine from start to finish:

```
int main( void ) {
    unsigned char *buffer =
                        (unsigned char*)big_random_block( SIZE );

    cudaEvent_t     start, stop;
    HANDLE_ERROR( cudaEventCreate( &start ) );
    HANDLE_ERROR( cudaEventCreate( &stop ) );
    HANDLE_ERROR( cudaEventRecord( start, 0 ) );

    // allocate memory on the GPU for the file's data
    unsigned char *dev_buffer;
    unsigned int  *dev_histo;
    HANDLE_ERROR( cudaMalloc( (void**)&dev_buffer, SIZE ) );
    HANDLE_ERROR( cudaMemcpy( dev_buffer, buffer, SIZE,
                                cudaMemcpyHostToDevice ) );

    HANDLE_ERROR( cudaMalloc( (void**)&dev_histo,
                                256 * sizeof( long ) ) );
    HANDLE_ERROR( cudaMemset( dev_histo, 0,
                                256 * sizeof( int ) ) );
```

```
cudaDeviceProp  prop;
HANDLE_ERROR( cudaGetDeviceProperties( &prop, 0 ) );
int blocks = prop.multiProcessorCount;
histo_kernel<<<blocks*2,256>>>( dev_buffer, SIZE, dev_histo );

unsigned int    histo[256];
HANDLE_ERROR( cudaMemcpy( histo, dev_histo,
                          256 * sizeof( int ),
                          cudaMemcpyDeviceToHost ) );

// get stop time, and display the timing results
HANDLE_ERROR( cudaEventRecord( stop, 0 ) );
HANDLE_ERROR( cudaEventSynchronize( stop ) );
float    elapsedTime;
HANDLE_ERROR( cudaEventElapsedTime( &elapsedTime,
                                    start, stop ) );
printf( "Time to generate:  %3.1f ms\n", elapsedTime );

long histoCount = 0;
for (int i=0; i<256; i++) {
    histoCount += histo[i];
}
printf( "Histogram Sum:  %ld\n", histoCount );

// verify that we have the same counts via CPU
for (int i=0; i<SIZE; i++)
    histo[buffer[i]]--;
for (int i=0; i<256; i++) {
    if (histo[i] != 0)
        printf( "Failure at %d!\n", i );
}

HANDLE_ERROR( cudaEventDestroy( start ) );
HANDLE_ERROR( cudaEventDestroy( stop ) );
```

```
        cudaFree( dev_histo );
        cudaFree( dev_buffer );
        free( buffer );
        return 0;
    }
```

HISTOGRAM KERNEL USING GLOBAL MEMORY ATOMICS

And now for the fun part: the GPU code that computes the histogram! The kernel that computes the histogram itself needs to be given a pointer to the input data array, the length of the input array, and a pointer to the output histogram. The first thing our kernel needs to compute is a linearized offset into the input data array. Each thread will start with an offset between 0 and the number of threads minus 1. It will then stride by the total number of threads that have been launched. We hope you remember this technique; we used the same logic to add vectors of arbitrary length when you first learned about threads.

```
#include "../common/book.h"


#define SIZE     (100*1024*1024)


__global__ void histo_kernel( unsigned char *buffer,
                              long size,
                              unsigned int *histo ) {
    int i = threadIdx.x + blockIdx.x * blockDim.x;
    int stride = blockDim.x * gridDim.x;
```

Once each thread knows its starting offset i and the stride it should use, the code walks through the input array incrementing the corresponding histogram bin.

```
    while (i < size) {
        atomicAdd( &(histo[buffer[i]]), 1 );
        i += stride;
    }
}
```

The highlighted line represents the way we use atomic operations in CUDA C. The call `atomicAdd( addr, y );` generates an atomic sequence of operations that read the value at address `addr`, adds `y` to that value, and stores the result back to the memory address `addr`. The hardware guarantees us that no other thread can read or write the value at address `addr` while we perform these operations, thus ensuring predictable results. In our example, the address in question is the location of the histogram bin that corresponds to the current byte. If the current byte is `buffer[i]`, just like we saw in the CPU version, the corresponding histogram bin is `histo[buffer[i]]`. The atomic operation needs the address of this bin, so the first argument is therefore `&(histo[buffer[i]])`. Since we simply want to increment the value in that bin by one, the second argument is 1.

So after all that hullabaloo, our GPU histogram computation is fairly similar to the corresponding CPU version.

```
#include "../common/book.h"


#define SIZE     (100*1024*1024)


__global__ void histo_kernel( unsigned char *buffer,
                              long size,
                              unsigned int *histo ) {
    int i = threadIdx.x + blockIdx.x * blockDim.x;
    int stride = blockDim.x * gridDim.x;
    while (i < size) {
        atomicAdd( &(histo[buffer[i]]), 1 );
        i += stride;
    }
}
```

However, we need to save the celebrations for later. After running this example, we discover that a GeForce GTX 285 can construct a histogram from 100MB of input data in 1.752 seconds. If you read the section on CPU-based histograms, you will realize that this performance is terrible. In fact, this is more than four times slower than the CPU version! But this is why we always measure our baseline performance. It would be a shame to settle for such a low-performance implementation simply because it runs on the GPU.

Since we do very little work in the kernel, it is quite likely that the atomic operation on global memory is causing the problem. Essentially, when thousands of threads are trying to access a handful of memory locations, a great deal of contention for our 256 histogram bins can occur. To ensure atomicity of the increment operations, the hardware needs to serialize operations to the same memory location. This can result in a long queue of pending operations, and any performance gain we might have had will vanish. We will need to improve the algorithm itself in order to recover this performance.

HISTOGRAM KERNEL USING SHARED AND GLOBAL MEMORY ATOMICS

Ironically, despite that the atomic operations cause this performance degradation, alleviating the slowdown actually involves using *more* atomics, not fewer. The core problem was not the use of atomics so much as the fact that thousands of threads were competing for access to a relatively small number of memory addresses. To address this issue, we will split our histogram computation into two phases.

In phase one, each parallel block will compute a separate histogram of the data that its constituent threads examine. Since each block does this independently, we can compute these histograms in shared memory, saving us the time of sending each write-off chip to DRAM. Doing this does not free us from needing atomic operations, though, since multiple threads within the block can still examine data elements with the same value. However, the fact that only 256 threads will now be competing for 256 addresses will reduce contention from the global version where thousands of threads were competing.

The first phase then involves allocating and zeroing a shared memory buffer to hold each block's intermediate histogram. Recall from Chapter 5 that since the subsequent step will involve reading and modifying this buffer, we need a __syncthreads() call to ensure that every thread's write has completed before progressing.

```
__global__ void histo_kernel( unsigned char *buffer,
                              long size,
                              unsigned int *histo ) {

    __shared__ unsigned int temp[256];
    temp[threadIdx.x] = 0;
    __syncthreads();
```

After zeroing the histogram, the next step is remarkably similar to our original GPU histogram. The sole differences here are that we use the shared memory buffer `temp[]` instead of the global memory buffer `histo[]` and that we need a subsequent call to `__syncthreads()` to ensure the last of our writes have been committed.

```
int i = threadIdx.x + blockIdx.x * blockDim.x;
int offset = blockDim.x * gridDim.x;
while (i < size) {
    atomicAdd( &temp[buffer[i]], 1);
    i += offset;
}
__syncthreads();
```

The last step in our modified histogram example requires that we merge each block's temporary histogram into the global buffer `histo[]`. Suppose we split the input in half and two threads look at different halves and compute separate histograms. If thread A sees byte 0xFC 20 times in the input and thread B sees byte 0xFC 5 times, the byte 0xFC must have appeared 25 times in the input. Likewise, each bin of the final histogram is just the sum of the corresponding bin in thread A's histogram and thread B's histogram. This logic extends to any number of threads, so merging every block's histogram into a single final histogram involves adding each entry in the block's histogram to the corresponding entry in the final histogram. For all the reasons we've seen already, this needs to be done atomically:

```
    atomicAdd( &(histo[threadIdx.x]), temp[threadIdx.x] );
}
```

Since we have decided to use 256 threads and have 256 histogram bins, each thread atomically adds a single bin to the final histogram's total. If these numbers didn't match, this phase would be more complicated. Note that we have no guarantees about what order the blocks add their values to the final histogram, but since integer addition is commutative, we will always get the same answer provided that the additions occur atomically.

And with this, our two phase histogram computation kernel is complete. Here it is from start to finish:

```
__global__ void histo_kernel( unsigned char *buffer,
                              long size,
                              unsigned int *histo ) {
    __shared__ unsigned int temp[256];
    temp[threadIdx.x] = 0;
    __syncthreads();

    int i = threadIdx.x + blockIdx.x * blockDim.x;
    int offset = blockDim.x * gridDim.x;
    while (i < size) {
        atomicAdd( &temp[buffer[i]], 1);
        i += offset;
    }

    __syncthreads();
    atomicAdd( &(histo[threadIdx.x]), temp[threadIdx.x] );
}
```

This version of our histogram example improves dramatically over the previous GPU version. Adding the shared memory component drops our running time on a GeForce GTX 285 to 0.057 seconds. Not only is this significantly better than the version that used global memory atomics only, but this beats our original CPU implementation by an order of magnitude (from 0.416 seconds to 0.057 seconds). This improvement represents greater than a sevenfold boost in speed over the CPU version. So despite the early setback in adapting the histogram to a GPU implementation, our version that uses both shared and global atomics should be considered a success.

9.5 Chapter Review

Although we have frequently spoken at length about how easy parallel programming can be with CUDA C, we have largely ignored some of the situations when massively parallel architectures such as the GPU can make our lives as program-mers more difficult. Trying to cope with potentially tens of thousands of threads simultaneously modifying the same memory addresses is a common situation where a massively parallel machine can seem burdensome. Fortunately, we have hardware-supported atomic operations available to help ease this pain.

However, as you saw with the histogram computation, sometimes reliance on atomic operations introduces performance issues that can be resolved only by rethinking parts of the algorithm. In the histogram example, we moved to a two-stage algorithm that alleviated contention for global memory addresses. In general, this strategy of looking to lessen memory contention tends to work well, and you should keep it in mind when using atomics in your own applications.

Chapter 10

Streams

Time and time again in this book we have seen how the massively data-parallel execution engine on a GPU can provide stunning performance gains over comparable CPU code. However, there is yet another class of parallelism to be exploited on NVIDIA graphics processors. This parallelism is similar to the *task parallelism* that is found in multithreaded CPU applications. Rather than simultaneously computing the same function on lots of data elements as one does with data parallelism, task parallelism involves doing two or more completely different tasks in parallel.

In the context of parallelism, a *task* could be any number of things. For example, an application could be executing two tasks: redrawing its GUI with one thread while downloading an update over the network with another thread. These tasks proceed in parallel, despite having nothing in common. Although the task parallelism on GPUs is not currently as flexible as a general-purpose processor's, it still provides opportunities for us as programmers to extract even more speed from our GPU-based implementations. In this chapter, we will look at CUDA streams and the ways in which their careful use will enable us to execute certain operations simultaneously on the GPU.

10.1 Chapter Objectives

Through the course of this chapter, you will accomplish the following:

- You will learn about allocating page-locked host memory.

- You will learn what CUDA *streams* are.

- You will learn how to use CUDA streams to accelerate your applications.

10.2 Page-Locked Host Memory

In every example over the course of nine chapters, you have seen us allocate memory on the GPU with cudaMalloc(). On the host, we have always allocated memory with the vanilla, C library routine malloc(). However, the CUDA runtime offers its own mechanism for allocating host memory: cudaHostAlloc(). Why would you bother using this function when malloc() has served you quite well since day one of your life as a C programmer?

In fact, there is a significant difference between the memory that malloc() will allocate and the memory that cudaHostAlloc() allocates. The C library function malloc() allocates standard, pageable host memory, while cudaHostAlloc() allocates a buffer of *page-locked* host memory. Sometimes called *pinned* memory, page-locked buffers have an important property: The operating system guarantees us that it will never page this memory out to disk, which ensures its residency in physical memory. The corollary to this is that it becomes safe for the OS to allow an application access to the physical address of the memory, since the buffer will not be evicted or relocated.

Knowing the physical address of a buffer, the GPU can then use direct memory access (DMA) to copy data to or from the host. Since DMA copies proceed without intervention from the CPU, it also means that the CPU could be simultaneously paging these buffers out to disk or relocating their physical address by updating the operating system's pagetables. The possibility of the CPU moving pageable data means that using pinned memory for a DMA copy is essential. In fact, even when you attempt to perform a memory copy with pageable memory, the CUDA driver still uses DMA to transfer the buffer to the GPU. Therefore, your copy happens twice, first from a pageable system buffer to a page-locked "staging" buffer and then from the page-locked system buffer to the GPU.

As a result, whenever you perform memory copies from pageable memory, you guarantee that the copy speed will be bounded by the *lower* of the PCIE transfer speed and the system front-side bus speeds. A large disparity in bandwidth between these buses in some systems ensures that page-locked host memory enjoys roughly a twofold performance advantage over standard pageable memory when used for copying data between the GPU and the host. But even in a world where PCI Express and front-side bus speeds were identical, pageable buffers would still incur the overhead of an additional CPU-managed copy.

However, you should resist the temptation to simply do a search-and-replace on *malloc* to convert every one of your calls to use cudaHostAlloc(). Using pinned memory is a double-edged sword. By doing so, you have effectively opted out of all the nice features of virtual memory. Specifically, the computer running the application needs to have available physical memory for every page-locked buffer, since these buffers can never be swapped out to disk. This means that your system will run out of memory much faster than it would if you stuck to standard malloc() calls. Not only does this mean that your application might start to fail on machines with smaller amounts of physical memory, but it means that your application can affect the performance of other applications running on the system.

These warnings are not meant to scare you out of using cudaHostAlloc(), but you should remain aware of the implications of page-locking buffers. We suggest trying to restrict their use to memory that will be used as a source or destination in calls to cudaMemcpy() and freeing them when they are no longer needed rather than waiting until application shutdown to release the memory. The use of cudaHostAlloc() should be no more difficult than anything else you've studied so far, but let's take a look at an example that will both illustrate how pinned memory is allocated and demonstrate its performance advantage over standard pageable memory.

Our application will be very simple and serves primarily to benchmark cudaMemcpy() performance with both pageable and page-locked memory. All we endeavor to do is allocate a GPU buffer and a host buffer of matching sizes and then execute some number of copies between these two buffers. We'll allow the user of this benchmark to specify the direction of the copy, either "up" (from host to device) or "down" (from device to host). You will also notice that, in order to obtain accurate timings, we set up CUDA events for the start and stop of the sequence of copies. You probably remember how to do this from previous performance-testing examples, but in case you've forgotten, the following will jog your memory:

```
float cuda_malloc_test( int size, bool up ) {
    cudaEvent_t     start, stop;
    int             *a, *dev_a;
    float           elapsedTime;

    HANDLE_ERROR( cudaEventCreate( &start ) );
    HANDLE_ERROR( cudaEventCreate( &stop ) );

    a = (int*)malloc( size * sizeof( *a ) );
    HANDLE_NULL( a );
    HANDLE_ERROR( cudaMalloc( (void**)&dev_a,
                              size * sizeof( *dev_a ) ) );
```

Independent of the direction of the copies, we start by allocating a host and GPU buffer of size integers. After this, we do 100 copies in the direction specified by the argument up, stopping the timer after we've finished copying.

```
    HANDLE_ERROR( cudaEventRecord( start, 0 ) );
    for (int i=0; i<100; i++) {
        if (up)
            HANDLE_ERROR( cudaMemcpy( dev_a, a,
                                      size * sizeof( *dev_a ),
                                      cudaMemcpyHostToDevice ) );
        else
            HANDLE_ERROR( cudaMemcpy( a, dev_a,
                                      size * sizeof( *dev_a ),
                                      cudaMemcpyDeviceToHost ) );
    }
    HANDLE_ERROR( cudaEventRecord( stop, 0 ) );
    HANDLE_ERROR( cudaEventSynchronize( stop ) );
    HANDLE_ERROR( cudaEventElapsedTime( &elapsedTime,
                                        start, stop ) );
```

After the 100 copies, clean up by freeing the host and GPU buffers as well as destroying our timing events.

```
    free( a );
    HANDLE_ERROR( cudaFree( dev_a ) );
    HANDLE_ERROR( cudaEventDestroy( start ) );
    HANDLE_ERROR( cudaEventDestroy( stop ) );


    return elapsedTime;
}
```

If you didn't notice, the function cuda_malloc_test() allocated pageable host memory with the standard C malloc() routine. The pinned memory version uses cudaHostAlloc() to allocate a page-locked buffer.

```
float cuda_host_alloc_test( int size, bool up ) {
    cudaEvent_t     start, stop;
    int             *a, *dev_a;
    float           elapsedTime;

    HANDLE_ERROR( cudaEventCreate( &start ) );
    HANDLE_ERROR( cudaEventCreate( &stop ) );

    HANDLE_ERROR( cudaHostAlloc( (void**)&a,
                                 size * sizeof( *a ),
                                 cudaHostAllocDefault ) );
    HANDLE_ERROR( cudaMalloc( (void**)&dev_a,
                              size * sizeof( *dev_a ) ) );

    HANDLE_ERROR( cudaEventRecord( start, 0 ) );
    for (int i=0; i<100; i++) {
        if (up)
            HANDLE_ERROR( cudaMemcpy( dev_a, a,
                                      size * sizeof( *a ),
                                      cudaMemcpyHostToDevice ) );

        else
```

```
            HANDLE_ERROR( cudaMemcpy( a, dev_a,
                                      size * sizeof( *a ),
                                      cudaMemcpyDeviceToHost ) );
    }
    HANDLE_ERROR( cudaEventRecord( stop, 0 ) );
    HANDLE_ERROR( cudaEventSynchronize( stop ) );
    HANDLE_ERROR( cudaEventElapsedTime( &elapsedTime,
                                        start, stop ) );


    HANDLE_ERROR( cudaFreeHost( a ) );
    HANDLE_ERROR( cudaFree( dev_a ) );
    HANDLE_ERROR( cudaEventDestroy( start ) );
    HANDLE_ERROR( cudaEventDestroy( stop ) );


    return elapsedTime;
}
```

As you can see, the buffer allocated by `cudaHostAlloc()` is used in the same way as a buffer allocated by `malloc()`. The other change from using `malloc()` lies in the last argument, the value `cudaHostAllocDefault`. This last argument stores a collection of flags that we can use to modify the behavior of `cudaHostAlloc()` in order to allocate other varieties of pinned host memory. In the next chapter, we'll see how to use the other possible values of these flags, but for now we're content to use the default, page-locked memory so we pass `cudaHostAllocDefault` in order to get the default behavior. To free a buffer that was allocated with `cudaHostAlloc()`, we have to use `cudaFreeHost()`. That is, every `malloc()` needs a `free()`, and every `cudaHostAlloc()` needs a `cudaFreeHost()`.

The body of `main()` proceeds not unlike what you would expect.

```
#include "../common/book.h"

#define SIZE    (10*1024*1024)

int main( void ) {
    float           elapsedTime;
    float           MB = (float)100*SIZE*sizeof(int)/1024/1024;
```

```
elapsedTime = cuda_malloc_test( SIZE, true );
printf( "Time using cudaMalloc:  %3.1f ms\n",
        elapsedTime );
printf( "\tMB/s during copy up:  %3.1f\n",
        MB/(elapsedTime/1000) );
```

Because the up argument to cuda_malloc_test() is true, the previous call tests the performance of copies from host to device, or "up" to the device. To benchmark the calls in the opposite direction, we execute the same calls but with false as the second argument.

```
elapsedTime = cuda_malloc_test( SIZE, false );
printf( "Time using cudaMalloc:  %3.1f ms\n",
        elapsedTime );
printf( "\tMB/s during copy down:  %3.1f\n",
        MB/(elapsedTime/1000) );
```

We perform the same set of steps to test the performance of cudaHostAlloc(). We call cuda_ host_alloc_test() twice, once with up as true and once with it false.

```
elapsedTime = cuda_host_alloc_test( SIZE, true );
printf( "Time using cudaHostAlloc:  %3.1f ms\n",
        elapsedTime );
printf( "\tMB/s during copy up:  %3.1f\n",
        MB/(elapsedTime/1000) );

elapsedTime = cuda_host_alloc_test( SIZE, false );
printf( "Time using cudaHostAlloc:  %3.1f ms\n",
        elapsedTime );
printf( "\tMB/s during copy down:  %3.1f\n",
        MB/(elapsedTime/1000) );
}
```

On a GeForce GTX 285, we observed copies from host to device improving from 2.77GB/s to 5.11GB/s when we use pinned memory instead of pageable memory.

Copies from the device down to the host improve similarly, from 2.43GB/s to 5.46GB/s. So, for most PCIE bandwidth-limited applications, you will notice a marked improvement when using pinned memory versus standard pageable memory. But page-locked memory is not solely for performance enhancements. As we'll see in the next sections, there are situations where we are *required* to use page-locked memory.

10.3 CUDA Streams

In Chapter 6, we introduced the concept of CUDA events. In doing so, we post-poned an in-depth discussion of the second argument to `cudaEventRecord()`, instead mentioning only that it specified the *stream* into which we were inserting the event.

```
cudaEvent_t start;
cudaEventCreate(&start);
cudaEventRecord( start, 0 );
```

CUDA streams can play an important role in accelerating your applications. A CUDA *stream* represents a queue of GPU operations that get executed in a specific order. We can add operations such as kernel launches, memory copies, and event starts and stops into a stream. The order in which operations are added to the stream specifies the order in which they will be executed. You can think of each stream as a *task* on the GPU, and there are opportunities for these tasks to execute in parallel. We'll first see how streams are used, and then we'll look at how you can use streams to accelerate your applications.

10.4 Using a Single CUDA Stream

As we'll see later, the real power of streams becomes apparent only when we use more than one of them, but we'll begin to illustrate the mechanics of their use within an application that employs just a single stream. Imagine that we have a CUDA C kernel that will take two input buffers of data, a and b. The kernel will compute some result based on a combination of values in these buffers to produce an output buffer c. Our vector addition example did something along these lines, but in this example we'll compute an average of three values in a and three values in b:

```
#include "../common/book.h"


#define N    (1024*1024)
#define FULL_DATA_SIZE    (N*20)


__global__ void kernel( int *a, int *b, int *c ) {
    int idx = threadIdx.x + blockIdx.x * blockDim.x;
    if (idx < N) {
        int idx1 = (idx + 1) % 256;
        int idx2 = (idx + 2) % 256;
        float   as = (a[idx] + a[idx1] + a[idx2]) / 3.0f;
        float   bs = (b[idx] + b[idx1] + b[idx2]) / 3.0f;
        c[idx] = (as + bs) / 2;
    }
}
```

This kernel is not incredibly important, so don't get too hung up on it if you aren't sure exactly what it's supposed to be computing. It's something of a placeholder since the important, stream-related component of this example resides in main().

```
int main( void ) {
    cudaDeviceProp  prop;
    int whichDevice;
    HANDLE_ERROR( cudaGetDevice( &whichDevice ) );
    HANDLE_ERROR( cudaGetDeviceProperties( &prop, whichDevice ) );
    if (!prop.deviceOverlap) {
        printf( "Device will not handle overlaps, so no "
                "speed up from streams\n" );

        return 0;
    }
```

The first thing we do is choose a device and check to see whether it supports a feature known as *device overlap*. A GPU supporting device overlap possesses the capacity to simultaneously execute a CUDA C kernel while performing a copy between device and host memory. As we've promised before, we'll use multiple streams to achieve this overlap of computation and data transfer, but first we'll see how to create and use a single stream. As with all of our examples that aim to measure performance improvements (or regressions), we begin by creating and starting an event timer:

```
cudaEvent_t      start, stop;
float            elapsedTime;

// start the timers
HANDLE_ERROR( cudaEventCreate( &start ) );
HANDLE_ERROR( cudaEventCreate( &stop ) );
HANDLE_ERROR( cudaEventRecord( start, 0 ) );
```

After starting our timer, we create the stream we want to use for this application:

```
// initialize the stream
cudaStream_t      stream;
HANDLE_ERROR( cudaStreamCreate( &stream ) );
```

Yeah, that's pretty much all it takes to create a stream. It's not really worth dwelling on, so let's press on to the data allocation.

```
int *host_a, *host_b, *host_c;
int *dev_a, *dev_b, *dev_c;

// allocate the memory on the GPU
HANDLE_ERROR( cudaMalloc( (void**)&dev_a,
                          N * sizeof(int) ) );
HANDLE_ERROR( cudaMalloc( (void**)&dev_b,
                          N * sizeof(int) ) );
HANDLE_ERROR( cudaMalloc( (void**)&dev_c,
                          N * sizeof(int) ) );
```

```
    // allocate page-locked memory, used to stream
    HANDLE_ERROR( cudaHostAlloc( (void**)&host_a,
                                 FULL_DATA_SIZE * sizeof(int),
                                 cudaHostAllocDefault ) );
    HANDLE_ERROR( cudaHostAlloc( (void**)&host_b,
                                 FULL_DATA_SIZE * sizeof(int),
                                 cudaHostAllocDefault ) );
    HANDLE_ERROR( cudaHostAlloc( (void**)&host_c,
                                 FULL_DATA_SIZE * sizeof(int),
                                 cudaHostAllocDefault ) );

    for (int i=0; i<FULL_DATA_SIZE; i++) {
        host_a[i] = rand();
        host_b[i] = rand();
    }
```

We have allocated our input and output buffers on both the GPU and the host. Notice that we've decided to use pinned memory on the host by using cudaHostAlloc() to perform the allocations. There is a very good reason for using pinned memory, and it's not strictly because it makes copies faster. We'll see in detail momentarily, but we will be using a new kind of cudaMemcpy() function, and this new function *requires* that the host memory be page-locked. After allocating the input buffers, we fill the host allocations with random integers using the C library call rand().

With our stream and our timing events created and our device and host buffers allocated, we're ready to perform some computations! Typically we blast through this stage by copying the two input buffers to the GPU, launching our kernel, and copying the output buffer back to the host. We will follow this pattern again, but this time with some small changes.

First, we will opt *not* to copy the input buffers in their entirety to the GPU. Rather, we will split our inputs into smaller chunks and perform the three-step process on each chunk. That is, we will take some fraction of the input buffers, copy them to the GPU, execute our kernel on that fraction of the buffers, and copy the resulting fraction of the output buffer back to the host. Imagine that we need to do this because our GPU has much less memory than our host does, so the computation needs to be staged in chunks because the entire buffer can't fit on the GPU at once. The code to perform this "chunkified" sequence of computations will look like this:

```
    // now loop over full data, in bite-sized chunks
    for (int i=0; i<FULL_DATA_SIZE; i+= N) {
        // copy the locked memory to the device, async
        HANDLE_ERROR( cudaMemcpyAsync( dev_a, host_a+i,
                                        N * sizeof(int),
                                        cudaMemcpyHostToDevice,
                                        stream ) );
        HANDLE_ERROR( cudaMemcpyAsync( dev_b, host_b+i,
                                        N * sizeof(int),
                                        cudaMemcpyHostToDevice,
                                        stream ) );

        kernel<<<N/256,256,0,stream>>>( dev_a, dev_b, dev_c );

        // copy the data from device to locked memory
        HANDLE_ERROR( cudaMemcpyAsync( host_c+i, dev_c,
                                        N * sizeof(int),
                                        cudaMemcpyDeviceToHost,
                                        stream ) );

    }
```

But you will notice two other unexpected shifts from the norm in the preceding excerpt. First, instead of using the familiar cudaMemcpy(), we're copying the data to and from the GPU with a new routine, cudaMemcpyAsync(). The difference between these functions is subtle yet significant. The original cudaMemcpy() behaves like the C library function memcpy(). Specifically, this function executes *synchronously*, meaning that when the function returns, the copy has completed, and the output buffer now contains the contents that were supposed to be copied into it.

The opposite of a *synchronous* function is an *asynchronous* function, which inspired the name `cudaMemcpyAsync()`. The call to `cudaMemcpyAsync()` simply places a *request* to perform a memory copy into the stream specified by the argument `stream`. When the call returns, there is no guarantee that the copy has even started yet, much less that it has finished. The guarantee that we have is that the copy will definitely be performed before the next operation placed into the same stream. It is required that any host memory pointers passed to `cudaMemcpyAsync()` have been allocated by `cudaHostAlloc()`. That is, you are only allowed to schedule asynchronous copies to or from page-locked memory.

Notice that the angle-bracketed kernel launch also takes an optional stream argument. This kernel launch is asynchronous, just like the preceding two memory copies to the GPU and the trailing memory copy back from the GPU. Technically, we can end an iteration of this loop without having actually started any of the memory copies or kernel execution. As we mentioned, all that we are guaranteed is that the first copy placed into the stream will execute before the second copy. Moreover, the second copy will complete before the kernel starts, and the kernel will complete before the third copy starts. So as we've mentioned earlier in this chapter, a stream acts just like an ordered queue of work for the GPU to perform.

When the `for()` loop has terminated, there could still be quite a bit of work queued up for the GPU to finish. If we would like to guarantee that the GPU is done with its computations and memory copies, we need to synchronize it with the host. That is, we basically want to tell the host to sit around and wait for the GPU to finish before proceeding. We accomplish that by calling `cudaStreamSynchronize()` and specifying the stream that we want to wait for:

```
    // copy result chunk from locked to full buffer
    HANDLE_ERROR( cudaStreamSynchronize( stream ) );
```

Since the computations and copies have completed after synchronizing `stream` with the host, we can stop our timer, collect our performance data, and free our input and output buffers.

```
          HANDLE_ERROR( cudaEventRecord( stop, 0 ) );

          HANDLE_ERROR( cudaEventSynchronize( stop ) );
          HANDLE_ERROR( cudaEventElapsedTime( &elapsedTime,
                                              start, stop ) );
          printf( "Time taken:  %3.1f ms\n", elapsedTime );

          // cleanup the streams and memory
          HANDLE_ERROR( cudaFreeHost( host_a ) );
          HANDLE_ERROR( cudaFreeHost( host_b ) );
          HANDLE_ERROR( cudaFreeHost( host_c ) );
          HANDLE_ERROR( cudaFree( dev_a ) );
          HANDLE_ERROR( cudaFree( dev_b ) );
          HANDLE_ERROR( cudaFree( dev_c ) );
```

Finally, before exiting the application, we destroy the stream that we were using to queue the GPU operations.

```
          HANDLE_ERROR( cudaStreamDestroy( stream ) );

          return 0;
      }
```

To be honest, this example has done very little to demonstrate the power of streams. Of course, even using a single stream can help speed up an application if we have work we want to complete on the host while the GPU is busy churning through the work we've stuffed into a stream. But assuming that we don't have much to do on the host, we can still speed up applications by using streams, and in the next section we'll take a look at how this can be accomplished.

10.5 Using Multiple CUDA Streams

Let's adapt the single-stream example from Section 10.3: Using a Single CUDA Stream to perform its work in two different streams. At the beginning of the previous example, we checked that the device indeed supported *overlap* and broke the computation into chunks. The idea underlying the improved version of this application is simple and relies on two things: the "chunked" computation and the overlap of memory copies with kernel execution. We endeavor to get stream 1 to copy its input buffers to the GPU while stream 0 is executing its kernel. Then stream 1 will execute its kernel while stream 0 copies its results to the host. Stream 1 will then copy its results to the host while stream 0 begins executing its kernel on the next chunk of data. Assuming that our memory copies and kernel executions take roughly the same amount of time, our application's execution timeline might look something like Figure 10.1. The figure assumes that the GPU can perform a memory copy and a kernel execution at the same time, so empty boxes represent time when one stream is waiting to execute an operation that it cannot overlap with the other stream's operation. Note also that calls to `cudaMemcpyAsync()` are abbreviated in the remaining figures in this chapter, represented simply as "`memcpy`."

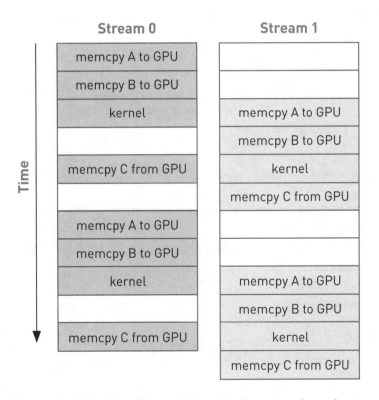

Figure 10.1 Timeline of intended application execution using two independent streams

In fact, the execution timeline can be even more favorable than this; some newer NVIDIA GPUs support simultaneous kernel execution and *two* memory copies, one *to* the device and one *from* the device. But on any device that supports the overlap of memory copies and kernel execution, the overall application should accelerate when we use multiple streams.

Despite these grand plans to accelerate our application, the computation kernel will remain unchanged.

```
#include "../common/book.h"


#define N      (1024*1024)
#define FULL_DATA_SIZE     (N*20)


__global__ void kernel( int *a, int *b, int *c ) {
    int idx = threadIdx.x + blockIdx.x * blockDim.x;
    if (idx < N) {
        int idx1 = (idx + 1) % 256;
        int idx2 = (idx + 2) % 256;
        float   as = (a[idx] + a[idx1] + a[idx2]) / 3.0f;
        float   bs = (b[idx] + b[idx1] + b[idx2]) / 3.0f;
        c[idx] = (as + bs) / 2
    }
}
```

As with the single stream version, we will check that the device supports overlapping computation with memory copy. If the device *does* support overlap, we proceed as we did before by creating CUDA events to time the application.

```
int main( void ) {
    cudaDeviceProp  prop;
    int whichDevice;
    HANDLE_ERROR( cudaGetDevice( &whichDevice ) );
    HANDLE_ERROR( cudaGetDeviceProperties( &prop, whichDevice ) );
```

```
if (!prop.deviceOverlap) {
    printf( "Device will not handle overlaps, so no "
            "speed up from streams\n" );
    return 0;
}


cudaEvent_t    start, stop;
float          elapsedTime;

// start the timers
HANDLE_ERROR( cudaEventCreate( &start ) );
HANDLE_ERROR( cudaEventCreate( &stop ) );
HANDLE_ERROR( cudaEventRecord( start, 0 ) );
```

Next, we create our two streams exactly as we created the single stream in the previous section's version of the code.

```
// initialize the streams
cudaStream_t    stream0, stream1;
HANDLE_ERROR( cudaStreamCreate( &stream0 ) );
HANDLE_ERROR( cudaStreamCreate( &stream1 ) );
```

We will assume that we still have two input buffers and a single output buffer on the host. The input buffers are filled with random data exactly as they were in the single-stream version of this application. However, now that we intend to use two streams to process the data, we allocate two identical sets of GPU buffers so that each stream can independently work on chunks of the input.

```
int *host_a, *host_b, *host_c;
int *dev_a0, *dev_b0, *dev_c0; //GPU buffers for stream0
int *dev_a1, *dev_b1, *dev_c1; //GPU buffers for stream1

// allocate the memory on the GPU
HANDLE_ERROR( cudaMalloc( (void**)&dev_a0,
                          N * sizeof(int) ) );
```

```
HANDLE_ERROR( cudaMalloc( (void**)&dev_b0,
                           N * sizeof(int) ) );
HANDLE_ERROR( cudaMalloc( (void**)&dev_c0,
                           N * sizeof(int) ) );
HANDLE_ERROR( cudaMalloc( (void**)&dev_a1,
                           N * sizeof(int) ) );
HANDLE_ERROR( cudaMalloc( (void**)&dev_b1,
                           N * sizeof(int) ) );
HANDLE_ERROR( cudaMalloc( (void**)&dev_c1,
                           N * sizeof(int) ) );

// allocate page-locked memory, used to stream
HANDLE_ERROR( cudaHostAlloc( (void**)&host_a,
                           FULL_DATA_SIZE * sizeof(int),
                           cudaHostAllocDefault ) );
HANDLE_ERROR( cudaHostAlloc( (void**)&host_b,
                           FULL_DATA_SIZE * sizeof(int),
                           cudaHostAllocDefault ) );
HANDLE_ERROR( cudaHostAlloc( (void**)&host_c,
                           FULL_DATA_SIZE * sizeof(int),
                           cudaHostAllocDefault ) );

for (int i=0; i<FULL_DATA_SIZE; i++) {
    host_a[i] = rand();
    host_b[i] = rand();
}
```

We then loop over the chunks of input exactly as we did in the first attempt at this application. But now that we're using two streams, we process twice as much data in each iteration of the for() loop. In stream0, we queue asynchronous copies of a and b to the GPU, queue a kernel execution, and then queue a copy back to c:

```
    // now loop over full data, in bite-sized chunks
    for (int i=0; i<FULL_DATA_SIZE; i+= N*2) {
        // copy the locked memory to the device, async
        HANDLE_ERROR( cudaMemcpyAsync( dev_a0, host_a+i,
                                        N * sizeof(int),
                                        cudaMemcpyHostToDevice,
                                        stream0 ) );
        HANDLE_ERROR( cudaMemcpyAsync( dev_b0, host_b+i,
                                        N * sizeof(int),
                                        cudaMemcpyHostToDevice,
                                        stream0 ) );

        kernel<<<N/256,256,0,stream0>>>( dev_a0, dev_b0, dev_c0 );

        // copy the data from device to locked memory
        HANDLE_ERROR( cudaMemcpyAsync( host_c+i, dev_c0,
                                        N * sizeof(int),
                                        cudaMemcpyDeviceToHost,
                                        stream0 ) );
```

After queuing these operations in `stream0`, we queue identical operations on the next chunk of data, but this time in `stream1`.

```
        // copy the locked memory to the device, async
        HANDLE_ERROR( cudaMemcpyAsync( dev_a1, host_a+i+N,
                                        N * sizeof(int),
                                        cudaMemcpyHostToDevice,
                                        stream1 ) );
        HANDLE_ERROR( cudaMemcpyAsync( dev_b1, host_b+i+N,
                                        N * sizeof(int),
                                        cudaMemcpyHostToDevice,
                                        stream1 ) );
```

```
        kernel<<<N/256,256,0,stream1>>>( dev_a1, dev_b1, dev_c1 );

        // copy the data from device to locked memory
        HANDLE_ERROR( cudaMemcpyAsync( host_c+i+N, dev_c1,
                                       N * sizeof(int),
                                       cudaMemcpyDeviceToHost,
                                       stream1 ) );
    }
```

And so our `for()` loop proceeds, alternating the streams to which it queues each chunk of data until it has queued every piece of input data for processing. After terminating the `for()` loop, we synchronize the GPU with the CPU before we stop our application timers. Since we are working in two streams, we need to synchronize both.

```
    HANDLE_ERROR( cudaStreamSynchronize( stream0 ) );
    HANDLE_ERROR( cudaStreamSynchronize( stream1 ) );
```

We wrap up `main()` the same way we concluded our single-stream implementation. We stop our timers, display the elapsed time, and clean up after ourselves. Of course, we remember that we now need to destroy two streams and free twice as many GPU buffers, but aside from that, this code is identical to what we've seen already:

```
    HANDLE_ERROR( cudaEventRecord( stop, 0 ) );

    HANDLE_ERROR( cudaEventSynchronize( stop ) );
    HANDLE_ERROR( cudaEventElapsedTime( &elapsedTime,
                                        start, stop ) );
    printf( "Time taken:  %3.1f ms\n", elapsedTime );

    // cleanup the streams and memory
    HANDLE_ERROR( cudaFreeHost( host_a ) );
    HANDLE_ERROR( cudaFreeHost( host_b ) );
    HANDLE_ERROR( cudaFreeHost( host_c ) );
```

```
        HANDLE_ERROR( cudaFree( dev_a0 ) );
        HANDLE_ERROR( cudaFree( dev_b0 ) );
        HANDLE_ERROR( cudaFree( dev_c0 ) );
        HANDLE_ERROR( cudaFree( dev_a1 ) );
        HANDLE_ERROR( cudaFree( dev_b1 ) );
        HANDLE_ERROR( cudaFree( dev_c1 ) );
        HANDLE_ERROR( cudaStreamDestroy( stream0 ) );
        HANDLE_ERROR( cudaStreamDestroy( stream1 ) );

        return 0;
}
```

We benchmarked both the original, single-stream implementation from Section 10.3: Using a Single CUDA Stream and the improved double-stream version on a GeForce GTX 285. The original version takes 62ms to run to completion. After modifying it to use two streams, it takes 61ms.

Uh-oh.

Well, the good news is that this is the reason we bother to time our applications. Sometimes, our most well-intended performance "enhancements" do nothing more than introduce unnecessary complications to the code.

But why didn't this application get any faster? We even said that it would get faster! Don't lose hope yet, though, because we actually *can* accelerate the single-stream version with a second stream, but we need to understand a bit more about how streams are handled by the CUDA driver in order to reap the rewards of device overlap. To understand how streams work behind the scenes, we'll need to look at both the CUDA driver and how the CUDA hardware architecture works.

10.6 GPU Work Scheduling

Although streams are logically independent queues of operations to be executed on the GPU, it turns out that this abstraction does not exactly match the GPU's queuing mechanism. As programmers, we think about our streams as ordered sequences of operations composed of a mixture of memory copies and kernel invocations. However, the hardware has no notion of streams. Rather, it has one or more engines to perform memory copies and an engine to execute kernels. These engines queue commands independently from each other, resulting in a task-scheduling scenario like the one shown in Figure 10.2. The arrows in the figure illustrate how operations that have been queued into streams get scheduled on the hardware engines that actually execute them.

So, the user and the hardware have somewhat orthogonal notions of how to queue GPU work, and the burden of keeping both the user and hardware sides of this equation happy falls on the CUDA driver. First and foremost, there are important dependencies specified by the order in which operations are added to streams. For example, in Figure 10.2, stream 0's memory copy of A needs to be completed before its memory copy of B, which in turn needs to be completed before kernel A is launched. But once these operations are placed into the hardware's copy engine and kernel engine queues, these dependencies are lost, so the CUDA driver needs to keep everyone happy by ensuring that the intrastream dependencies remain satisfied by the hardware's execution units.

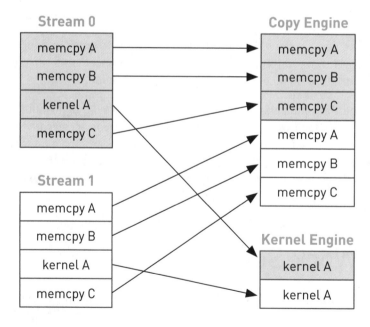

Figure 10.2 Mapping of CUDA streams onto GPU engines

What does this mean to us? Well, let's look at what's actually happening with our example in Section 10.4: Using Multiple CUDA Streams. If we review the code, we see that our application basically amounts to a `cudaMemcpyAsync()` of a, `cudaMemcpyAsync()` of b, our kernel execution, and then a `cudaMemcpyAsync()` of c back to the host. The application enqueues all the operations from stream 0 followed by all the operations from stream 1. The CUDA driver schedules these operations on the hardware for us in the order they were specified, keeping the interengine dependencies straight. These dependencies are illustrated in Figure 10.3 where an arrow from a copy to a kernel indicates that the copy depends on the kernel completing execution before it can begin.

Given our newfound understanding of how the GPU schedules work, we can look at a timeline of how these get executed on the hardware in Figure 10.4.

Because stream 0's copy of c back to the host depends on its kernel execution completing, stream 1's completely independent copies of a and b to the GPU get blocked because the GPU's engines execute work in the order it's provided. This inefficiency explains why the two-stream version of our application showed absolutely no speedup. The lack of improvement is a direct result of our assumption that the hardware works in the same manner as the CUDA stream programming model implies.

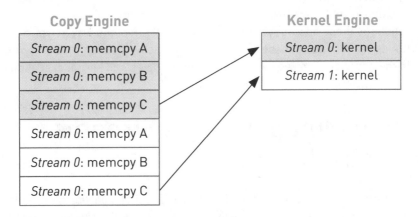

Figure 10.3 Arrows depicting the dependency of `cudaMemcpyAsync()` calls on kernel executions in the example from Section 10.4: Using Multiple CUDA Streams

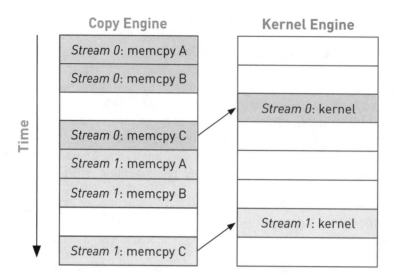

Figure 10.4 Execution timeline of the example from Section 10.4: Using Multiple CUDA Streams

The moral of this story is that we as programmers need to help out when it comes to ensuring that independent streams actually get executed in parallel. Keeping in mind that the hardware has independent engines that handle memory copies and kernel executions, we need to remain aware that the order in which we enqueue these operations in our streams will affect the way in which the CUDA driver schedules these for execution. In the next section, we'll see how to help the hardware achieve overlap of memory copies and kernel execution.

10.7 Using Multiple CUDA Streams Effectively

As we saw in the previous section, if we schedule all of a particular stream's operations at once, it's very easy to inadvertently block the copies or kernel executions of another stream. To alleviate this problem, it suffices to enqueue our operations breadth-first across streams rather than depth-first. That is, rather than add the copy of a, copy of b, kernel execution, and copy of c to stream 0 before starting to schedule on stream 1, we bounce back and forth between the streams assigning work. We add the copy of a to stream 0, and then we add the copy of a to stream 1. Then we add the copy of b to stream 0, and then we add the copy of b to stream 1. We enqueue the kernel invocation in stream 0, and then we enqueue one in stream 1. Finally, we enqueue the copy of c back to the host in stream 0 followed by the copy of c in stream 1.

To make this more concrete, let's take a look at the code. All we've changed is the order in which operations get assigned to each of our two streams, so this will be strictly a copy-and-paste optimization. Everything else in the application will remain unchanged, which means that our improvements are localized to the for() loop. The new, breadth-first assignment to the two streams looks like this:

```
for (int i=0; i<FULL_DATA_SIZE; i+= N*2) {
    // enqueue copies of a in stream0 and stream1
    HANDLE_ERROR( cudaMemcpyAsync( dev_a0, host_a+i,
                                    N * sizeof(int),
                                    cudaMemcpyHostToDevice,
                                    stream0 ) );
    HANDLE_ERROR( cudaMemcpyAsync( dev_a1, host_a+i+N,
                                    N * sizeof(int),
                                    cudaMemcpyHostToDevice,
                                    stream1 ) );
    // enqueue copies of b in stream0 and stream1
    HANDLE_ERROR( cudaMemcpyAsync( dev_b0, host_b+i,
                                    N * sizeof(int),
                                    cudaMemcpyHostToDevice,
                                    stream0 ) );
    HANDLE_ERROR( cudaMemcpyAsync( dev_b1, host_b+i+N,
                                    N * sizeof(int),
                                    cudaMemcpyHostToDevice,
                                    stream1 ) );

    // enqueue kernels in stream0 and stream1
    kernel<<<N/256,256,0,stream0>>>( dev_a0, dev_b0, dev_c0 );
    kernel<<<N/256,256,0,stream1>>>( dev_a1, dev_b1, dev_c1 );
```

```
        // enqueue copies of c from device to locked memory
        HANDLE_ERROR( cudaMemcpyAsync( host_c+i, dev_c0,
                                    N * sizeof(int),
                                    cudaMemcpyDeviceToHost,
                                    stream0 ) );
        HANDLE_ERROR( cudaMemcpyAsync( host_c+i+N, dev_c1,
                                    N * sizeof(int),
                                    cudaMemcpyDeviceToHost,
                                    stream1 ) );
    }
```

If we assume that our memory copies and kernel executions are roughly comparable in execution time, our new execution timeline will look like Figure 10.5. The interengine dependencies are highlighted with arrows simply to illustrate that they are still satisfied with this new scheduling order.

Because we have queued our operations breadth-first across streams, we no longer have stream 0's copy of c blocking stream 1's initial memory copies of a and b. This allows the GPU to execute copies and kernels in parallel, allowing our application to run significantly faster. The new code runs in 48ms, a 21 percent improvement over our original, naïve double-stream implementation. For applications that can overlap nearly all computation and memory copies, you can approach a nearly twofold improvement in performance because the copy and kernel engines will be cranking the entire time.

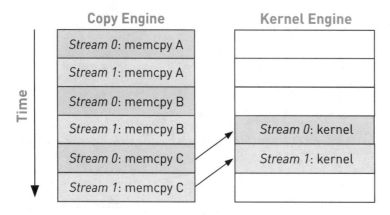

Figure 10.5 Execution timeline of the improved example with arrows indicating interengine dependencies

10.8 Chapter Review

In this chapter, we looked at a method for achieving a kind of task-level paral-lelism in CUDA C applications. By using two (or more) CUDA streams, we can allow the GPU to simultaneously execute a kernel while performing a copy between the host and GPU. We need to be careful about two things when we endeavor to do this, though. First, the host memory involved needs to be allo-cated using `cudaHostAlloc()` since we will queue our memory copies with `cudaMemcpyAsync()`, and asynchronous copies need to be performed with pinned buffers. Second, we need to be aware that the order in which we add oper-ations to our streams will affect our capacity to achieve overlapping of copies and kernel executions. The general guideline involves a breadth-first, or round-robin, assignment of work to the streams you intend to use. This can be counterintuitive if you don't understand how the hardware queuing works, so it's a good thing to remember when you go about writing your own applications.

Chapter 11

CUDA C on Multiple GPUs

There is an old saying that goes something like this: "The only thing better than computing on a GPU is computing on two GPUs." Systems containing multiple graphics processors have become more and more common in recent years. Of course, in some ways multi-GPU systems are similar to multi-CPU systems in that they are still far from the common system configuration, but it has gotten quite easy to end up with more than one GPU in your system. Products such as the GeForce GTX 295 contain two GPUs on a single card. NVIDIA's Tesla S1070 contains a whopping four CUDA-capable graphics processors in it. Systems built around a recent NVIDIA chipset will have an integrated, CUDA-capable GPU on the motherboard. Adding a discrete NVIDIA GPU in one of the PCI Express slots will make this system multi-GPU. Neither of these scenarios is very farfetched, so we would be best served by learning to exploit the resources of a system with multiple GPUs in it.

11.1 Chapter Objectives

Through the course of this chapter, you will accomplish the following:

• You will learn how to allocate and use *zero-copy* memory.

• You will learn how to use multiple GPUs within the same application.

• You will learn how to allocate and use *portable* pinned memory.

11.2 Zero-Copy Host Memory

In Chapter 10, we examined pinned or page-locked memory, a new type of host memory that came with the guarantee that the buffer would never be swapped out of physical memory. If you recall, we allocated this memory by making a call to `cudaHostAlloc()` and passing `cudaHostAllocDefault` to get default, pinned memory. We promised that in the next chapter, you would see other more exciting means by which you can allocate pinned memory. Assuming that this is the only reason you've continued reading, you will be glad to know that the wait is over. The flag `cudaHostAllocMapped` can be passed instead of `cudaHostAllocDefault`. The host memory allocated using `cudaHostAllocMapped` is *pinned* in the same sense that memory allocated with `cudaHostAllocDefault` is pinned, specifically that it cannot be paged out of or relocated within physical memory. But in addition to using this memory from the host for memory copies to and from the GPU, this new kind of host memory allows us to violate one of the first rules we presented in Chapter 3 concerning host memory: We can access this host memory directly from within CUDA C kernels. Because this memory does not require copies to and from the GPU, we refer to it as *zero-copy* memory.

11.2.1 ZERO-COPY DOT PRODUCT

Typically, our GPU accesses only GPU memory, and our CPU accesses only host memory. But in some circumstances, it's better to break these rules. To see an instance where it's better to have the GPU manipulate host memory, we'll revisit our favorite reduction: the vector dot product. If you've managed to read this entire book, you may recall our first attempt at the dot product. We copied the two input vectors to the GPU, performed the computation, copied the intermediate results back to the host, and completed the computation on the CPU.

In this version, we'll skip the explicit copies of our input up to the GPU and instead use zero-copy memory to access the data directly from the GPU. This version of dot product will be set up exactly like our pinned memory test. Specifically, we'll write two functions; one will perform the test with standard host memory, and the other will finish the reduction on the GPU using zero-copy memory to hold the input and output buffers. First let's take a look at the standard host memory version of the dot product. We start in the usual fashion by creating timing events, allocating input and output buffers, and filling our input buffers with data.

```
float malloc_test( int size ) {
    cudaEvent_t      start, stop;
    float            *a, *b, c, *partial_c;
    float            *dev_a, *dev_b, *dev_partial_c;
    float            elapsedTime;

    HANDLE_ERROR( cudaEventCreate( &start ) );
    HANDLE_ERROR( cudaEventCreate( &stop ) );

    // allocate memory on the CPU side
    a = (float*)malloc( size*sizeof(float) );
    b = (float*)malloc( size*sizeof(float) );
    partial_c = (float*)malloc( blocksPerGrid*sizeof(float) );

    // allocate the memory on the GPU
    HANDLE_ERROR( cudaMalloc( (void**)&dev_a,
                              size*sizeof(float) ) );
    HANDLE_ERROR( cudaMalloc( (void**)&dev_b,
                              size*sizeof(float) ) );
    HANDLE_ERROR( cudaMalloc( (void**)&dev_partial_c,
                              blocksPerGrid*sizeof(float) ) );

    // fill in the host memory with data
    for (int i=0; i<size; i++) {
        a[i] = i;
        b[i] = i*2;
    }
```

After the allocations and data creation, we can begin the computations. We start our timer, copy our inputs to the GPU, execute the dot product kernel, and copy the partial results back to the host.

```
HANDLE_ERROR( cudaEventRecord( start, 0 ) );
// copy the arrays 'a' and 'b' to the GPU
HANDLE_ERROR( cudaMemcpy( dev_a, a, size*sizeof(float),
                          cudaMemcpyHostToDevice ) );
HANDLE_ERROR( cudaMemcpy( dev_b, b, size*sizeof(float),
                          cudaMemcpyHostToDevice ) );

dot<<<blocksPerGrid,threadsPerBlock>>>( size, dev_a, dev_b,
                                        dev_partial_c );

// copy the array 'c' back from the GPU to the CPU
HANDLE_ERROR( cudaMemcpy( partial_c, dev_partial_c,
                          blocksPerGrid*sizeof(float),
                          cudaMemcpyDeviceToHost ) );
```

Now we need to finish up our computations on the CPU as we did in Chapter 5. Before doing this, we'll stop our event timer because it only measures work that's being performed on the GPU:

```
HANDLE_ERROR( cudaEventRecord( stop, 0 ) );
HANDLE_ERROR( cudaEventSynchronize( stop ) );
HANDLE_ERROR( cudaEventElapsedTime( &elapsedTime,
                                    start, stop ) );
```

Finally, we sum our partial results and free our input and output buffers.

```
// finish up on the CPU side
c = 0;
for (int i=0; i<blocksPerGrid; i++) {
    c += partial_c[i];
}
```

```
        HANDLE_ERROR( cudaFree( dev_a ) );
        HANDLE_ERROR( cudaFree( dev_b ) );
        HANDLE_ERROR( cudaFree( dev_partial_c ) );

        // free memory on the CPU side
        free( a );
        free( b );
        free( partial_c );

        // free events
        HANDLE_ERROR( cudaEventDestroy( start ) );
        HANDLE_ERROR( cudaEventDestroy( stop ) );

        printf( "Value calculated:  %f\n", c );

        return elapsedTime;
    }
```

The version that uses zero-copy memory will be remarkably similar, with the exception of memory allocation. So, we start by allocating our input and output, filling the input memory with data as before:

```
float cuda_host_alloc_test( int size ) {
    cudaEvent_t      start, stop;
    float            *a, *b, c, *partial_c;
    float            *dev_a, *dev_b, *dev_partial_c;
    float            elapsedTime;

    HANDLE_ERROR( cudaEventCreate( &start ) );
    HANDLE_ERROR( cudaEventCreate( &stop ) );

    // allocate the memory on the CPU
    HANDLE_ERROR( cudaHostAlloc( (void**)&a,
                            size*sizeof(float),
                            cudaHostAllocWriteCombined |
                            cudaHostAllocMapped ) );
```

```
HANDLE_ERROR( cudaHostAlloc( (void**)&b,
                             size*sizeof(float),
                             cudaHostAllocWriteCombined |
                             cudaHostAllocMapped ) );
HANDLE_ERROR( cudaHostAlloc( (void**)&partial_c,
                             blocksPerGrid*sizeof(float),
                             cudaHostAllocMapped ) );

// fill in the host memory with data
for (int i=0; i<size; i++) {
    a[i] = i;
    b[i] = i*2;
}
```

As with Chapter 10, we see cudaHostAlloc() in action again, although we're now using the flags argument to specify more than just default behavior. The flag cudaHostAllocMapped tells the runtime that we intend to access this buffer from the GPU. In other words, this flag is what makes our buffer *zero-copy*. For the two input buffers, we specify the flag cudaHostAllocWriteCombined. This flag indicates that the runtime should allocate the buffer as write-combined with respect to the CPU cache. This flag will not change functionality in our application but represents an important performance enhancement for buffers that will be read only by the GPU. However, write-combined memory can be extremely inefficient in scenarios where the CPU also needs to perform reads from the buffer, so you will have to consider your application's likely access patterns when making this decision.

Since we've allocated our host memory with the flag cudaHostAllocMapped, the buffers can be accessed from the GPU. However, the GPU has a different virtual memory space than the CPU, so the buffers will have different addresses when they're accessed on the GPU as compared to the CPU. The call to cudaHostAlloc() returns the CPU pointer for the memory, so we need to call cudaHostGetDevicePointer() in order to get a valid GPU pointer for the memory. These pointers will be passed to the kernel and then used by the GPU to read from and write to our host allocations:

```
HANDLE_ERROR( cudaHostGetDevicePointer( &dev_a, a, 0 ) );
HANDLE_ERROR( cudaHostGetDevicePointer( &dev_b, b, 0 ) );
HANDLE_ERROR( cudaHostGetDevicePointer( &dev_partial_c,
                                        partial_c, 0 ) );
```

With valid device pointers in hand, we're ready to start our timer and launch our kernel.

```
HANDLE_ERROR( cudaEventRecord( start, 0 ) );

dot<<<blocksPerGrid,threadsPerBlock>>>( size, dev_a, dev_b,
                                        dev_partial_c );
HANDLE_ERROR( cudaThreadSynchronize() );
```

Even though the pointers dev_a, dev_b, and dev_partial_c all reside on the host, they will look to our kernel as if they are GPU memory, thanks to our calls to cudaHostGetDevicePointer(). Since our partial results are already on the host, we don't need to bother with a cudaMemcpy() from the device. However, you will notice that we're synchronizing the CPU with the GPU by calling cudaThreadSynchronize(). The contents of zero-copy memory are undefined during the execution of a kernel that potentially makes changes to its contents. After synchronizing, we're sure that the kernel has completed and that our zero-copy buffer contains the results so we can stop our timer and finish the computation on the CPU as we did before.

```
HANDLE_ERROR( cudaEventRecord( stop, 0 ) );
HANDLE_ERROR( cudaEventSynchronize( stop ) );
HANDLE_ERROR( cudaEventElapsedTime( &elapsedTime,
                                    start, stop ) );

// finish up on the CPU side
c = 0;
for (int i=0; i<blocksPerGrid; i++) {
    c += partial_c[i];
}
```

The only thing remaining in the `cudaHostAlloc()` version of the dot product is cleanup.

```
        HANDLE_ERROR( cudaFreeHost( a ) );
        HANDLE_ERROR( cudaFreeHost( b ) );
        HANDLE_ERROR( cudaFreeHost( partial_c ) );

        // free events
        HANDLE_ERROR( cudaEventDestroy( start ) );
        HANDLE_ERROR( cudaEventDestroy( stop ) );

        printf( "Value calculated:  %f\n", c );

        return elapsedTime;
    }
```

You will notice that no matter what flags we use with `cudaHostAlloc()`, the memory always gets freed in the same way. Specifically, a call to `cudaFreeHost()` does the trick.

And that's that! All that remains is to look at how `main()` ties all of this together. The first thing we need to check is whether our device supports mapping host memory. We do this the same way we checked for device overlap in the previous chapter, with a call to `cudaGetDeviceProperties()`.

```
int main( void ) {
    cudaDeviceProp  prop;
    int whichDevice;
    HANDLE_ERROR( cudaGetDevice( &whichDevice ) );
    HANDLE_ERROR( cudaGetDeviceProperties( &prop, whichDevice ) );
    if (prop.canMapHostMemory != 1) {
        printf( "Device cannot map memory.\n" );
        return 0;
    }
```

Assuming that our device supports zero-copy memory, we place the runtime into a state where it will be able to allocate zero-copy buffers for us. We accomplish this by a call to `cudaSetDeviceFlags()` and by passing the flag `cudaDeviceMapHost` to indicate that we want the device to be allowed to map host memory:

```
HANDLE_ERROR( cudaSetDeviceFlags( cudaDeviceMapHost ) );
```

That's really all there is to `main()`. We run our two tests, display the elapsed time, and exit the application:

```
    float elapsedTime = malloc_test( N );
    printf( "Time using cudaMalloc:  %3.1f ms\n",
            elapsedTime );

    elapsedTime = cuda_host_alloc_test( N );
    printf( "Time using cudaHostAlloc:  %3.1f ms\n",
            elapsedTime );
}
```

The kernel itself is unchanged from Chapter 5, but for the sake of completeness, here it is in its entirety:

```
#define imin(a,b)  (a<b?a:b)

const int N = 33 * 1024 * 1024;
const int threadsPerBlock = 256;
const int blocksPerGrid =
            imin( 32, (N+threadsPerBlock-1) / threadsPerBlock );

__global__ void dot( int size, float *a, float *b, float *c ) {
    __shared__ float cache[threadsPerBlock];
    int tid = threadIdx.x + blockIdx.x * blockDim.x;
    int cacheIndex = threadIdx.x;
```

```
float   temp = 0;
while (tid < size) {
    temp += a[tid] * b[tid];
    tid += blockDim.x * gridDim.x;
}


// set the cache values
cache[cacheIndex] = temp;


// synchronize threads in this block
__syncthreads();


// for reductions, threadsPerBlock must be a power of 2
// because of the following code
int i = blockDim.x/2;
while (i != 0) {
    if (cacheIndex < i)
        cache[cacheIndex] += cache[cacheIndex + i];
    __syncthreads();
    i /= 2;
}


if (cacheIndex == 0)
    c[blockIdx.x] = cache[0];
}
```

11.2.2 ZERO-COPY PERFORMANCE

What should we expect to gain from using zero-copy memory? The answer to this question is different for discrete GPUs and integrated GPUs. *Discrete GPUs* are graphics processors that have their own dedicated DRAMs and typically sit on separate circuit boards from the CPU. For example, if you have ever installed a graphics card into your desktop, this GPU is a discrete GPU. *Integrated GPUs* are graphics processors built into a system's chipset and usually share regular system memory with the CPU. Many recent systems built with NVIDIA's nForce media and communications processors (MCPs) contain CUDA-capable integrated GPUs. In addition to nForce MCPs, all the netbook, notebook, and desktop computers based on NVIDIA's new ION platform contain integrated, CUDA-capable GPUs. For integrated GPUs, the use of zero-copy memory is *always* a performance win because the memory is physically shared with the host anyway. Declaring a buffer as zero-copy has the sole effect of preventing unnecessary copies of data. But remember that nothing is free and that zero-copy buffers are still constrained in the same way that all pinned memory allocations are constrained: Each pinned allocation carves into the system's available physical memory, which will eventually degrade system performance.

In cases where inputs and outputs are used exactly once, we will even see a performance enhancement when using zero-copy memory with a discrete GPU. Since GPUs are designed to excel at hiding the latencies associated with memory access, performing reads and writes over the PCI Express bus can be mitigated to some degree by this mechanism, yielding a noticeable performance advantage. But since the zero-copy memory is not cached on the GPU, in situations where the memory gets read multiple times, we will end up paying a large penalty that could be avoided by simply copying the data to the GPU first.

How do you determine whether a GPU is integrated or discrete? Well, you can open up your computer and look, but this solution is fairly unworkable for your CUDA C application. Your code can check this property of a GPU by, not surprisingly, looking at the structure returned by `cudaGetDeviceProperties()`. This structure has a field named `integrated`, which will be `true` if the device is an integrated GPU and `false` if it's not.

Since our dot product application satisfies the "read and/or write exactly once" constraint, it's possible that it will enjoy a performance boost when run with zero-copy memory. And in fact, it does enjoy a slight boost in performance. On a GeForce GTX 285, the execution time improves by more than 45 percent, dropping from 98.1ms to 52.1ms when migrated to zero-copy memory. A GeForce GTX 280 enjoys a similar improvement, speeding up by 34 percent from 143.9 ms to 94.7ms. Of course, different GPUs will exhibit different performance characteristics because of varying ratios of computation to bandwidth, as well as because of variations in effective PCI Express bandwidth across chipsets.

11.3 Using Multiple GPUs

In the previous section, we mentioned how devices are either integrated or discrete GPUs, where the former is built into the system's chipset and the latter is typically an expansion card in a PCI Express slot. More and more systems contain *both* integrated and discrete GPUs, meaning that they also have multiple CUDA-capable processors. NVIDIA also sells products, such as the GeForce GTX 295, that contain more than one GPU. A GeForce GTX 295, while physically occupying a single expansion slot, will appear to your CUDA applications as two separate GPUs. Furthermore, users can also add multiple GPUs to separate PCI Express slots, connecting them with bridges using NVIDIA's *scalable link interface* (SLI) technology. As a result of these trends, it has become relatively common to have a CUDA application running on a system with multiple graphics processors. Since our CUDA applications tend to be very parallelizable to begin with, it would be excellent if we could use every CUDA device in the system to achieve maximum throughput. So, let's figure out how we can accomplish this.

To avoid learning a new example, let's convert our dot product to use multiple GPUs. To make our lives easier, we will summarize all the data necessary to compute a dot product in a single structure. You'll see momentarily exactly why this will make our lives easier.

```
struct DataStruct {
    int      deviceID;
    int      size;
    float    *a;
    float    *b;
    float    returnValue;
};
```

This structure contains the identification for the device on which the dot product will be computed; it contains the size of the input buffers as well as pointers to the two inputs a and b. Finally, it has an entry to store the value computed as the dot product of a and b.

To use N GPUs, we first would like to know exactly what value of N we're dealing with. So, we start our application with a call to cudaGetDeviceCount() in order to determine how many CUDA-capable processors have been installed in our system.

```
int main( void ) {
    int deviceCount;
    HANDLE_ERROR( cudaGetDeviceCount( &deviceCount ) );
    if (deviceCount < 2) {
        printf( "We need at least two compute 1.0 or greater "
                "devices, but only found %d\n", deviceCount );
        return 0;
    }
```

This example is designed to show multi-GPU usage, so you'll notice that we simply exit if the system has only one CUDA device (not that there's anything wrong with that). This is not encouraged as a best practice for obvious reasons. To keep things as simple as possible, we'll allocate standard host memory for our inputs and fill them with data exactly how we've done in the past.

```
    float   *a = (float*)malloc( sizeof(float) * N );
    HANDLE_NULL( a );
    float   *b = (float*)malloc( sizeof(float) * N );
    HANDLE_NULL( b );

    // fill in the host memory with data
    for (int i=0; i<N; i++) {
        a[i] = i;
        b[i] = i*2;
    }
```

We're now ready to dive into the multi-GPU code. The trick to using multiple GPUs with the CUDA runtime API is realizing that each GPU needs to be controlled by a different CPU thread. Since we have used only a single GPU before, we haven't needed to worry about this. We have moved a lot of the annoyance of multithreaded code to our file of auxiliary code, book.h. With this code tucked away, all we need to do is fill a structure with data necessary to perform the computations. Although the system could have any number of GPUs greater than one, we will use only two of them for clarity:

```
DataStruct   data[2];

data[0].deviceID = 0;
data[0].size = N/2;
data[0].a = a;
data[0].b = b;

data[1].deviceID = 1;
data[1].size = N/2;
data[1].a = a + N/2;
data[1].b = b + N/2;
```

To proceed, we pass one of the DataStruct variables to a utility function we've named start_thread(). We also pass start_thread() a pointer to a function to be called by the newly created thread; this example's thread function is called routine(). The function start_thread() will create a new thread that then calls the specified function, passing the DataStruct to this function. The other call to routine() gets made from the default application thread (so we've created only one *additional* thread).

```
CUTThread   thread = start_thread( routine, &(data[0]) );
routine( &(data[1]) );
```

Before we proceed, we have the main application thread wait for the other thread to finish by calling end_thread().

```
end_thread( thread );
```

Since both threads have completed at this point in main(), it's safe to clean up and display the result.

```
        free( a );
        free( b );


        printf( "Value calculated:  %f\n",
                data[0].returnValue + data[1].returnValue );


        return 0;
    }
```

Notice that we sum the results computed by each thread. This is the last step in our dot product reduction. In another algorithm, this combination of multiple results may involve other steps. In fact, in some applications, the two GPUs may be executing completely different code on completely different data sets. For simplicity's sake, this is not the case in our dot product example.

Since the dot product routine is identical to the other versions you've seen, we'll omit it from this section. However, the contents of routine() may be of interest. We declare routine() as taking and returning a void* so that you can reuse the start_thread() code with arbitrary implementations of a thread function. Although we'd love to take credit for this idea, it's fairly standard procedure for callback functions in C:

```
    void* routine( void *pvoidData ) {
        DataStruct  *data = (DataStruct*)pvoidData;
        HANDLE_ERROR( cudaSetDevice( data->deviceID ) );
```

Each thread calls cudaSetDevice(), and each passes a different ID to this function. As a result, we know each thread will be manipulating a different GPU. These GPUs may have identical performance, as with the dual-GPU GeForce GTX 295, or they may be different GPUs as would be the case in a system that has both an integrated GPU and a discrete GPU. These details are not important to our application, though they might be of interest to you. Particularly, these details prove useful if you depend on a certain minimum compute capability to launch your kernels or if you have a serious desire to load balance your application across the system's GPUs. If the GPUs are different, you will need to do some work to partition the computations so that each GPU is occupied for roughly the same amount of time. For our purposes in this example, however, these are piddling details with which we won't worry.

Outside the call to `cudaSetDevice()` to specify which CUDA device we intend to use, this implementation of `routine()` is remarkably similar to the vanilla `malloc_test()` from Section 11.1.1: Zero-Copy Dot Product. We allocate buffers for our GPU copies of the input and a buffer for our partial results followed by a `cudaMemcpy()` of each input array to the GPU.

```
int      size = data->size;
float    *a, *b, c, *partial_c;
float    *dev_a, *dev_b, *dev_partial_c;

// allocate memory on the CPU side
a = data->a;
b = data->b;
partial_c = (float*)malloc( blocksPerGrid*sizeof(float) );

// allocate the memory on the GPU
HANDLE_ERROR( cudaMalloc( (void**)&dev_a,
                          size*sizeof(float) ) );
HANDLE_ERROR( cudaMalloc( (void**)&dev_b,
                          size*sizeof(float) ) );
HANDLE_ERROR( cudaMalloc( (void**)&dev_partial_c,
                          blocksPerGrid*sizeof(float) ) );

// copy the arrays 'a' and 'b' to the GPU
HANDLE_ERROR( cudaMemcpy( dev_a, a, size*sizeof(float),
                          cudaMemcpyHostToDevice ) );
HANDLE_ERROR( cudaMemcpy( dev_b, b, size*sizeof(float),
                          cudaMemcpyHostToDevice ) );
```

We then launch our dot product kernel, copy the results back, and finish the computation on the CPU.

```
        dot<<<blocksPerGrid,threadsPerBlock>>>( size, dev_a, dev_b,
                                              dev_partial_c );
        // copy the array 'c' back from the GPU to the CPU
        HANDLE_ERROR( cudaMemcpy( partial_c, dev_partial_c,
                                  blocksPerGrid*sizeof(float),
                                  cudaMemcpyDeviceToHost ) );


        // finish up on the CPU side
        c = 0;
        for (int i=0; i<blocksPerGrid; i++) {
            c += partial_c[i];
        }
```

As usual, we clean up our GPU buffers and return the dot product we've computed in the `returnValue` field of our `DataStruct`.

```
        HANDLE_ERROR( cudaFree( dev_a ) );
        HANDLE_ERROR( cudaFree( dev_b ) );
        HANDLE_ERROR( cudaFree( dev_partial_c ) );

        // free memory on the CPU side
        free( partial_c );

        data->returnValue = c;
        return 0;
    }
```

So when we get down to it, outside of the host thread management issue, using multiple GPUs is not too much tougher than using a single GPU. Using our helper code to create a thread and execute a function on that thread, this becomes significantly more manageable. If you have your own thread libraries, you should feel free to use them in your own applications. You just need to remember that each GPU gets its own thread, and everything else is cream cheese.

11.4 Portable Pinned Memory

The last important piece to using multiple GPUs involves the use of pinned memory. We learned in Chapter 10 that pinned memory is actually host memory that has its pages locked in physical memory to prevent it from being paged out or relocated. However, it turns out that pages can appear pinned to a single CPU thread only. That is, they will remain page-locked if *any* thread has allocated them as pinned memory, but they will only *appear* page-locked to the thread that allocated them. If the pointer to this memory is shared between threads, the other threads will see the buffer as standard, pageable data.

As a side effect of this behavior, when a thread that did not allocate a pinned buffer attempts to perform a cudaMemcpy() using it, the copy will be performed at standard pageable memory speeds. As we saw in Chapter 10, this speed can be roughly 50 percent of the maximum attainable transfer speed. What's worse, if the thread attempts to enqueue a cudaMemcpyAsync() call into a CUDA stream, this operation will fail because it requires a pinned buffer to proceed. Since the buffer appears pageable from the thread that didn't allocate it, the call dies a grisly death. Even in the future nothing works!

But there is a remedy to this problem. We can allocate pinned memory as *portable*, meaning that we will be allowed to migrate it between host threads and allow any thread to view it as a pinned buffer. To do so, we use our trusty cudaHostAlloc() to allocate the memory, but we call it with a new flag: cudaHostAllocPortable. This flag can be used in concert with the other flags you've seen, such as cudaHostAllocWriteCombined and cudaHostAllocMapped. This means that you can allocate your host buffers as any combination of portable, zero-copy and write-combined.

To demonstrate portable pinned memory, we'll enhance our multi-GPU dot product application. We'll adapt our original zero-copy version of the dot product, so this version begins as something of a mash-up of the zero-copy and multi-GPU versions. As we have throughout this chapter, we need to verify that there are at least two CUDA-capable GPUs and that both can handle zero-copy buffers.

```
int main( void ) {
    int deviceCount;
    HANDLE_ERROR( cudaGetDeviceCount( &deviceCount ) );
    if (deviceCount < 2) {
        printf( "We need at least two compute 1.0 or greater "
                "devices, but only found %d\n", deviceCount );
        return 0;
    }


    cudaDeviceProp  prop;
    for (int i=0; i<2; i++) {
        HANDLE_ERROR( cudaGetDeviceProperties( &prop, i ) );
        if (prop.canMapHostMemory != 1) {
            printf( "Device %d cannot map memory.\n", i );
            return 0;
        }
    }
```

In previous examples, we'd be ready to start allocating memory on the host to hold our input vectors. To allocate portable pinned memory, however, it's necessary to first set the CUDA device on which we intend to run. Since we intend to use the device for zero-copy memory as well, we follow the `cudaSetDevice()` call with a call to `cudaSetDeviceFlags()`, as we did in Section 11.1.1: Zero-Copy Dot Product.

```
float *a, *b;
HANDLE_ERROR( cudaSetDevice( 0 ) );
HANDLE_ERROR( cudaSetDeviceFlags( cudaDeviceMapHost ) );
HANDLE_ERROR( cudaHostAlloc( (void**)&a, N*sizeof(float),
                            cudaHostAllocWriteCombined |
                            cudaHostAllocPortable |
                            cudaHostAllocMapped ) );
HANDLE_ERROR( cudaHostAlloc( (void**)&b, N*sizeof(float),
                            cudaHostAllocWriteCombined |
                            cudaHostAllocPortable      |
                            cudaHostAllocMapped ) );
```

Earlier in this chapter, we called cudaSetDevice() but not until we had already allocated our memory and created our threads. One of the requirements of allocating page-locked memory with cudaHostAlloc(), though, is that we have initialized the device first by calling cudaSetDevice(). You will also notice that we pass our newly learned flag, cudaHostAllocPortable, to both allocations. Since these were allocated after calling cudaSetDevice(0), only CUDA device zero would see these buffers as pinned memory if we had not specified that they were to be portable allocations.

We continue the application as we have in the past, generating data for our input vectors and preparing our DataStruct structures as we did in the multi-GPU example in Section 11.2: Zero-Copy Performance.

```
// fill in the host memory with data
for (int i=0; i<N; i++) {
    a[i] = i;
    b[i] = i*2;
}


// prepare for multithread
DataStruct   data[2];
data[0].deviceID = 0;
data[0].offset = 0;
data[0].size = N/2;
data[0].a = a;
data[0].b = b;


data[1].deviceID = 1;
data[1].offset = N/2;
data[1].size = N/2;
data[1].a = a;
data[1].b = b;
```

We can then create our secondary thread and call routine() to begin computing on each device.

```
CUTThread   thread = start_thread( routine, &(data[1]) );
routine( &(data[0]) );
end_thread( thread );
```

Because our host memory was allocated by the CUDA runtime, we use `cudaFreeHost()` to free it. Other than no longer calling `free()`, we have seen all there is to see in `main()`.

```
    // free memory on the CPU side
    HANDLE_ERROR( cudaFreeHost( a ) );
    HANDLE_ERROR( cudaFreeHost( b ) );

    printf( "Value calculated:  %f\n",
            data[0].returnValue + data[1].returnValue );

    return 0;
}
```

To support portable pinned memory and zero-copy memory in our multi-GPU application, we need to make two notable changes in the code for `routine()`. The first is a bit subtle, and in no way should this have been obvious.

```
void* routine( void *pvoidData ) {
    DataStruct  *data = (DataStruct*)pvoidData;
    if (data->deviceID != 0) {
        HANDLE_ERROR( cudaSetDevice( data->deviceID ) );
        HANDLE_ERROR( cudaSetDeviceFlags( cudaDeviceMapHost ) );
    }
```

You may recall in our multi-GPU version of this code, we need a call to `cudaSetDevice()` in `routine()` in order to ensure that each participating thread controls a different GPU. On the other hand, in this example we have already made a call to `cudaSetDevice()` from the main thread. We did so in order to allocate pinned memory in `main()`. As a result, we only want to call cudaSetDevice() and cudaSetDeviceFlags() on devices where we have not made this call. That is, we call these two functions if the deviceID is not zero. Although it would yield cleaner code to simply repeat these calls on device zero, it turns out that this is in fact an error. Once you have set the device on a particular thread, you cannot call cudaSetDevice() again, even if you pass the same device identifier. The highlighted if() statement helps us avoid this little nasty-gram from the CUDA runtime, so we move on to the next important change to routine().

In addition to using portable pinned memory for the host-side memory, we are using zero-copy in order to access these buffers directly from the GPU. Consequently, we no longer use cudaMemcpy() as we did in the original multi-GPU application, but we use cudaHostGetDevicePointer() to get valid device pointers for the host memory as we did in the zero-copy example. However, you will notice that we use standard GPU memory for the partial results. As always, this memory gets allocated using cudaMalloc().

```
int      size = data->size;
float    *a, *b, c, *partial_c;
float    *dev_a, *dev_b, *dev_partial_c;

// allocate memory on the CPU side
a = data->a;
b = data->b;
partial_c = (float*)malloc( blocksPerGrid*sizeof(float) );

HANDLE_ERROR( cudaHostGetDevicePointer( &dev_a, a, 0 ) );
HANDLE_ERROR( cudaHostGetDevicePointer( &dev_b, b, 0 ) );
HANDLE_ERROR( cudaMalloc( (void**)&dev_partial_c,
                          blocksPerGrid*sizeof(float) ) );

// offset 'a' and 'b' to where this GPU is gets it data
dev_a += data->offset;
dev_b += data->offset;
```

At this point, we're pretty much ready to go, so we launch our kernel and copy our results back from the GPU.

```
        dot<<<blocksPerGrid,threadsPerBlock>>>( size, dev_a, dev_b,
                                      dev_partial_c );
        // copy the array 'c' back from the GPU to the CPU
        HANDLE_ERROR( cudaMemcpy( partial_c, dev_partial_c,
                          blocksPerGrid*sizeof(float),
                          cudaMemcpyDeviceToHost ) );
```

We conclude as we always have in our dot product example by summing our partial results on the CPU, freeing our temporary storage, and returning to main().

```
        // finish up on the CPU side
        c = 0;
        for (int i=0; i<blocksPerGrid; i++) {
            c += partial_c[i];
        }

        HANDLE_ERROR( cudaFree( dev_partial_c ) );

        // free memory on the CPU side
        free( partial_c );

        data->returnValue = c;
        return 0;
    }
```

11.5 Chapter Review

We have seen some new types of host memory allocations, all of which get allocated with a single call, cudaHostAlloc(). Using a combination of this one entry point and a set of argument flags, we can allocate memory as any combination of zero-copy, portable, and/or write-combined. We used *zero-copy* buffers to avoid making explicit copies of data to and from the GPU, a maneuver that potentially speeds up a wide class of applications. Using a support library for threading, we manipulated multiple GPUs from the same application, allowing our dot product computation to be performed across multiple devices. Finally, we saw how multiple GPUs could share pinned memory allocations by allocating them as *portable* pinned memory. Our last example used portable pinned memory, multiple GPUs, and zero-copy buffers in order to demonstrate a turbocharged version of the dot product we started toying with back in Chapter 5. As multiple-device systems gain popularity, these techniques should serve you well in harnessing the computational power of your target platform in its entirety.

Chapter 12

The Final Countdown

Congratulations! We hope you've enjoyed learning about CUDA C and experimenting some with GPU computing. It's been a long trip, so let's take a moment to review where we started and how much ground we've covered. Starting with a background in C or C++ programming, we've learned how to use the CUDA runtime's angle bracket syntax to easily launch multiple copies of kernels across any number of multiprocessors. We expanded these concepts to use collections of threads *and* blocks, operating on arbitrarily large inputs. These more complex launches exploited interthread communication using the GPU's special, on-chip shared memory, and they employed dedicated synchronization primitives to ensure correct operation in an environment that supports (and encourages) thousands upon thousands of parallel threads.

Armed with basic concepts about parallel programming using CUDA C on NVIDIA's CUDA Architecture, we explored some of the more advanced concepts and APIs that NVIDIA provides. The GPU's dedicated graphics hardware proves useful for GPU computing, so we learned how to exploit texture memory to accelerate some common patterns of memory access. Because many users add GPU computing to their interactive graphics applications, we explored the interoperation of CUDA C kernels with industry-standard graphics APIs such as OpenGL and DirectX. Atomic operations on both global and shared memory allowed safe, multithreaded access to common memory locations. Moving steadily into more and more advanced topics, streams enabled us to keep our entire system as busy as possible, allowing kernels to execute simultaneously with memory copies between the host and GPU. Finally, we looked at the ways in which we could allocate and use zero-copy memory to accelerate applications on integrated GPUs. Moreover, we learned to initialize multiple devices and allocate portable pinned memory in order to write CUDA C that fully utilizes increasingly common, multi-GPU environments.

12.1 Chapter Objectives

Through the course of this chapter, you will accomplish the following:

- You will learn about some of the tools available to aid your CUDA C development.

- You will learn about additional written and code resources to take your CUDA C development to the next level.

12.2 CUDA Tools

Through the course of this book, we have relied upon several components of the CUDA C software system. The applications we wrote made heavy use of the CUDA C compiler in order to convert our CUDA C kernels into code that could be executed on NVIDIA GPUs. We also used the CUDA runtime in order to perform much of the setup and dirty work behind launching kernels and communicating with the GPU. The CUDA runtime, in turn, uses the CUDA driver to talk directly to the hardware in your system. In addition to these components that we have already used at length, NVIDIA makes available a host of other software in order to ease the development of CUDA C applications. This section does not serve well as a user's manual to these products, but rather, it aims solely to inform you of the existence and utility of these packages.

12.2.1 CUDA TOOLKIT

You almost certainly already have the CUDA Toolkit collection of software on your development machine. We can be so sure of this because the set of CUDA C compiler tools comprises one of the principal components of this package. If you don't have the CUDA Toolkit on your machine, then it's a veritable certainty that you haven't tried to write or compile any CUDA C code. We're on to you now, sucker! Actually, this is no big deal (but it does make us wonder why you've read this entire book). On the other hand, if you *have* been working through the examples in this book, then you should possess the libraries we're about to discuss.

12.2.2 CUFFT

The CUDA Toolkit comes with two very important utility libraries if you plan to pursue GPU computing in your own applications. First, NVIDIA provides a tuned Fast Fourier Transform library known as *CUFFT*. As of release 3.0, the CUFFT library supports a number of useful features, including the following:

- One-, two-, and three-dimensional transforms of both real-valued and complex-valued input data

- Batch execution for performing multiple one-dimensional transforms in parallel

- 2D and 3D transforms with sizes ranging from 2 to 16,384 in any dimension

- 1D transforms of inputs up to 8 million elements in size

- In-place and out-of-place transforms for both real-valued and complex-valued data

NVIDIA provides the CUFFT library free of charge with an accompanying license that allows for use in any application, regardless of whether it's for personal, academic, or professional development.

12.2.3 CUBLAS

In addition to a Fast Fourier Transform library, NVIDIA also provides a library of linear algebra routines that implements the well-known package of Basic Linear Algebra Subprograms (BLAS). This library, named *CUBLAS*, is also freely available and supports a large subset of the full BLAS package. This includes versions of each routine that accept both single- and double-precision inputs as well as real- and complex-valued data. Because BLAS was originally a FORTRAN-implemented library of linear algebra routines, NVIDIA attempts to maximize compatibility with the requirements and expectations of these implementations. Specifically, the CUBLAS library uses a column-major storage layout for arrays, rather than the row-major layout natively used by C and C++. In practice, this is not typically a concern, but it does allow for current users of BLAS to adapt their applications to exploit the GPU-accelerated CUBLAS with minimal effort. NVIDIA also distributes FORTRAN bindings to CUBLAS in order to demonstrate how to link existing FORTRAN applications to CUDA libraries.

12.2.4 NVIDIA GPU COMPUTING SDK

Available separately from the NVIDIA drivers and CUDA Toolkit, the optional *GPU Computing SDK* download contains a package of dozens and dozens of sample GPU computing applications. We mentioned this SDK earlier in the book because its samples serve as an excellent complement to the material we've covered in the first 11 chapters. But if you haven't taken a look yet, NVIDIA has geared these samples toward varying levels of CUDA C competency as well as spreading them over a broad spectrum of subject material. The samples are roughly categorized into the following sections:

CUDA Basic Topics

CUDA Advanced Topics

CUDA Systems Integration

Data-Parallel Algorithms

Graphics Interoperability

Texture

Performance Strategies

Linear Algebra

Image/Video Processing

Computational Finance

Data Compression

Physically-Based Simulation

The examples work on any platform that CUDA C works on and can serve as excellent jumping-off points for your own applications. For readers who have considerable experience in some of these areas, we warn you against expecting to see state-of-the-art implementations of your favorite algorithms in the NVIDIA

GPU Computing SDK. These code samples should not be treated as production-worthy library code but rather as educational illustrations of functioning CUDA C programs, not unlike the examples in this book.

12.2.5 NVIDIA PERFORMANCE PRIMITIVES

In addition to the routines offered in the CUFFT and CUBLAS libraries, NVIDIA also maintains a library of functions for performing CUDA-accelerated data processing known as the NVIDIA Performance Primitives (NPP). Currently, NPP's initial set of functionality focuses specifically on imaging and video processing and is widely applicable for developers in these areas. NVIDIA intends for NPP to evolve over time to address a greater number of computing tasks in a wider range of domains. If you have an interest in high-performance imaging or video applications, you should make it a priority to look into NPP, available as a free download at www.nvidia.com/object/npp.html (or accessible from your favorite web search engine).

12.2.6 DEBUGGING CUDA C

We have heard from a variety of sources that, in rare instances, computer software does not work exactly as intended when first executed. Some code computes incorrect values, some fails to terminate execution, and some code even puts the computer into a state that only a flip of the power switch can remedy. Although having clearly *never* written code like this personally, the authors of this book recognize that some software engineers may desire resources to debug their CUDA C kernels. Fortunately, NVIDIA provides tools to make this painful process significantly less troublesome.

CUDA-GDB

A tool known as *CUDA-GDB* is one of the most useful CUDA downloads available to CUDA C programmers who develop their code on Linux-based systems. NVIDIA extended the open source GNU debugger (gdb) to transparently support debugging device code in real time while maintaining the familiar interface of gdb. Prior to CUDA-GDB, there existed no good way to debug device code outside of using the CPU to simulate the way in which it was expected to run. This method yielded extremely slow debugging, and in fact, it was frequently a very poor approximation of the exact GPU execution of the kernel. NVIDIA's CUDA-GDB enables programmers to debug their kernels directly on the GPU, affording them all of the control that they've grown accustomed to with CPU debuggers. Some of the highlights of CUDA-GDB include the following:

- Viewing CUDA state, such as information regarding installed GPUs and their capabilities

- Setting breakpoints in CUDA C source code

- Inspecting GPU memory, including all global and shared memory

- Inspecting the blocks and threads currently resident on the GPU

- Single-stepping a warp of threads

- Breaking into currently running applications, including hung or deadlocked applications

Along with the debugger, NVIDIA provides the CUDA Memory Checker whose functionality can be accessed through CUDA-GDB or the stand-alone tool, cuda-memcheck. Because the CUDA Architecture includes a sophisticated memory management unit built directly into the hardware, all illegal memory accesses will be detected and prevented by the hardware. As a result of a memory violation, your program will cease functioning as expected, so you will certainly want visibility into these types of errors. When enabled, the CUDA Memory Checker will detect any global memory violations or misaligned global memory accesses that your kernel attempts to make, reporting them to you in a far more helpful and verbose manner than previously possible.

NVIDIA PARALLEL NSIGHT

Although CUDA-GDB is a mature and fantastic tool for debugging your CUDA C kernels on hardware in real time, NVIDIA recognizes that not every developer is over the moon about Linux. So, unless Windows users are hedging their bets by saving up to open their own pet stores, they need a way to debug their applications, too. Toward the end of 2009, NVIDIA introduced NVIDIA Parallel Nsight (originally code-named Nexus), the first integrated GPU/CPU debugger for Microsoft Visual Studio. Like CUDA-GDB, Parallel Nsight supports debugging CUDA applications with thousands of threads. Users can place breakpoints anywhere in their CUDA C source code, including breakpoints that trigger on writes to arbitrary memory locations. They can inspect GPU memory directly from the Visual Studio Memory window and check for out-of-bounds memory accesses. This tool has been made publicly available in a beta program as of press time, and the final version should be released shortly.

12.2.7 CUDA VISUAL PROFILER

We often tout the CUDA Architecture as a wonderful foundation for high-performance computing applications. Unfortunately, the reality is that after ferreting out all the bugs from your applications, even the most well-meaning "high-performance computing" applications are more accurately referred to as simply "computing" applications. We have often been in the position where we wonder, "Why in the Sam Hill is my code performing so poorly?" In situations like this, it helps to be able to execute the kernels in question under the watchful gaze of a profiling tool. NVIDIA provides just such a tool, available as a separate download on the CUDA Zone website. Figure 12.1 shows the Visual Profiler being used to compare two implementations of a matrix transpose operation. Despite not looking at a line of code, it becomes quite easy to determine that both memory and instruction throughput of the `transpose()` kernel outstrip that of the `transpose_naive()` kernel. (But then again, it would be unfair to expect much more from a function with *naive* in the name.)

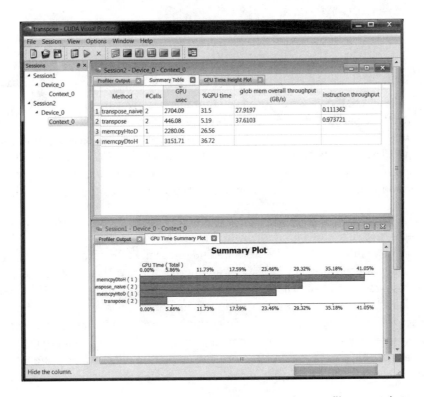

Figure 12.1 The CUDA Visual Profiler being used to profile a matrix transpose application

The CUDA Visual Profiler will execute your application, examining special performance counters built into the GPU. After execution, the profiler can compile data based on these counters and present you with reports based on what it observed. It can verify how long your application spends executing each kernel as well as determine the number of blocks launched, whether your kernel's memory accesses are coalesced, the number of divergent branches the warps in your code execute, and so on. We encourage you to look into the CUDA Visual Profiler if you have some subtle performance problems in need of resolution.

12.3 Written Resources

If you haven't already grown queasy from all the prose in this book, then it's possible you might actually be interested in reading more. We know that some of you are more likely to want to play with code in order to continue your learning, but for the rest of you, there are additional written resources to maintain your growth as a CUDA C coder.

12.3.1 PROGRAMMING MASSIVELY PARALLEL PROCESSORS: A HANDS-ON APPROACH

If you read Chapter 1, we assured you that this book was most decidedly *not* a textbook on parallel architectures. Sure, we bandied about terms such as *multiprocessor* and *warp*, but this book strives to teach the softer side of programming with CUDA C and its attendant APIs. We learned the CUDA C language within the programming model set forth in the *NVIDIA CUDA Programming Guide*, largely ignoring the way NVIDIA's hardware actually accomplishes the tasks we give it.

But to truly become an advanced, well-rounded CUDA C programmer, you will need a more intimate familiarity with the CUDA Architecture and some of the nuances of how NVIDIA GPUs work behind the scenes. To accomplish this, we recommend working your way through *Programming Massively Parallel Processors: A Hands-on Approach*. To write it, David Kirk, formerly NVIDIA's chief scientist, collaborated with Wen-mei W. Hwu, the W.J. Sanders III chairman in electrical and computer engineering at University of Illinois. You'll encounter a number of familiar terms and concepts, but you will learn about the gritty details of NVIDIA's CUDA Architecture, including thread scheduling and latency tolerance, memory bandwidth usage and efficiency, specifics on floating-point handling, and much more. The book also addresses parallel programming in a more general sense than this book, so you will gain a better overall understanding of how to engineer parallel solutions to large, complex problems.

12.3.2 CUDA U

Some of us were unlucky enough to have attended university prior to the exciting world of GPU computing. For those who are fortunate enough to be attending college now or in the near future, about 300 universities across the world currently teach courses involving CUDA. But before you start a crash diet to fit back into your college gear, there's an alternative! On the CUDA Zone website, you will find a link for *CUDA U*, which is essentially an online university for CUDA education. Or you can navigate directly there with the URL www.nvidia.com/object/cuda_education. Although you will be able to learn quite a bit about GPU computing if you attend some of the online lectures at CUDA U, as of press time there are still no online fraternities for partying after class.

UNIVERSITY COURSE MATERIALS

Among the myriad sources of CUDA education, one of the highlights includes an entire course from the University of Illinois on programming in CUDA C. NVIDIA and the University of Illinois provide this content free of charge in the M4V video format for your iPod, iPhones, or compatible video players. We know what you're thinking: "Finally, a way to learn CUDA while I wait in line at the Department of Motor Vehicles!" You may also be wondering why we waited until the very end of this book to inform you of the existence of what is essentially a movie version of this book. We're sorry for holding out on you, but the movie is hardly ever as good as the book anyway, right? In addition to actual course materials from the University of Illinois and from the University of California Davis, you will also find materials from CUDA Training Podcasts and links to third-party training and consultancy services.

DR. DOBB'S

For more than 30 years, *Dr. Dobb's* has covered nearly every major development in computing technology, and NVIDIA's CUDA is no exception. As part of an ongoing series, *Dr. Dobb's* has published an extensive series of articles cutting a broad swath through the CUDA landscape. Entitled *CUDA, Supercomputing for the Masses*, the series starts with an introduction to GPU computing and progresses quickly from a first kernel to other pieces of the CUDA programming model. The articles in *Dr. Dobb's* cover error handling, global memory performance, shared memory, the CUDA Visual Profiler, texture memory, CUDA-GDB, and the CUDPP library of data-parallel CUDA primitives, as well as many other topics. This series of articles is an excellent place to get additional information about some of the material we've attempted to convey in this book. Furthermore, you'll find practical information concerning some of the tools that we've only had time to glance over in this text, such as the profiling and debugging options available to you. The series of articles is linked from the CUDA Zone web page but is readily accessible through a web search for *Dr Dobbs CUDA*.

12.3.3 NVIDIA FORUMS

Even after digging around all of NVIDIA's documentation, you may find yourself with an unanswered or particularly intriguing question. Perhaps you're wondering whether anyone else has seen some funky behavior you're experiencing. Or maybe you're throwing a CUDA celebration party and wanted to assemble a group of like-minded individuals. For anything you're interested in asking, we strongly recommend the forums on NVIDIA's website. Located at http://forums.nvidia.com, the forums are a great place to ask questions of other CUDA users. In fact, after reading this book, you're in a position to potentially help others if you want! NVIDIA employees regularly prowl the forums, too, so the trickiest questions will prompt authoritative advice right from the source. We also love to get suggestions for new features and feedback on the good, bad, and ugly things that we at NVIDIA do.

12.4 Code Resources

Although the NVIDIA GPU Computing SDK is a treasure trove of how-to samples, it's not designed to be used for much more than pedagogy. If you're hunting for production-caliber, CUDA-powered libraries or source code, you'll need to look a bit further. Fortunately, there is a large community of CUDA developers who have produced top-notch solutions. A couple of these tools and libraries are presented here, but you are encouraged to search the Web for whatever solutions you need. And hey, maybe you'll contribute some of your own to the CUDA C community some day!

12.4.1 CUDA DATA PARALLEL PRIMITIVES LIBRARY

NVIDIA, with the help of researchers at the University of California Davis, has released a library known as the CUDA Data Parallel Primitives Library (CUDPP). CUDPP, as the name indicates, is a library of data-parallel algorithm primitives. Some of these primitives include parallel prefix-sum (*scan*), parallel sort, and parallel reduction. Primitives such as these form the foundation of a wide variety of data-parallel algorithms, including sorting, stream compaction, building data structures, and many others. If you're looking to write an even moderately complex algorithms, chances are good that either CUDPP already has what you need or it can get you significantly closer to where you want to be. Download it at http://code.google.com/p/cudpp.

12.4.2 CULATOOLS

As we mentioned in Section 12.1.3: CUBLAS, NVIDIA provides an implementation of the BLAS packaged along with the CUDA Toolkit download. For readers who need a broader solution for linear algebra, take a look at EM Photonics' CUDA implementation of the industry-standard Linear Algebra Package (LAPACK). Its LAPACK implementation is known as *CULAtools* and offers more complex linear algebra routines that are built on NVIDIA's CUBLAS technology. The freely available Basic package offers LU decomposition, QR factorization, linear system solver, and singular value decomposition, as well as least squares and constrained least squares solvers. You can obtain the Basic download at www.culatools.com/versions/basic. You will also notice that EM Photonics offers Premium and Commercial licenses, which contain a far greater fraction of the LAPACK routines, as well as licensing terms that will allow you to distribute your own commercial applications based on CULAtools.

12.4.3 LANGUAGE WRAPPERS

This book has primarily been concerned with C and C++, but clearly hundreds of projects exist that don't employ these languages. Fortunately, third parties have written wrappers to allow access to CUDA technology from languages not officially supported by NVIDIA. NVIDIA itself provides FORTRAN bindings for its CUBLAS library, but you can also find Java bindings for several of the CUDA libraries at www.jcuda.org. Likewise, Python wrappers to allow the use of CUDA C kernels from Python applications are available from the PyCUDA project at http://mathema.tician.de/software/pycuda. Finally, there are bindings for the Microsoft .NET environment available from the CUDA.NET project at www.hoopoe-cloud.com/Solutions/CUDA.NET.

Although these projects are not officially supported by NVIDIA, they have been around for several versions of CUDA, are all freely available, and each has many successful customers. The moral of this story is, if your language of choice (or your boss's choice) is not C or C++, you should not rule out GPU computing until you've first looked to see whether the necessary bindings are available.

12.5 Chapter Review

And there you have it. Even after 11 chapters of CUDA C, there are still loads of resources to download, read, watch, and compile. This is a remarkably interesting time to be learning GPU computing, as the era of heterogeneous computing platforms matures. We hope that you have enjoyed learning about one of the most pervasive parallel programming environments in existence. Moreover, we hope that you leave this experience excited about the possibilities to develop new and exciting means for interacting with computers and for processing the ever-increasing amount of information available to your software. It's your ideas and the amazing technologies you develop that will push GPU computing to the next level.

Appendix

Advanced Atomics

Chapter 9 covered some of the ways in which we can use atomic operations to enable hundreds of threads to safely make concurrent modifications to shared data. In this appendix, we'll look at an advanced method for using atomics to implement locking data structures. On its surface, this topic does not seem much more complicated than anything else we've examined. And in reality, this is accurate. You've learned a lot of complex topics through this book, and locking data structures are no more challenging than these. So, why is this material hiding in the appendix? We don't want to reveal any spoilers, so if you're intrigued, read on, and we'll discuss this through the course of the appendix.

A.1 Dot Product Revisited

In Chapter 5, we looked at the implementation of a vector dot product using CUDA C. This algorithm was one of a large family of algorithms known as *reductions*. If you recall, the algorithm computed the dot product of two input vectors by doing the following:

1. Each thread in each block multiplies two corresponding elements of the input vectors and stores the products in shared memory.

2. Although a block has more than one product, a thread adds two of the products and stores the result back to shared memory. Each step results in half as many values as it started with (this is where the term *reduction* comes from)

3. When every block has a final sum, each one writes its value to global memory and exits.

4. If the kernel ran with N parallel blocks, the CPU sums these remaining N values to generate the final dot product.

This high-level look at the dot product algorithm is intended to be review, so if it's been a while or you've had a couple glasses of Chardonnay, it may be worth the time to review Chapter 5. If you feel comfortable enough with the dot product code to continue, draw your attention to step 4 in the algorithm. Although it doesn't involve copying much data to the host or performing many calculations on the CPU, moving the computation back to the CPU to finish is indeed as awkward as it sounds.

But it's more than an issue of an awkward step to the algorithm or the inelegance of the solution. Consider a scenario where a dot product computation is just one step in a long sequence of operations. If you want to perform *every* operation on the GPU because your CPU is busy with other tasks or computations, you're out of luck. As it stands, you'll be forced to stop computing on the GPU, copy intermediate results back to the host, finish the computation with the CPU, and finally upload that result back to the GPU and resume computing with your next kernel.

Since this is an appendix on atomics and we have gone to such lengths to explain what a pain our original dot product algorithm is, you should see where we're heading. We intend to fix our dot product using atomics so the entire computation can stay on the GPU, leaving your CPU free to perform other tasks. Ideally, instead of exiting the kernel in step 3 and returning to the CPU in step 4, we want each block to add its final result to a total in global memory. If each value were added atomically, we would not have to worry about potential collisions or indeterminate results. Since we have already used an `atomicAdd()` operation in the histogram operation, this seems like an obvious choice.

Unfortunately, prior to compute capability 2.0, `atomicAdd()` operated only on integers. Although this might be fine if you plan to compute dot products of vectors with integer components, it is significantly more common to use floating-point components. However, the majority of NVIDIA hardware does not support atomic arithmetic on floating-point numbers! But there's a reasonable explanation for this, so don't throw your GPU in the garbage just yet.

Atomic operations on a value in memory guarantee only that each thread's read-modify-write sequence will complete without other threads reading or writing the target value while in process. There is no stipulation about the order in which the threads will perform their operations, so in the case of three threads performing addition, sometimes the hardware will perform $(A+B)+C$ and sometimes it will compute $A+(B+C)$. This is acceptable for integers because integer math is associative, so $(A+B)+C = A+(B+C)$. Floating-point arithmetic is *not* associative because of the rounding of intermediate results, so $(A+B)+C$ often does not equal $A+(B+C)$. As a result, atomic arithmetic on floating-point values is of dubious utility because it gives rise to nondeterministic results in a highly multithreaded environment such as on the GPU. There are many applications where it is simply unacceptable to get two different results from two runs of an application, so the support of floating-point atomic arithmetic was not a priority for earlier hardware.

However, if we are willing to tolerate some nondeterminism in the results, we can still accomplish the reduction entirely on the GPU. But we'll first need to develop a way to work around the lack of atomic floating-point arithmetic. The solution will still use atomic operations, but not for the arithmetic itself.

A.1.1 ATOMIC LOCKS

The `atomicAdd()` function we used to build GPU histograms performed a read-modify-write operation without interruption from other threads. At a low level, you can imagine the hardware locking the target memory location while this operation is underway, and while locked, no other threads can read or write the value at the location. If we had a way of emulating this lock in our CUDA C kernels, we could perform arbitrary operations on an associated memory location or data structure. The locking mechanism itself will operate exactly like a typical CPU *mutex*. If you are unfamiliar with mutual exclusion (*mutex*), don't fret. It's not any more complicated than the things you've already learned.

The basic idea is that we allocate a small piece memory to be used as a *mutex*. The mutex will act like something of a traffic signal that governs access to some resource. The resource could be a data structure, a buffer, or simply a memory location we want to modify atomically. When a thread reads a 0 from the mutex, it interprets this value as a "green light" indicating that no other thread is using the memory. Therefore, the thread is free to lock the memory and make whatever changes it desires, free of interference from other threads. To lock the memory location in question, the thread writes a 1 to the mutex. This 1 will act as a "red light" for potentially competing threads. The competing threads must then wait until the owner has written a 0 to the mutex before they can attempt to modify the locked memory.

A simple code sequence to accomplish this locking process might look like this:

```
void lock( void ) {
    if( *mutex == 0 ) {
        *mutex = 1; //store a 1 to lock
    }
}
```

Unfortunately, there's a problem with this code. Fortunately, it's a familiar problem: What happens if another thread writes a 1 to the mutex after our thread has read the value to be zero? That is, both threads check the value at `mutex` and see that it's zero. They then both write a 1 to this location to signify to other threads that the structure is locked and unavailable for modification. After doing so, both threads think they own the associated memory or data structure and begin making unsafe modifications. Catastrophe ensues!

The operation we want to complete is fairly simple: We need to compare the value at `mutex` to 0 and store a 1 at that location if and only if the `mutex` was 0. To accomplish this correctly, this entire operation needs to be performed atomically so we know that no other thread can interfere while our thread examines and updates the value at `mutex`. In CUDA C, this operation can be performed with the function `atomicCAS()`, an atomic compare-and-swap. The function `atomicCAS()` takes a pointer to memory, a value with which to compare the value at that location, and a value to store in that location if the comparison is successful. Using this operation, we can implement a GPU lock function as follows:

```
__device__ void lock( void ) {
    while( atomicCAS( mutex, 0, 1 ) != 0 );
}
```

The call to `atomicCAS()` returns the value that it found at the address `mutex`. As a result, the `while()` loop will continue to run until `atomicCAS()` sees a 0 at `mutex`. When it sees a 0, the comparison is successful, and the thread writes a 1 to `mutex`. Essentially, the thread will spin in the `while()` loop until it has successfully locked the data structure. We'll use this locking mechanism to implement our GPU hash table. But first, we dress the code up in a structure so it will be cleaner to use in the dot product application:

```
struct Lock {
    int *mutex;
    Lock( void ) {
        int state = 0;
        HANDLE_ERROR( cudaMalloc( (void**)& mutex,
                                  sizeof(int) ) );
        HANDLE_ERROR( cudaMemcpy( mutex, &state, sizeof(int),
                                  cudaMemcpyHostToDevice ) );
    }

    ~Lock( void ) {
        cudaFree( mutex );
    }

    __device__ void lock( void ) {
        while( atomicCAS( mutex, 0, 1 ) != 0 );
    }

    __device__ void unlock( void ) {
        atomicExch( mutex, 1 );
    }
};
```

Notice that we restore the value of `mutex` with `atomicExch( mutex, 1 )`. The function `atomicExch()` reads the value that is located at `mutex`, exchanges

253

it with the second argument (a 1 in this case), and returns the original value it read. Why would we use an atomic function for this rather than the more obvious method to reset the value at `mutex`?

```
*mutex = 1;
```

If you're expecting some subtle, hidden reason why this method fails, we hate to disappoint you, but this would work as well. So, why not use this more obvious method? Atomic transactions and generic global memory operations follow different paths through the GPU. Using both atomics and standard global memory operations could therefore lead to an `unlock()` seeming out of sync with a subsequent attempt to `lock()` the mutex. The behavior would still be function-ally correct, but to ensure consistently intuitive behavior from the application's perspective, it's best to use the same pathway for all accesses to the mutex. Because we're required to use an atomic to lock the resource, we have chosen to also use an atomic to unlock the resource.

A.1.2 DOT PRODUCT REDUX: ATOMIC LOCKS

The only piece of our earlier dot product example that we endeavor to change is the final CPU-based portion of the reduction. In the previous section, we described how we implement a mutex on the GPU. The `Lock` structure that implements this mutex is located in `lock.h` and included at the beginning of our improved dot product example:

```c
#include "../common/book.h"
#include "lock.h"


#define imin(a,b) (a<b?a:b)


const int N = 33 * 1024 * 1024;
const int threadsPerBlock = 256;
const int blocksPerGrid =
            imin( 32, (N+threadsPerBlock-1) / threadsPerBlock );
```

With two exceptions, the beginning of our dot product kernel is identical to the kernel we used in Chapter 5. Both exceptions involve the kernel's signature:

```c
__global__ void dot( Lock lock, float *a, float *b, float *c )
```

In our updated dot product, we pass a `Lock` to the kernel in addition to input vectors and the output buffer. The `Lock` will govern access to the output buffer during the final accumulation step. The other change is not *noticeable* from the signature but involves the signature. Previously, the `float *c` argument was a buffer for `N` floats where each of the `N` blocks could store its partial result. This buffer was copied back to the CPU to compute the final sum. Now, the argument `c` no longer points to a temporary buffer but to a single floating-point value that will store the dot product of the vectors in `a` and `b`. But even with these changes, the kernel starts out exactly as it did in Chapter 5:

```
__global__ void dot( Lock lock, float *a,
                     float *b, float *c ) {
    __shared__ float cache[threadsPerBlock];
    int tid = threadIdx.x + blockIdx.x * blockDim.x;
    int cacheIndex = threadIdx.x;

    float   temp = 0;
    while (tid < N) {
        temp += a[tid] * b[tid];
        tid += blockDim.x * gridDim.x;
    }

    // set the cache values
    cache[cacheIndex] = temp;

    // synchronize threads in this block
    __syncthreads();

    // for reductions, threadsPerBlock must be a power of 2
    // because of the following code
    int i = blockDim.x/2;
    while (i != 0) {
        if (cacheIndex < i)
            cache[cacheIndex] += cache[cacheIndex + i];
        __syncthreads();
        i /= 2;
    }
```

At this point in execution, the 256 threads in each block have summed their 256 pairwise products and computed a single value that's sitting in `cache[0]`. Each thread block now needs to add its final value to the value at c. To do this safely, we'll use the lock to govern access to this memory location, so each thread needs to acquire the lock before updating the value *c. After adding the block's partial sum to the value at c, it unlocks the mutex so other threads can accumulate their values. After adding its value to the final result, the block has nothing remaining to compute and can return from the kernel.

```
    if (cacheIndex == 0) {
        lock.lock();
        *c += cache[0];
        lock.unlock();
    }
}
```

The `main()` routine is very similar to our original implementation, though it does have a couple differences. First, we no longer need to allocate a buffer for partial results as we did in Chapter 5. We now allocate space for only a single floating-point result:

```
int main( void ) {
    float   *a, *b, c = 0;
    float   *dev_a, *dev_b, *dev_c;

    // allocate memory on the CPU side
    a = (float*)malloc( N*sizeof(float) );
    b = (float*)malloc( N*sizeof(float) );

    // allocate the memory on the GPU
    HANDLE_ERROR( cudaMalloc( (void**)&dev_a,
                              N*sizeof(float) ) );
    HANDLE_ERROR( cudaMalloc( (void**)&dev_b,
                              N*sizeof(float) ) );
    HANDLE_ERROR( cudaMalloc( (void**)&dev_c,
                              sizeof(float) ) );
```

As we did in Chapter 5, we initialize our input arrays and copy them to the GPU. But you'll notice an additional copy in this example: We're also copying a zero to `dev_c`, the location that we intend to use to accumulate our final dot product. Since each block wants to read this value, add its partial sum, and store the result back, we need the initial value to be zero in order to get the correct result.

```
// fill in the host memory with data
for (int i=0; i<N; i++) {
    a[i] = i;
    b[i] = i*2;
}


// copy the arrays 'a' and 'b' to the GPU
HANDLE_ERROR( cudaMemcpy( dev_a, a, N*sizeof(float),
                          cudaMemcpyHostToDevice ) );
HANDLE_ERROR( cudaMemcpy( dev_b, b, N*sizeof(float),
                          cudaMemcpyHostToDevice ) );
HANDLE_ERROR( cudaMemcpy( dev_c, &c, sizeof(float),
                          cudaMemcpyHostToDevice ) );
```

All that remains is declaring our `Lock`, invoking the kernel, and copying the result back to the CPU.

```
Lock    lock;
dot<<<blocksPerGrid,threadsPerBlock>>>( lock, dev_a,
                                        dev_b, dev_c );


// copy c back from the GPU to the CPU
HANDLE_ERROR( cudaMemcpy( &c, dev_c,
                          sizeof(float),
                          cudaMemcpyDeviceToHost ) );
```

In Chapter 5, this is when we would do a final `for()` loop to add the partial sums. Since this is done on the GPU using atomic locks, we can skip right to the answer-checking and cleanup code:

```
#define sum_squares(x)   (x*(x+1)*(2*x+1)/6)
printf( "Does GPU value %.6g = %.6g?\n", c,
        2 * sum_squares( (float)(N - 1) ) );


// free memory on the GPU side
cudaFree( dev_a );
cudaFree( dev_b );
cudaFree( dev_c );


// free memory on the CPU side
free( a );
free( b );
}
```

Because there is no way to precisely predict the order in which each block will add its partial sum to the final total, it is very likely (almost certain) that the final result will be summed in a different order than the CPU will sum it. Because of the nonassociativity of floating-point addition, it's therefore quite probable that the final result will be slightly different between the GPU and CPU. There is not much that can be done about this without adding a nontrivial chunk of code to ensure that the blocks acquire the lock in a deterministic order that matches the summation order on the CPU. If you feel extraordinarily motivated, give this a try. Otherwise, we'll move on to see how these atomic locks can be used to implement a multithreaded data structure.

A.2 Implementing a Hash Table

The hash table is one of the most important and commonly used data structures in computer science, playing an important role in a wide variety of applications. For readers not already familiar with hash tables, we'll provide a quick primer here. The study of data structures warrants more in-depth study than we intend to provide, but in the interest of making forward progress, we will keep this brief. If you already feel comfortable with the concepts behind hash tables, you should skip to the hash table implementation in Section A.2.2: A CPU Hash Table.

A.2.1 HASH TABLE OVERVIEW

A hash table is essentially a structure that is designed to store pairs of *keys* and *values*. For example, you could think of a dictionary as a hash table. Every word in the dictionary is a *key*, and each word has a definition associated with it. The definition is the *value* associated with the word, and thus every word and definition in the dictionary form a key/value pair. For this data structure to be useful, though, it is important that we minimize the time it takes to find a particular value if we're given a key. In general, this should be a constant amount of time. That is, the time to look up a value given a key should be the same, regardless of how many key/ value pairs are in the hash table.

At an abstract level, our hash table will place values in "buckets" based on the value's corresponding key. The method by which we map keys to buckets is often called the *hash function*. A good hash function will map the set of possible keys uniformly across all the buckets because this will help satisfy our requirement that it take constant time to find any value, regardless of the number of values we've added to the hash table.

For example, consider our dictionary hash table. One obvious hash function would involve using 26 buckets, one for each letter of the alphabet. This simple hash function might simply look at the first letter of the key and put the value in one of the 26 buckets based on this letter. Figure A.1 shows how this hash function would assign few sample words.

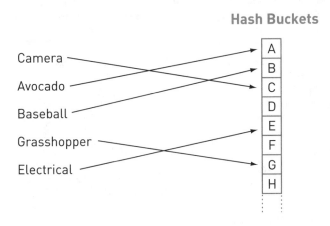

Hash Buckets

Figure A.1 Hashing of words into buckets

Given what we know about the distribution of words in the English language, this hash function leaves much to be desired because it will not map words uniformly across the 26 buckets. Some of the buckets will contain very few key/value pairs, and some of the buckets will contain a large number of pairs. Accordingly, it will take much longer to find the value associated with a word that begins with a common letter such as S than it would take to find the value associated with a word that begins with the letter X. Since we are looking for hash functions that will give us constant-time retrieval of any value, this consequence is fairly undesirable. An immense amount of research has gone into the study of hash functions, but even a brief survey of these techniques is beyond the scope of this book.

The last component of our hash table data structure involves the buckets. If we had a perfect hash function, every key would map to a different bucket. In this case, we can simply store the key/value pairs in an array where each entry in the array is what we've been calling a *bucket*. However, even with an excellent hash function, in most situations we will have to deal with *collisions*. A collision occurs when more than one key maps to a bucket, such as when we add both the words *avocado* and *aardvark* to our dictionary hash table. The simplest way to store all of the values that map to a given bucket is simply to maintain a list of values in the bucket. When we encounter a collision, such as adding *aardvark* to a dictionary that already contains *avocado*, we put the value associated with *aardvark* at the end of the list we're maintaining in the "A" bucket, as shown in Figure A.2.

After adding the word *avocado* in Figure A.2, the first bucket has a single key/value pair in its list. Later in this imaginary application we add the word *aardvark*, a word that collides with *avocado* because they both start with the letter A. You will notice in Figure A.3 that it simply gets placed at the end of the list in the first bucket:

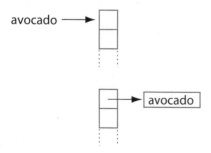

Figure A.2 Inserting the word *avocado* into the hash table

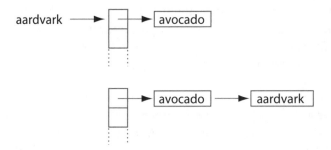

Figure A.3 Resolving the conflict when adding the word *aardvark*

Armed with some background on the notions of a *hash function* and *collision resolution*, we're ready to take a look at implementing our own hash table.

A.2.2 A CPU HASH TABLE

As described in the previous section, our hash table will consist of essentially two parts: a hash function and a data structure of buckets. Our buckets will be implemented exactly as before: We will allocate an array of length N, and each entry in the array holds a list of key/value pairs. Before concerning ourselves with a hash function, we will take a look at the data structures involved:

```
#include "../common/book.h"

struct Entry {
    unsigned int    key;
    void*           value;
    Entry           *next;
};

struct Table {
    size_t  count;
    Entry   **entries;
    Entry   *pool;
    Entry   *firstFree;
};
```

As described in the introductory section, the structure `Entry` holds both a key and a value. In our application, we will use unsigned integer keys to store our key/value pairs. The value associated with this key can be any data, so we have declared `value` as a `void*` to indicate this. Our application will primarily be concerned with creating the hash table data structure, so we won't actually store anything in the `value` field. We have included it in the structure for completeness, in case you want to use this code in your own applications. The last piece of data in our hash table `Entry` is a pointer to the next `Entry`. After collisions, we'll have multiple entries in the same bucket, and we have decided to store these entries as a list. So, each entry will point to the next entry in the bucket, thereby forming a list of entries that have hashed to the same location in the table. The last entry will have a `NULL` next pointer.

At its heart, the `Table` structure itself is an array of "buckets." This bucket array is just an array of length `count`, where each bucket in `entries` is just a pointer to an `Entry`. To avoid incurring the complication and performance hit of allocating memory every time we want to add an `Entry` to the table, the table will maintain a large array of available entries in `pool`. The field `firstFree` points to the next available `Entry` for use, so when we need to add an entry to the table, we can simply use the `Entry` pointed to by `firstFree` and increment that pointer. Note that this will also simplify our cleanup code because we can free all of these entries with a single call to `free()`. If we had allocated every entry as we went, we would have to walk through the table and free every entry one by one.

After understanding the data structures involved, let's take a look at some of the other support code:

```
void initialize_table( Table &table, int entries,
                       int elements ) {
    table.count = entries;
    table.entries = (Entry**)calloc( entries, sizeof(Entry*) );
    table.pool = (Entry*)malloc( elements * sizeof( Entry ) );
    table.firstFree = table.pool;
}
```

Table initialization consists primarily of allocating memory and clearing memory for the bucket array entries. We also allocate storage for a pool of entries and initialize the firstFree pointer to be the first entry in the pool array.

At the end of the application, we'll want to free the memory we've allocated, so our cleanup routine frees the bucket array and the pool of free entries:

```
void free_table( Table &table ) {
    free( table.entries );
    free( table.pool );
}
```

In our introduction, we spoke quite a bit about the hash function. Specifically, we discussed how a good hash function can make the difference between an excellent hash table implementation and poor one. In this example, we're using unsigned integers as our keys, and we need to map these to the indices of our bucket array. The simplest way to do this would be to select the bucket with an index equal to the key. That is, we could store the entry e in table.entries[e.key]. However, we have no way of guaranteeing that every key will be less than the length of the array of buckets. Fortunately, this problem can be solved relatively painlessly:

```
size_t hash( unsigned int key, size_t count ) {
    return key % count;
}
```

If the hash function is so important, how can we get away with such a simple one? Ideally, we want the keys to map uniformly across all the buckets in our table, and all we're doing here is taking the key modulo the array length. In reality, hash functions may not normally be this simple, but because this is just an example program, we will be randomly generating our keys. If we assume that the random number generator generates values roughly uniformly, this hash function should map these keys uniformly across all of the buckets of the hash table. In your own hash table implementation, you may require a more complicated hash function.

Having seen the hash table structures and the hash function, we're ready to look at the process of adding a key/value pair to the table. The process involves three basic steps:

1. Compute the hash function on the input key to determine the new entry's bucket.

2. Take a preallocated Entry from the pool and initialize its key and value fields.

3. Insert the entry at the front of the proper bucket's list.

We translate these steps to code in a fairly straightforward way.

```
void add_to_table( Table &table, unsigned int key, void* value )
{
    //Step 1
    size_t hashValue = hash( key, table.count );

    //Step 2
    Entry *location = table.firstFree++;
    location->key = key;
    location->value = value;

    //Step 3
    location->next = table.entries[hashValue];
    table.entries[hashValue] = location;
}
```

If you have never seen linked lists (or it's been a while), step 3 may be tricky to understand at first. The existing list has its first node stored at table. entries[hashValue]. With this in mind, we can insert a new node at the head of the list in two steps: First, we set our new entry's next pointer to point to the first node in the existing list. Then, we store the new entry in the bucket array so *it* becomes the first node of the new list.

Since it's a good idea to have some idea whether the code you've written works, we've implemented a routine to perform a sanity check on a hash table. The check involves first walking through the table and examining every node. We compute the hash function on the node's key and confirm that the node is stored in the correct bucket. After checking every node, we verify that the number of nodes *actually* in the table is indeed equal to the number of elements we *intended* to add to the table. If these numbers don't agree, then either we've added a node accidentally to multiple buckets or we haven't inserted it correctly.

```c
#define SIZE      (100*1024*1024)
#define ELEMENTS    (SIZE / sizeof(unsigned int))

void verify_table( const Table &table ) {
    int count = 0;
    for (size_t i=0; i<table.count; i++) {
        Entry   *current = table.entries[i];
        while (current != NULL) {
            ++count;
            if (hash( current->value, table.count ) != i)
                printf( "%d hashed to %ld, but was located "
                        "at %ld\n", current->value,
                        hash( current->value, table.count ), i );
            current = current->next;
        }
    }
    if (count != ELEMENTS)
        printf( "%d elements found in hash table.  Should be %ld\n",
                count, ELEMENTS );
    else
        printf( "All %d elements found in hash table.\n", count);
}
```

With all the infrastructure code out of the way, we can look at `main()`. As with many of this book's examples, a lot of the heavy lifting has been done in helper functions, so we hope that `main()` will be relatively easy to follow:

```c
#define HASH_ENTRIES    1024

int main( void ) {
    unsigned int *buffer =
                    (unsigned int*)big_random_block( SIZE );

    clock_t start, stop;
    start = clock();

    Table table;
    initialize_table( table, HASH_ENTRIES, ELEMENTS );

    for (int i=0; i<ELEMENTS; i++) {
        add_to_table( table, buffer[i], (void*)NULL );
    }

    stop = clock();
    float   elapsedTime = (float)(stop - start) /
                            (float)CLOCKS_PER_SEC * 1000.0f;
    printf( "Time to hash:  %3.1f ms\n", elapsedTime );

    verify_table( table );

    free_table( table );
    free( buffer );
    return 0;
}
```

As you can see, we start by allocating a big chunk of random numbers. These randomly generated unsigned integers will be the keys we insert into our hash table. After generating the numbers, we read the system time in order to measure the performance of our implementation. We initialize the hash table and then insert each random key into the table using a `for()` loop. After adding all the keys, we read the system time again to compute the elapsed time to initialize and add the keys. Finally, we verify the hash table with our sanity check routine and free the buffers we've allocated.

You probably noticed that we are using NULL as the value for every key/value pair. In a typical application, you would likely store some useful data with the key, but because we are primarily concerned with the hash table implementation itself, we're storing a meaningless value with each key.

A.2.3 MULTITHREADED HASH TABLE

There are some assumptions built into our CPU hash table that will no longer be valid when we move to the GPU. First, we have assumed that only one node can be added to the table at a time in order to make the addition of a node simpler. If more than one thread were trying to add a node to the table at once, we could end up with problems similar to the multithreaded addition problems in the example from Chapter 9.

For example, let's revisit our "avocado and aardvark" example and imagine that threads A and B are trying to add these entries to the table. Thread A computes a hash function on *avocado*, and thread B computes the function on *aardvark*. They both decide their keys belong in the same bucket. To add the new entry to the list, thread A and B start by setting their new entry's next pointer to the first node of the existing list as in Figure A.4.

Then, both threads try to replace the entry in the bucket array with their new entry. However, the thread that finishes second is the only thread that has its update preserved because it overwrites the work of the previous thread. So consider the scenario where thread A replaces the entry *altitude* with its entry for *avocado*. Immediately after finishing, thread B replaces what it believe to be the entry for *altitude* with its entry for *aardvark*. Unfortunately, it's replacing *avocado* instead of *altitude*, resulting in the situation illustrated in Figure A.5.

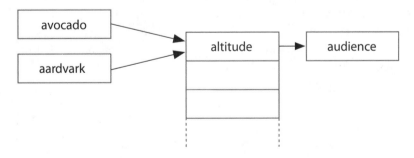

Figure A.4 Multiple threads attempting to add a node to the same bucket

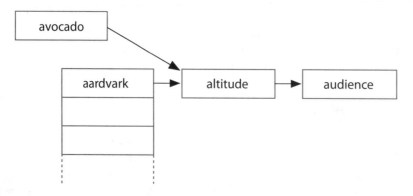

Figure A.5 The hash table after an unsuccessful concurrent modification by two threads

Thread A's entry is tragically "floating" outside of the hash table. Fortunately, our sanity check routine would catch this and alert us to the presence of a problem because it would count fewer nodes than we expected. But we still need to answer this question: How do we build a hash table on the GPU?! The key observation here involves the fact that only one thread can safely make modifications to a bucket at a time. This is similar to our dot product example where only one thread at a time could safely add its value to the final result. If each bucket had an atomic lock associated with it, we could ensure that only a single thread was making changes to a given bucket at a time.

A.2.4 A GPU HASH TABLE

Armed with a method to ensure safe multithreaded access to the hash table, we can proceed with a GPU implementation of the hash table application we wrote in Section A.2.2: A CPU Hash Table. We'll need to include `lock.h`, the implementation of our GPU `Lock` structure from Section A.1.1 Atomic Locks, and we'll need to declare the hash function as a `__device__` function. Aside from these changes, the fundamental data structures and hash function are identical to the CPU implementation.

```
#include "../common/book.h"
#include "lock.h"

struct Entry {
    unsigned int    key;
    void*           value;
    Entry           *next;
};

struct Table {
    size_t  count;
    Entry   **entries;
    Entry   *pool;
};


__device__ __host__ size_t hash( unsigned int value,
                                 size_t count ) {
    return value % count;
}
```

Initializing and freeing the hash table consists of the same steps as we performed on the CPU, but as with previous examples, we use CUDA runtime functions to accomplish this. We use cudaMalloc() to allocate a bucket array and a pool of entries, and we use cudaMemset() to set the bucket array entries to zero. To free the memory upon application completion, we use cudaFree().

```
void initialize_table( Table &table, int entries,
                       int elements ) {
    table.count = entries;
    HANDLE_ERROR( cudaMalloc( (void**)&table.entries,
                              entries * sizeof(Entry*)) );
    HANDLE_ERROR( cudaMemset( table.entries, 0,
                              entries * sizeof(Entry*) ) );
    HANDLE_ERROR( cudaMalloc( (void**)&table.pool,
                              elements * sizeof(Entry)) );
}
```

```
void free_table( Table &table ) {
    cudaFree( table.pool );
    cudaFree( table.entries );
}
```

We used a routine to check our hash table for correctness in the CPU implementation. We need a similar routine for the GPU version, so we have two options. We could write a GPU-based version of verify_table(), or we could use the same code we used in the CPU version and add a function that copies a hash table from the GPU to the CPU. Although either option gets us what we need, the second option seems superior for two reasons: First, it involves reusing our CPU version of verify_table(). As with code reuse in general, this saves time and ensures that future changes to the code would need to be made in only one place for both versions of the hash table. Second, implementing a copy function will uncover an interesting problem, the solution to which may be very useful to you in the future.

As promised, verify_table() is identical to the CPU implementation and is reprinted here for your convenience:

```
#define SIZE      (100*1024*1024)
#define ELEMENTS    (SIZE / sizeof(unsigned int))
#define HASH_ENTRIES    1024

void verify_table( const Table &dev_table ) {
    Table   table;
    copy_table_to_host( dev_table, table );

    int count = 0;
    for (size_t i=0; i<table.count; i++) {
        Entry   *current = table.entries[i];
        while (current != NULL) {
            ++count;
            if (hash( current->value, table.count ) != i)
                printf( "%d hashed to %ld, but was located "
                        "at %ld\n", current->value,
                        hash(current->value, table.count), i );
            current = current->next;
        }
    }
}
```

```
    if (count != ELEMENTS)
        printf( "%d elements found in hash table.  Should be %ld\n",
                count, ELEMENTS );
    else
        printf( "All %d elements found in hash table.\n", count );


    free( table.pool );
    free( table.entries );
}
```

Since we chose to reuse our CPU implementation of verify_table(), we need a function to copy the table from GPU memory to host memory. There are three steps to this function, two relatively obvious steps and a third, trickier step. The first two steps involve allocating host memory for the hash table data and performing a copy of the GPU data structures into this memory with cudaMemcpy(). We have done this many times previously, so this should come as no surprise.

```
void copy_table_to_host( const Table &table, Table &hostTable) {
    hostTable.count = table.count;
    hostTable.entries = (Entry**)calloc( table.count,
                                          sizeof(Entry*) );
    hostTable.pool = (Entry*)malloc( ELEMENTS *
                                         sizeof( Entry ) );


    HANDLE_ERROR( cudaMemcpy( hostTable.entries, table.entries,
                              table.count * sizeof(Entry*),
                              cudaMemcpyDeviceToHost ) );
    HANDLE_ERROR( cudaMemcpy( hostTable.pool, table.pool,
                              ELEMENTS * sizeof( Entry ),
                              cudaMemcpyDeviceToHost ) );
```

The tricky portion of this routine involves the fact that some of the data we have copied are pointers. We cannot simply copy these pointers to the host because they are addresses on the GPU; they will no longer be valid pointers on the host. However, the relative offsets of the pointers *will* still be valid. Every GPU pointer to an `Entry` points somewhere within the `table.pool[]` array, but for the hash table to be usable on the host, we need them to point to the same `Entry` in the `hostTable.pool[]` array.

Given a GPU pointer X, we therefore need to add the pointer's offset from `table.pool` to `hostTable.pool` to get a valid host pointer. That is, the new pointer should be computed as follows:

```
(X - table.pool) + hostTable.pool
```

We perform this update for every `Entry` pointer we've copied from the GPU: the `Entry` pointers in `hostTable.entries` and the `next` pointer of every `Entry` in the table's pool of entries:

```
for (int i=0; i<table.count; i++) {
    if (hostTable.entries[i] != NULL)
        hostTable.entries[i] =
            (Entry*)((size_t)hostTable.entries[i] -
            (size_t)table.pool + (size_t)hostTable.pool);
}
for (int i=0; i<ELEMENTS; i++) {
    if (hostTable.pool[i].next != NULL)
        hostTable.pool[i].next =
            (Entry*)((size_t)hostTable.pool[i].next -
            (size_t)table.pool + (size_t)hostTable.pool);
}
}
```

Having seen the data structures, hash function, initialization, cleanup, and verification code, the most important piece remaining is the one that actually involves CUDA C atomics. As arguments, the `add_to_table()` kernel will take an array of keys and values to be added to the hash table. Its next argument is the hash table itself, and the final argument is an array of locks that will be used to lock each of the table's buckets. Since our input is two arrays that our threads will need to index, we also need our all-too-common index linearization:

```
__global__ void add_to_table( unsigned int *keys, void **values,
                               Table table, Lock *lock ) {
    int tid = threadIdx.x + blockIdx.x * blockDim.x;
    int stride = blockDim.x * gridDim.x;
```

Our threads walk through the input arrays exactly like they did in the dot product example. For each key in the keys[] array, the thread will compute the hash function in order to determine which bucket the key/value pair belongs in. After determining the target bucket, the thread locks the bucket, adds its key/value pair, and unlocks the bucket.

```
while (tid < ELEMENTS) {
    unsigned int key = keys[tid];
    size_t hashValue = hash( key, table.count );
    for (int i=0; i<32; i++) {
        if ((tid % 32) == i) {
            Entry *location = &(table.pool[tid]);
            location->key = key;
            location->value = values[tid];
            lock[hashValue].lock();
            location->next = table.entries[hashValue];
            table.entries[hashValue] = location;
            lock[hashValue].unlock();
        }
    }
    tid += stride;
}
}
```

There is something remarkably peculiar about this bit of code, however. The for() loop and subsequent if() statement seem decidedly unnecessary. In Chapter 6, we introduced the concept of a *warp*. If you've forgotten, a warp is a collection of 32 threads that execute together in lockstep. Although the nuances of how this gets implemented in the GPU are beyond the scope of this book, only one thread in the warp can acquire the lock at a time, and we will suffer many a headache if we let all 32 threads in the warp contend for the lock simultaneously. In this situation, we've found that it's best to do some of the work in software and simply walk through each thread in the warp, giving each a chance to acquire the data structure's lock, do its work, and subsequently release the lock.

The flow of main() should appear identical to the CPU implementation. We start by allocating a large chunk of random data for our hash table keys. Then we create start and stop CUDA events and record the start event for our performance measurements. We proceed to allocate GPU memory for our array of random keys, copy the array up to the device, and initialize our hash table:

```
int main( void ) {
    unsigned int *buffer =
                      (unsigned int *)big_random_block( SIZE );

    cudaEvent_t    start, stop;
    HANDLE_ERROR( cudaEventCreate( &start ) );
    HANDLE_ERROR( cudaEventCreate( &stop ) );
    HANDLE_ERROR( cudaEventRecord( start, 0 ) );

    unsigned int *dev_keys;
    void         **dev_values;
    HANDLE_ERROR( cudaMalloc( (void**)&dev_keys, SIZE ) );
    HANDLE_ERROR( cudaMalloc( (void**)&dev_values, SIZE ) );
    HANDLE_ERROR( cudaMemcpy( dev_keys, buffer, SIZE,
                              cudaMemcpyHostToDevice ) );

    // copy the values to dev_values here
    // filled in by user of this code example

    Table table;
    initialize_table( table, HASH_ENTRIES, ELEMENTS );
```

The last step of preparation to build our hash table involves preparing locks for the hash table's buckets. We allocate one lock for each bucket in the hash table. Conceivably we could save a lot of memory by using only one lock for the whole table. But doing so would utterly destroy performance because every thread would have to compete for the table lock whenever a group of threads tries to simultaneously add entries to the table. So we declare an array of locks, one for every bucket in the array. We then allocate a GPU array for the locks and copy them up to the device:

```
Lock     lock[HASH_ENTRIES];
Lock     *dev_lock;
HANDLE_ERROR( cudaMalloc( (void**)&dev_lock,
                          HASH_ENTRIES * sizeof( Lock ) ) );
HANDLE_ERROR( cudaMemcpy( dev_lock, lock,
                          HASH_ENTRIES * sizeof( Lock ),
                          cudaMemcpyHostToDevice ) );
```

The rest of main() is similar to the CPU version: We add all of our keys to the hash table, stop the performance timer, verify the correctness of the hash table, and clean up after ourselves:

```
add_to_table<<<60,256>>>( dev_keys, dev_values,
                          table, dev_lock );

HANDLE_ERROR( cudaEventRecord( stop, 0 ) );
HANDLE_ERROR( cudaEventSynchronize( stop ) );
float    elapsedTime;
HANDLE_ERROR( cudaEventElapsedTime( &elapsedTime,
                                    start, stop ) );
printf( "Time to hash:  %3.1f ms\n", elapsedTime );

verify_table( table );

HANDLE_ERROR( cudaEventDestroy( start ) );
HANDLE_ERROR( cudaEventDestroy( stop ) );
free_table( table );
cudaFree( dev_lock );
cudaFree( dev_keys );
cudaFree( dev_values );
free( buffer );
return 0;
}
```

A.2.5 HASH TABLE PERFORMANCE

Using an Intel Core 2 Duo, the CPU hash table example in Section A.2.2: A CPU Hash Table takes 360ms to build a hash table from 100MB of data. The code was built with the option -O3 to ensure maximally optimized CPU code. The multithreaded GPU hash table in Section A.2.4: A GPU Hash Table takes 375ms to complete the same task. Differing by less than 5 percent, these are roughly comparable execution times, which raises an excellent question: Why would such a massively parallel machine such as a GPU get beaten by a single-threaded CPU version of the same application? Frankly, this is because GPUs were not designed to excel at multithreaded access to complex data structures such as a hash table. For this reason, there are very few performance motivations to build a data structure such as a hash table on the GPU. So if *all* your application needs to do is build a hash table or similar data structure, you would likely be better off doing this on your CPU.

On the other hand, you will sometimes find yourself in a situation where a long computation pipeline involves one or two stages that the GPU does not enjoy a performance advantage over comparable CPU implementations. In these situations, you have three (somewhat obvious) options:

- Perform every step of the pipeline on the GPU

- Perform every step of the pipeline on the CPU

- Perform some pipeline steps on the GPU and some on the CPU

The last option sounds like the best of both worlds; however, it implies that you will need to synchronize your CPU and GPU at any point in your application where you want to move computation from the GPU to CPU or back. This synchronization and subsequent data transfer between host and GPU can often kill any performance advantage you might have derived from employing a hybrid approach in the first place.

In such a situation, it may be worth your time to perform every phase of computation on the GPU, even if the GPU is not ideally suited for some steps of the algorithm. In this vein, the GPU hash table can potentially prevent a CPU/GPU synchronization point, minimize data transfer between the host and GPU and free the CPU to perform other computations. In such a scenario, it's possible that the overall performance of a GPU implementation would exceed a CPU/GPU hybrid approach, despite the GPU being no faster than the CPU on certain steps (or potentially even getting trounced by the CPU in some cases).

A.3 Appendix Review

We saw how to use atomic compare-and-swap operations to implement a GPU mutex. Using a lock built with this mutex, we saw how to improve our original dot product application to run entirely on the GPU. We carried this idea further by implementing a multithreaded hash table that used an array of locks to prevent unsafe simultaneous modifications by multiple threads. In fact, the mutex we developed could be used for any manner of parallel data structures, and we hope that you'll find it useful in your own experimentation and application development. Of course, the performance of applications that use the GPU to implement mutex-based data structures needs careful study. Our GPU hash table gets beaten by a single-threaded CPU version of the same code, so it will make sense to use the GPU for this type of application only in certain situations. There is no blanket rule that can be used to determine whether a GPU-only, CPU-only, or hybrid approach will work best, but knowing how to use atomics will allow you to make that decision on a case-by-case basis.

Index

H